SOCIAL JUSTICE FOR WOMEN

SOCIAL JUSTICE
FOR WOMEN

The International Labor Organization

and Women

Carol Riegelman Lubin and Anne Winslow

Duke University Press   Durham and London   1990

© 1990 by Duke University Press. All rights reserved
Printed in the United States of America on acid-free paper ∞

Library of Congress Cataloging-in-Publication Data
Lubin, Carol Riegelman.
Social justice for women : the International Labor Organization
and women / Carol Riegelman Lubin and Anne Winslow.
p.   cm.
Includes bibliographical references and index.
ISBN 0-8223-1062-7
1. International Labor Organization—History.   2. Women—
Employment—History—20th century.   3. Women in trade-unions—
History—20th century.   I. Winslow, Anne.   II. Title.
HD6475.A2169735   1991
341.7′63′082—dc20   MB   90-2003
                                                       CIP

Contents

Contents

Foreword

The authors, Carol Lubin and Anne Winslow, in writing this history of the role of women in the International Labor Organization are to be congratulated on making a unique contribution. The book illustrates by a case study—covering the seventy years of the organization's life to date—the difficulty inherent in the struggle for women's rights. The value of this record is not only in its focusing on the problems of protecting and achieving this human right, but on how the International Labor Organization has influenced and affected the United Nations System in this vital effort.

As Director-General of the International Labor Organization from 1948 to 1970, I can testify to the formidable barriers that had to be overcome during that period in making any progress to recognize and protect the status of women. This book, while based on solid fact and history, reads as dramatically as fiction. It belongs in every school and household and will encourage those who believe in a world free of discrimination to continue their efforts for social justice. The authors have illuminated and put into perspective where the experience of the International Labor Organization places the status of women. They conclude: "There is certainly a growing awareness of women throughout the world that they are not necessarily condemned to be beasts of burden or procreators. In many but by no means all parts of the world the status of women has improved, and they are beginning to assert themselves as partners in a common enterprise. The avalanche moves, even though slowly, eroding the habit of centuries toward the achievement of the impossible dream." This message gives society a solid base to build on. We must be grateful to the authors and those who labored with them in producing this history and in giving us the understanding upon which further progress must be made.

David A. Morse, New York City

Preface

The present study presents the results of new research in an important area—the role of international agencies in promoting women's equality on a global basis. By focusing on the International Labor Organization (ILO) the authors have selected one of the central organizations involved in women's projects over the last seven decades and one that allows them to address the critical issue of the role of women both as technical experts and as policy makers.

The study was initially conceived as an analysis of the problems facing women staff members and of the contribution of a few outstanding women delegates to ILO meetings, such as Margaret Bondfield of the United Kingdom and Frances Perkins of the United States, in shaping ILO policies. However, its emphasis gradually changed to its present focus on a global approach to women's problems and successes as reflected in the ILO, in other international bodies and in feminist and other women's movements. Impetus for the global focus of the study was provided by the United Nations Decade for Women, culminating in the Nairobi Conference of 1985.

The study was conducted, inter alia, through interviews and correspondence both with current and former members of the staff and with representatives to ILO meetings and to other international organizations. The representatives interviewed came from a wide range of geographic areas, and those connected with the ILO came from all three groups—governments, employers, and labor. To them we owe a deep debt of gratitude for their willingness to find the time—sometimes at length—to talk or write to us.

The authors wish to acknowledge and express their thanks for the access they have been given to basic material contained in both public and private archives and libraries. We were enabled to use unpublished memoranda, internal instructions, minutes of meetings, and reports on missions as well as correspondence in the Library and the Central Archives of the ILO in Geneva. The documentation in the Paris, London, and Washington branch offices and the New York Liaison Office to the United Nations was consulted at length, and the good offices of the Directors and Deputy Directors were invaluable both in guiding us through the maze of files and in arranging for interviews with women participants in appropriate meetings.

The Library of the United Nations, and especially its League of Nations Collection and its Specialized Agencies Collection, was another widely used source of information, as was the Information Department of the European Community in Brussels.

The resources of the National Archives of the United States and those of the U.S. Department of Labor were drawn upon extensively, under the guidance of Jerry Hess at the Archives and Joseph Goldberg of the Bureau of Labor Statistics. Many interviews and access to files were provided through the Office of International Labor Affairs and the Historian's Office of the Department of Labor.

The most relevant private collections consulted were those at the Schlesinger Library at Radcliffe, the Mudd Library at Princeton, the Rare Book and Manuscript Library at Columbia, and those deposited in the Presidential Library at Hyde Park. In each case we wish to thank the staff concerned who gave us endless personal assistance and time, thus enabling us to take full advantage of the resources available.

A Radcliffe Research Support grant awarded under a joint Murray Center/Schlesinger Library program was especially helpful in facilitating the use of the collections at the Schlesinger Library. Particular thanks for assistance in the use of the Library are extended to Eva Moseley for all her help and advice. The collection of papers from Pauline Newman provides an invaluable resource for understanding the role of women trade unionists in the early years of the twentieth century in the United States. They include minutes and reports of meetings of the National Women's Trade Union League, issues of its periodical, *Life and Labor Bulletin,* and correspondence between Pauline Newman and many of her American and British colleagues. This material has been drawn upon extensively as background information.

The most useful papers covering the period from the late 1920s until the 1980s are those of Frieda S. Miller. While the collection deals with a much wider range of activities than those bearing directly on the ILO, its pages document her extensive influence both in the United States and in the ILO. They include minutes and reports on almost all the sessions of the conferences she attended, as well as sessions of the Governing Body and its wartime Emergency Committee, memoranda to David Morse when she served under him as Director of the Women's Bureau of the Department of Labor, and correspondence with her colleagues in the United States and from many other countries. This material has been used extensively in the development of the relevant sections of the manuscript, but it is most useful in supporting the narrative provided for the war and early postwar periods and the regional approach.

The papers, and Oral History, of Clara M. Beyer cover much the same period as those of Frieda Miller, but they provide a different approach since her position, more than that of policy maker, was frequently as a legislative specialist, administrator, and behind-the-scenes implementer of U.S. policies. As a young research assistant she had attended the first ILO Conference in Washington, D.C., and served as a member of the U.S. delegation to ILO conferences from 1935, when the United States joined the organization, until the 1960s. She continued to attend regional conferences as an expert for the U.S. Agency for International Development, and her papers include reports and correspondence bearing on each of these activities.

The Women's Rights Collection (WRC) contains some of the most valuable of Frances Perkins's papers dealing with the ILO. They include the originals of much of her correspondence and instructions that one would have expected to find in the National Archives or the Department of Labor papers. These papers were used extensively in putting together both the story of the U.S. entry and the wartime role of the ILO. They corroborate the reasons why she could not obtain authorization from the President to permit the ILO to locate its wartime working center in the United States. Her correspondence also reinforces her public statements concerning support for the ILO and its usefulness to the United States.

The Oral History and collected papers of Esther Peterson are the most important resource for the period—approximately 1960–1975—when Peterson was the moving spirit and major decision maker with respect to the role of women in the U.S. government and in its relations with the ILO. Because of her trade union background she also, as is evident from her papers, greatly influenced U.S. women's participation in the labor movement. Finally, papers fully document the establishment by President Kennedy of the U.S. Committee on the Status of Women, his appointments of senior women in his administration, and the influence attributed to women by President Johnson.

A number of other collections, some in the Women's Rights Collection and some in the Women in the Federal Government Collection, have also provided substantial resources and background material. These include the papers and autobiography of Mary Anderson, the papers of Ethel M. Johnson, and in particular an unpublished study on women in the ILO, 1919–1946; the papers and Oral History of Aryness Joy Wickens; the papers of Alice Leopold (especially with respect to labor legislation and status of women); and the Oral Histories of Mary Dublin Keyserling and Martha Elliot.

The papers of David A. Morse, the former Director-General of the ILO, are at the Seelye G. Mudd Library at Princeton University. They provide a wealth of information on the role of women during his time of office. The papers include his Oral History, correspondence, memoranda, and rough, handwritten drafts of memoranda as well as documentation related to his work as Deputy and Acting Secretary of Labor, when he represented the United States on the Governing Body of the ILO and as head of the U.S. delegation to the 1947 and 1948 annual Conferences. Finally, other vital papers concern the years when he was Director-General of the ILO and include telegrams, letters, and memoranda concerning his decisions to resign or continue to serve as Director-General at the conclusion of his term.

The Franklin D. Roosevelt Library at Hyde Park, New York, contains, in addition to the papers of Eleanor and Franklin D. Roosevelt and those of many of their advisers and consultants, the papers of John G. Winant and of Isador Lubin. These papers provide invaluable information concerning the entry of the United States into the ILO; the operations of the ILO from 1934 to the end of the 1940s are also included. The collections at Columbia University—in particular the papers of Lewis Lorwin, Carter Goodrich, and Dean Gildersleeve—document the activities of both the ILO itself and of many of the women participants from the entry of the United States in 1934 until 1946. They provide the minutes of meetings of the economic and social committee of the San Francisco Conference, illuminating the background and events that led to arrangements for specialized agencies to be associated with the UN and for the establishment of the UN's Commission on the Status of Women.

If the book achieves its objectives in any large measure, and if it is an accurate account of the role played by women in the ILO, it will be the result of the incalculable support and assistance of Antoinette Waelbroeck Béguin, a former Assistant Director-General of the ILO. Her detailed criticisms at each stage, corrections of emphasis as well as of facts, and suggestions for reorganization have been of inestimable value. Other members of the staff have made major contributions both in editing texts and in opening up channels of information—historical and current. To name only two, Angela Butler, former staff member and officer of the Federation of Associations of Former International Civil Servants (of the UN family, including the ILO), and Mrs. Hong-Trang Perret-Nguyen, currently a senior ILO official and formerly spokesman for the Staff Union, revised the manuscript of the chapter dealing with staff negotiations to improve the status of women so as to ensure an accurate presentation. Without the assistance of these and many other members of the staff and members of delegations, completion of this study would not have been possible.

Finally, special thanks to Duke University Press and its staff for patient editing and invaluable comments.

Glossary

ILO International Labor Organization, established by the 1919 Peace Treaties

Annual Conference The ILO's legislative organ

Bureaus of the Conference Each of the three groups (governments, employers, workers) has its own bureau for the purpose of nominations and elections as well as discussion of group policy

CIADFOR Inter-African Center for Vocational Training (French acronym)

CINTERFOR Inter-American Centre for Research and Documentation on Vocational Training (Spanish acronym)

Conference Plenary A meeting of the delegates as a whole for general discussion and adoption of reports

Correspondence Committee A group of individuals appointed by the Governing Body to advise the Office on issues relating to women

Director-General The chief administrative officer of the ILO, appointed by the Governing Body; the Director-General appoints the staff, pursuant to regulations approved by the Governing Body

Governing Body The executive organ of the ILO

Office The staff which, under the Director-General, implements policies

Reporter A member of a committee elected to prepare the report of the committee

Tripartite Structure Governments, employers, and workers participating in ILO meetings; members from the last two categories are nominated by the most representative organizations in their countries

Visiting Ministers Ministers of government, or the equivalent, who participate in Plenary Debates and are not delegates

WEP World Employment Program of the ILO

NGO   Non Governmental Organization

ACWW   Associated Country Women of the World (International Non Governmental Organization)

AFL-CIO   American Federation of Labor–Congress of Industrial Organizations

CLUW   Coalition of Labor Union Women

CONGO   Conference of Non Governmental Organizations accredited to the UN Economic and Social Council to provide a more coordinated approach to UN bodies

ICFTU   International Confederation of Free Trade Unions

ICW   International Council of Women (International Non Governmental Organization)

ILGWU   International Ladies Garment Workers Union (U.S.)

NGO Forum or Tribune   A meeting organized by NGOs in conjunction with an intergovernmental meeting

NWTUL   National Women's Trade Union League (U.S.)

OCAM   Communal African and Mauritanian Organization (French acronym)

TUC   Trades Union Congress (U.K.)

TUP   Trickle Up Program (U.S.)

WTUL   Women's Trade Union League (U.K.)

WWB   Women's World Banking (International Non Governmental Organization)

Specialized Agency   An intergovernmental organization with formal association with the United Nations)

FAO   Food and Agriculture Organization

FICSA   Federation of International Civil Servants Associations

IAEA   International Atomic Energy Agency

UNESCO   United Nations Educational, Scientific and Cultural Organization

UNIDO   United Nations Industrial Development Organization

WHO   World Health Organization

UN   United Nations

ECE   United Nations Economic Commission for Europe

INSTRAW   United Nations International Research and Training Institute
for the Advancement of Women

UNDP   United Nations Development Programme

UNFPA   United Nations Fund for Population Activities

UNHCR   United Nations High Commissioner for Refugees

UNICEF   United Nations Childrens Fund

UNIFEM   United Nations Development Fund for Women

SOCIAL JUSTICE FOR WOMEN

Introduction

One of the notable features of the past seventy years has been the ever-increasing insistence by women on full equality with men. This has been the subject of numerous articles and books but one aspect has, so far, been neglected. The role of intergovernmental organizations in fostering, or sometimes hindering, this development has still to be explored. Only one of the constitutions of the international organizations established prior to or shortly after the Second World War mentioned women at all—perhaps because it never occurred to their founding fathers that women had any place in the big arenas. The only exception, apart from the League of Nations, was the International Labor Organization (ILO), established in 1919 at the Paris Peace Conference which formally ended the Second World War.[1] (The ILO Constitution became Part XIII of the Treaties of Peace. The Covenant of the League of Nations was Part I.)

The Preamble to the Constitution of the ILO provided for the "protection of children, young persons and women." Its statement of objectives, known as the Labor Charter, affirms the "principle that men and women should receive equal remuneration for work of equal value," an objective strongly supported by the American Federation of Labor. The charter also calls for "a system of inspection in which women should take part." This was a direct concession to the demands of an international women's lobby all too familiar with enforcement problems arising in the implementation of their own national legislation.

The Constitution further declared that, when the Conference considered a question affecting women, "at least one of the advisers should be a woman." This provision subsequently came in for considerable criticism. Why "should" and not "must"? Why adviser and not delegate? Why only one? Advisers are usually technicians, despite certain exceptions, and only speak or vote in the absence of a delegate. Another provision in the Constitution which raises different kinds of questions is the one stating that "a certain number of the staff should be women." At what grades and how many? The Constitution is silent. Even the inclusion of such a provision was due to the insistence of the women's groups lobbying at the Peace Conference.

The existence of these provisions, the fact that the ILO has had close to seventy years of experience—functioning in very diverse climates— between wars, during war, and after the Second World War provides a good vantage point from which to appraise what the ILO has done for women and what they have done for it.

The initiative for establishing the ILO had two very different roots. One was the desire of governments to defend themselves from unfair competition, resulting from different labor standards, and the other the pressures from labor to be rewarded for their wartime efforts.

By the end of the nineteenth century and the beginning of the twentieth, efforts to improve working conditions had become a matter of concern to governments. Protective labor legislation was enacted in a number of countries in the 1890s and 1900s prohibiting employment of women in night work and dangerous occupations and limiting (to some degree) the hours of work of women and young persons. However, to protect their own trade against unfair competition, governments recognized that international treaties were needed. Initially they were negotiated on a bilateral basis between neighboring countries or between countries whose products were in direct competition. Then in 1891 the German government called an international conference in Berlin with a broad agenda covering virtually the whole field of labor legislation. This agenda had been proposed earlier by the Swiss government. Although this conference failed to reach agreement, the event led indirectly to the International Congress on Labor Legislation, held in Brussels in 1897, which resulted in the founding of the International Association for Labor Legislation in 1900, with headquarters in Basle. Two conferences held under the auspices of the Association in Berne in 1905 and 1906 resulted in the first multinational agreements dealing with the prohibition of the use of white phosphorous in the manufacture of matches and of night work for women. In 1913 another technical conference drafted two new conventions, one limiting the hours of work for women and young persons, and the other prohibiting night work for young persons. The war intervened before these conventions could be acted upon, but they were placed on the agenda of the annual ILO conference (held in Washington in 1919). It was experience with these conferences which led members of the British Ministry of Labour and the Home Office to prepare a draft proposal for establishing at the Peace Conference a new kind of international organization to deal with labor legislation.

The second motivating force came from labor. "Organized labor, throughout the nineteenth century, tended to transcend national frontiers, or at least to recognize similar interests in the working class of the population the world over. While the left wing of the labor movement developed a militant revolutionary internationalism, the orthodox trade-union movement had also an international organization which kept the leaders of the various countries in contact with each other, and to some extent made common cause in the struggle for higher wages and better conditions of livelihood. When the war came, labor, no less than other sections of society, found its international organization broken and its ideal of international class solidarity shattered. Nevertheless, throughout the War, although organized labor movements in warring countries loyally supported the national cause, the memory of their past relationship across frontiers did not wholly fade: even in the midst of disillusionment labor attempted to preserve something of its pre-war structure and to keep the way open to restore its own international organization, once peace was secured."[2] Thus labor representatives came to the Peace Conference determined to press their demands for the rights of workers. The Preamble of the labor section of the peace treaties reflects much of the program laid down by the various labor conferences held during the war.[3]

Another element which helped to shape the ILO was the existence of employer coalitions. The first Congress of Industrial and Agricultural Employers' Organizations was held in 1911. Three years later another meeting in Paris, designed to establish an international employers' information center, was frustrated by the onset of the First World War. When the ILO was created the existence of employer groups which had been active in collective bargaining and arbitration led to their inclusion as one of the three elements of tripartism. This, in turn, led to a permanent International Federation of Employers after the first ILO conference in 1919.

The structure of the ILO was—and still is—unique in the history of intergovernmental bodies. It provides not only for participation by governmental representatives—the normal pattern—but also for workers' and employers' organizations voting independently. Each member nation is authorized to have four delegates—two government and one each from employer and labor organizations, as well as one adviser for each delegate on each item on the agenda. In other intergovernmental organizations women participate in the decisionmaking process primarily if governments decide to include them in their delegations. In ILO the tripartite structure provides a channel for women employers and, more importantly, for working women who have long spearheaded the drive for the objectives of the ILO. Thus, both because of its subject matter and the opportunities it provides, the ILO is of special importance to women.

The principal aim of the Organization is the promotion of social justice as a precondition for universal peace. From the beginning this has involved the setting of standards for national governments to follow in regard to "the well-being, physical, moral and intellectual of industrial wage earners" throughout the world.[4] An annual tripartite International Labor Conference is the legislative organ. The Conference operates through a plenary and a series of committees. The Plenary provides an opportunity for an exchange of views on social and economic issues, based largely on annual reports by the Director-General and by the Governing Body. This debate is often the occasion for visiting ministers and other high dignitaries to make known the position of their governments. In addition, representatives of the international labor or employer organizations also address the Plenary.

The Conference operates through two types of committees—standing committees which deal with such items as finance, rules of procedure, and credentials, and technical committees established to deal with each item on the agenda. These committees report to the Plenary. Depending on the circumstances, the Conference adopts conventions, recommendations, resolutions, or declarations. These legislative acts are commonly referred to as instruments and collectively constitute the International Labor Code. When there seems to be enough ground for formal action—and the subject matter is appropriate for national legislation—the conference adopts a convention. This places upon member governments a number of obligations. First, it must be submitted to the national authority or authorities for ratification. If ratified, the member is obliged to take suitable action to implement the convention and to report annually thereon. Even if a member does not ratify, it is required to report what action it has taken or intends to take. A tripartite conference committee and an independent Committee of Experts monitor the observance by governments of the obligations they have undertaken. Moreover, organizations of workers, of employers, or governments have the right to submit complaints which may lead to the dispatch of a commission of enquiry. Its report is then considered by the Governing Body and ultimately if no solution is found the issue may be submitted to the World Court for an Advisory Opinion.

Recommendations are adopted either when the subject matter is not suitable or opportune for a convention, or to complement a convention by administrative actions and detailed procedures that may be carried out by national or local governments. (Frequently, also, a recommendation is adopted as a preliminary step, looking to later adoption of a convention.)

Resolutions are much more general, and may contain statements of objectives, requests for further study or conference action. They may be addressed to particular countries or other organizations. Declarations are a relatively new phenomena, designed to make formal statements, often addressed to the world at large or to special groups. The first declaration was made by the 1939 regional meeting in Havana as a statement of support for the ILO in wartime. The Philadelphia Conference in 1944 used this form to enunciate the ILO Social Mandate in the postwar world. Most recently, a declaration was adopted with respect to the program of the UN Decade for Women.

The executive organ of the ILO is its tripartite Governing Body. Eight government seats were initially reserved for the eight states of chief industrial importance, while the remaining four government seats were chosen by the government group of the conference. All employer and worker seats were selected by their respective groups in the Conference. As will be seen in chapter 7, this composition has been modified over the years, rising from the original twenty-four to fifty-six and now based on a regional basis, selected by the respective groups.[5] The Governing Body decides on the site and agenda of the Conference, elects the Director of the International Labor Office, and acts on proposals of the Director with respect to both program and finance. The third entity is the International Labor Office. The Director appoints the staff which is responsible for initiating and carrying out programs and research and organizing technical assistance missions. The Office, as a result of the political wisdom of the first Director and of the backing it usually receives from the labor movement and, to a lesser extent, from employer organizations, has a greater power of initiative and independence than the staff of most other international, intergovernmental bodies.[6]

When this machinery was set in motion in 1919 the world it dealt with was primarily controlled by West European countries. Its focus was on their interests and their concerns. But as that world changed, so did the ILO. The tide of decolonization brought into being a host of newly independent nations from Africa, Asia, the Middle East, the Caribbean, as well as the most vocal Latin American countries. Their needs and demands were very different from those of the industrialized states and the differences within these groups were enormous. This had its effect on the legislative efforts of the ILO and, even more, on the nature of its activities. Research and technical assistance have assumed an ever greater importance. Technical cooperation provides a vehicle for practical assistance to countries emerging from barter economies and antiquated colonial structures and makes it possible to deal with the great diversity of problems by finding specific solutions to specific problems. Today ILO's 150 members come predominantly from developing countries. Meeting the new membership needs and problems has entailed decentralization of the ILO programs and structure and affected both the kinds of technical assistance rendered and the substance of its standard setting.

The extent of the change that has taken place was evident in Nairobi in 1985. That was the year the United Nations concluded a "Decade for Women." Ten years previously the first women's conference was held in Mexico City. There women from all over the world gave voluble expression to their demands for equality with men and for recognition of their rightful place in all spheres of activity. Five years later, in Copenhagen, women, both as delegates to the UN governmental conference and as members of a non-governmental forum, discussed the progress that had been made, noting the adoption by the 1979 UN General Assembly of the first comprehensive convention directed to the elimination of discrimination against women. This convention, now ratified by a hundred governments, is a wide-ranging document setting international standards in the fields of political rights, nationality, private and penal law, traffic in women, education, and economic and social rights.

In 1985, at the Annual Conference of the International Labor Organization, a resolution was adopted on "equal opportunities and equal treatment for men and women in employment" and this Resolution was submitted to the UN Nairobi Conference. Both the Resolution of the International Labor Conference and the Forward-Looking Strategies adopted at Nairobi "confirmed the proposition that the economic contribution of women is a key element in planning and implementing social policies." While the former "identified conceptual approaches to improving the conditions of women in society, the Forward-Looking Strategies provide a framework for a long-term vision of the future." Re-emphasizing the crucial role of women, the Strategies warned that "neglect or exclusion of women in decision-making processes could seriously jeopardise economic and social progress."[7]

These achievements were the culmination of the UN's long-term efforts on behalf of human rights and the rights of women. Article 55 of the UN Charter provided that the UN should promote "universal respect for, and observance of, human rights and fundamental freedoms for all without distinction as to race, *sex,* language, or religion" (italics added). Soon after the United Nations came into existence a Commission on Human Rights was established. Its mandate included the preparation of an international bill of rights and international declarations or conventions on civil liberties, the status of women, and similar matters. As a first order of business, the commission worked on the elaboration of the bill of rights. The specialized agencies concerned, such as the ILO and UNESCO (the United Nations Educational, Scientific, and Cultural Organization), as well as private organizations and a number of governments, took an active part in the drafting of the bill but the major credit goes to the first chairman, Eleanor Roosevelt and to her close collaborator, René Cassin of France. In December 1948 the UN General Assembly adopted the Universal Declaration of Human Rights.[8] Translated into forty-six languages, the text has been circulated throughout the world and a number of the articles have been incorporated verbatim in the constitutions of newly independent countries. While the Declaration is not specifically addressed to women, its provisions apply without distinction as to "sex." The provisions of particular concern to ILO constituencies are: the right to work, to protection against unemployment, and to join trade unions; the right to a standard of living adequate for health and well-being; the right to education and the right to rest and leisure. To implement the Declaration, two Covenants were adopted in 1967, one on civil and political rights, and the other on economic, social, and cultural rights. However, it took another thirty-one years for the adoption of a convention specifically addressed to the elimination of discrimination against women.

Despite the long road still ahead, the progress already achieved can be measured if one looks back to the early struggles, even in the developed world. Less than 150 years ago eight American women sought to attend the first Anti-Slavery Congress in London. They were refused admission on the ground that "God's clear intention would be violated if promiscuous female representation be allowed."[9] And in 1861 a French politician, Jules Simon, said that "a woman who becomes a worker is no longer a woman."[10]

How did we get from there to here? Whence came the impossible dream that has left such a mark on the last half of the twentieth century? Where are the roots that nourished it? Perhaps not unexpectedly, the roots are more economic than humanitarian, more reformist than activist, although suffragists played a part. Much of the change that ensued owes a depth of gratitude to the early British and American women trade union leaders.

Obviously, with such a broad canvas one can be little more than impressionistic. In trying to assess the role ILO played in regard to women we will try to address the following issues. How did the ILO's concern with women manifest itself and evolve over the years? To what extent did its activities reflect, influence, or be influenced by women's struggles on the world scene for greater equality? How did it deal with the growing dichotomy between the feminist demands in industrialized countries and the demands of Third World women, struggling both against tradition and the impact of technological advances from the West? How did it relate to other intergovernmental—women centered—bodies that began to emerge in 1946? Did it provide a leadership role or did that task fall to others and, if so, why?

Our study opens with a portrayal of the militant women, particularly in the British and U.S. labor movements, who played an active role in the early days of the ILO and before. We watch the gathering storm of war in the 1930s, culminating in the ILO taking refuge in Montreal, Canada. Then came the difficult war years and the effort to survive and plan for a very different postwar world. We discuss the role of the ILO in the UN Conference on International Organization and what the emergence of a plethora of new organizations boded for ILO's own programs for women, especially the UN Commission on the Status of Women.

The following chapters deal with the major ILO activities affecting women, their evolution over time, and their interaction with national and international women's movements. What has been the impact of ILO legislation on the position of women and their greater self-fulfillment? Who were the women, and what was their motivation, who served on delegations to ILO meetings or who joined the ILO staff? What kind of role did they play? Has technical assistance significantly improved the lot of women in the Third World? Have ILO conferences and seminars provided women with a meaningful platform for the expression of their concerns? And, finally, to what extent has the ILO lived up to its constitutional provisions in the treatment of its own staff. In the pages that follow we try to present the facts as they took place, to isolate the major trends, and tentatively attempt to answer some of the questions raised.

1. The Impossible Dream: Early Years

The International Labor Organization (ILO) was born into a world still struggling with the aftermath of the industrial revolution. That revolution put women into the lowest and most degrading positions, threatening family life and society as a whole. Sweatshops and the employment of children added new horrors. Efforts to mitigate some of the worst aspects of the situation, particularly in France, England, and Germany, were made during the nineteenth century. A body of legislation was adopted which "gradually encompassed many aspects of women's work: it established a limit first of twelve, then of eleven and, in some cases, of ten hours work per day; it prohibited most work at night, on Saturday afternoons, and in particularly dangerous places, such as underground mines; it set basic health and safety standards; and it forbade the rehiring of new mothers within four weeks of giving birth. From the 1890s the authorities appointed women factory inspectors."[1]

These measures, however, did little to soften the impact of the basic structural changes that were taking place. The introduction of machinery both reduced the number of workers needed and demanded new skills from the workers who remained. Women, mostly unskilled and with few opportunities to learn new techniques, were the first to be fired. One of their principal opportunities to work, aside from domestic service, was in the textile industry. When this became mechanized, men frequently took the place that many women had previously occupied. However in some instances, particularly in the United States, industrialization of industries such as textiles brought new low-wage jobs which were usually filled by women. Factories drew men into urban areas, leaving the women behind. More and more women became dependent for survival on home industry, the value of which shrank in the face of cheaper machine-made products. Moreover, the introduction of compulsory education and the growing role of the state meant that the state assumed many of the functions formerly the responsibility of the family, and the women's role declined commensurately. The psychological impact of these changes was felt by all members of the family. Prior to the industrial revolution all members of the family had their clearly defined and generally accepted roles. The industrial revolution disrupted traditional ways of life and cast women adrift to find their own means of economic survival and to maintain the life of the family.[2]

In the face of this onslaught on their way of life, women began to react. Middle-class women, particularly in England, France, and the United States, formed organizations to fight for the rights of women. Leaders of the antislavery movement, the world temperance movement and, above all, the women's suffrage movement provided the political and militant leadership that began to shape the international women's movement as a whole. The primary emphasis of these groups was on civil and political rights. Social reformers and those concerned with the economic and social needs of women also formed their own groups.

Women Organize

The first steps in organizing women were taken by the abolitionists, the temperance groups, and a wide variety of early feminists. The culmination of these early efforts came in 1848 with the holding of the First Women's Rights Convention at Seneca Falls, New York, to discuss the "social, civil and religious condition and rights of women." This meeting is frequently described as the beginning of the women's movement but, according to a recent study, Seneca Falls was "a magnificent transition point. The earlier movement had been diffuse and embryonic, still closely tied to abolitionism; in the future it would become more focused and visible, with a leadership clearly speaking for women." The Seneca Falls meeting issued a Declaration of Sentiments which became "the most publicized expression of nineteenth century ideology" but the "themes of the developing movement had been appearing in print for ten years before that." These were "the equal rights and responsibilities of women and men, the right of a woman to leave her prescribed 'sphere' in order to do a 'man's job' and the parallel positions of women and slaves."[3]

Interest in establishing links with women across national frontiers led in 1888 to the convening in Washington of an international congress.

Forty-nine delegates gathered from Great Britain, France, Denmark, Norway, Finland, India, Canada, and the United States. Goals included temperance, higher education for women, career opportunities, and charitable work, but major emphasis was on the right to vote as the key to progress in all other areas. This meeting set up the International Council of Women (ICW), a relatively nonmilitant organization designed to achieve social reform and improvement of women's status everywhere. A year later the ICW meeting in London was attended by 5,000 delegates. Its eleven affiliated councils, from the United States, Canada, Germany, Sweden, Great Britain, Ireland, Australia (New South Wales), Denmark, Holland, New Zealand, and Tasmania claimed memberships of 6 million.[4]

The basic purposes of the ICW reflected the interests not only of Elizabeth Cady Stanton and Susan B. Anthony, founders of the women's rights movement in the United States, but also the leadership of May Wright Sewall, a young educator and chairman of the National American Woman Suffrage Association. These American women dominated the ICW in its early years. Ishbel, Marchioness of Aberdeen and Temair, became president in 1893 and served initially until 1899. During this period national councils were organized in nine European countries. Lady Aberdeen resumed the presidency on two further occasions—1904 to 1920, and 1922 to 1936. She was an experienced organizer of women for social goals. With the help of her husband she founded Onward and Upward, an association for the recreation and education of young girls. Later, when she was in Canada, she organized the Victorian Order of Nurses, and when her husband served as Governor-General in Ireland she started the Women's National Health Association to crusade against infant mortality and tuberculosis. She was also a member of the executive board of the association of women connected with the Liberal Party. As president of the ICW she led a committee representing women's organizations at the Peace Conference.[5]

Meantime, in France 1870 saw the creation of two important women's organizations. One was the Association pour les Droits des Femmes which subsequently became La Société pour l'Amelioration du Sort de la Femme et la Revendication de Ses Droits; the other was la Ligue Française pour les Droits des Femmes. In 1889 the first Congrès des Oeuvres et Institutions Feminines was held under the auspices of the French government. May Wright Sewall participated in the congrès as the chairman of the U.S. National Council of Women. She was subsequently to become one of the presidents of the ICW.

Controversial issues developed around women's suffrage. At one extreme was Alice Paul, founder of the National Women's Party (NWP) which subsequently formulated the Equal Rights Amendment to the U.S. Constitution. She organized women voters, picketed the White House, and burned the president's war speeches. Less militant women founded another women's organization in 1902, the International Woman's Suffrage Alliance (later to become the International Alliance of Women). This new body, organized by an American, Carrie Chapman Catt, sought a compromise between the extreme militant suffrage leaders and those who wanted equal franchise rights for men and women to be achieved by legislative means. Its stated purpose was to act as a "central bureau for the collection, exchange and dissemination of information concerning the methods of suffrage work and the general status of women in the various countries" where it had members.[6] Until the United States entered the First World War, she was deeply concerned with organizing women for peace and seeking to stop the European war. She was later a participant in the delegation of women who lobbied at the Paris Peace Conference.

Meantime, in Great Britain, the Women's Labour League was set up in 1906 to work for labor representation in connection with the Labour Party and "to obtain direct Labour Representation of women in Parliament and in the local bodies." In an effort to internationalize these efforts the Labour League held a one-day conference in Stuttgart in August 1907, prior to the meeting of the International Trade Union Conference. At this meeting, in addition to establishing an international secretariat to further the work of the Women's Labour League, the socialist representatives appointed an International Socialist Women's Committee, with an international bureau to provide continuity. A *Labour Leaflet*—which subsequently became the *Labour Women* was initiated to maintain contact between the British Labour women and the European Socialist women. At its 1910 conference the Women's Labour League proclaimed an annual women's day as propaganda for women's suffrage. The next year the first International Socialist Women's Day was held in Vienna with the slogan "Equal Rights for Men and Women"—a goal, one might add, still being sought three-quarters of a century later.[7]

In Great Britain militant suffragettes heckled cabinet ministers during meetings and, disguised as messengers or waitresses, managed to circumvent the efforts of the police to keep them out of the House of Commons. "Once a party of women chained themselves to the railings in Downing Street; another was found chained to a statue in the lobby of the House of Commons."[8] Prominent among the British women who spearheaded this drive for the political rights of women were Millicent Garrett Fawcett, president of the Union of Women's Suffrage Societies of Great Britain, and Margaret Corbett Ashby, for many years its secretary, Emmeline Pankhurst of the ultra militant Women's Social and Political Union (founded in 1902), and Lady Aberdeen.

At about the same time U.S. suffragists stood at the White House gates with banners and sang songs, resulting in their imprisonment.[9] Women in Belgium, France, and Switzerland also participated in the growing movement for women's rights.[10]

During this period other sectors of society became actively involved in the industrial struggle and its impact on working women, particularly the influx of immigrant women. The leadership included heads of settlement houses, social workers, and social reformers. The Triangle Shirtwaist fire (see below) provided the rallying cry for such women as Jane Addams, Head Worker of Chicago's early settlement, Hull House, who became the mentor of the social workers and reformers. The latter included Mary Drier and her sister Margaret Drier Robins, Grace Abbott and her sister Edith, Frances Perkins, and Eleanor Roosevelt. Two other outstanding social reformers were Mary Van Kleek and Mary Anderson, the latter also being an early trade unionist.

These women and their British counterparts spearheaded the drive to provide women with the organizational strength to achieve their own demands. Meantime working women were fighting their battles on two fronts; against the weight of tradition and against employers. "There was yet a third battle front—the trade union itself—and it might have been the most important of all. Instead of recognizing women as workers and encouraging them to join in organizational struggles, male unionists insisted on women's primary function in the home and remained stubbornly ambivalent in their efforts."[11] To counter this situation, two women's organizations were established, first in Great Britain and then in the United States by joint action of reformers and women workers.

The Women's Trade Union League (WTUL), originally named the Women's Protective and Provident League, was set up in Great Britain in 1874 by Emma Patterson to promote the organization of women workers. One of its first actions was to protest the passing of laws that "it saw as inhibiting women's rights freely to compete with men." In 1880 it dropped its opposition to protective legislation, "realizing that the benefits it offered women outweighed the freedom of choice it imposed on

---

13

them."[12] It helped to found over thirty women's unions, and initiated contact with the Trades Union Congress, getting it to pass an equal pay resolution. By 1907, 15 percent of all British unions admitted women. The WTUL became the lobbyist for women workers with the government, supporting legislation to improve working conditions, and won the appointment of women factory inspectors. In 1920 it merged with the Trades Union Congress (TUC) on the basis of an agreement that women were to hold two protected seats on the TUC General Council. These two seats remained for fifty years the only representation of women until 1981 when the number was increased to five.[13] As of 1989, women at the TUC have twelve reserved seats and three by election from individual unions, bringing the current total number of representatives up to fifteen.

The National Women's Trade Union League of the United States had been created by a meeting of women trade unionists and likeminded women during the annual American Federation of Labor (AFL) Conference in 1903, using as the model its British counterpart. Its objectives were to help women to organize, and when organized to obtain better working conditions, promote facilities in big factories, and assist in avoiding jurisdictional conflicts when new organizations were being formed. It published, from 1911 to 1921, a periodic *Life and Labor Bulletin,* "covering the Activities of the National Women's Trade Union League and Some Happenings in the Labor Movement," and remained an influence in the women's labor movement until its dissolution in 1950. A New York and a Chicago League continued for several years longer.

The first president was Mrs. Mary Norton Kehew, a prominent Bostonian, with Jane Addams as vice president. Subsequently Margaret Drier Robins became president, with Rose Schneiderman as vice president. Margaret Drier Robins initially was president of the New York League, and after marrying Raymond Robins, a Chicago social reformer, moved to Chicago where she worked with Jane Addams and other members of the settlement house movement. She was one of the founders of the Chicago League. As a dominant figure in the Women's Trade Union League, she brought in as staff—in addition to Schneiderman—Mary Anderson, Pauline Newman, Frieda Miller, and other women later concerned with the ILO. Because of her interest in having the voice of American women represented at the Peace Conference, she financed the travel of Mary Anderson and Rose Schneiderman to the Paris Peace Conference. They brought with them a list of proposals that would ensure recognition of the rights of working women in the peace treaty. Unfortunately, they arrived too late for a full hearing but found that many of their proposals had already been included, partly as the result of an earlier Paris visit by Margaret Bondfield, their British colleague.[14]

Mary Van Kleek, another outstanding economist and social reformer, was one of the few women who assisted in the U.S. planning for labor participation at the Peace Conference—although she did not attend. During the war she had been the Ordinance Bureau's supervisor of women's work, and then first chief of a newly established Women in Industry Service in the U.S. Department of Labor. She later became director of the Russell Sage Foundation, an economic think tank and publishing house concerned with political and economic issues.

Trade Union Activists

Great Britain

Among the British women workers who took an early lead and who were later to play a substantial role in the ILO, one of the earliest was Julia Varley, born in Yorkshire in 1871, who was sent to work in the woolen mills as a child. When she was only twelve years old, she joined the Weavers and Textile Workers Union and was soon launched on a recruiting career. Her description of her first attempt vividly illustrates the uphill road women faced. "I stood on a table in the square and argued the merits of trade unionism to a few children, two cats and an occasional passerby." A fat old woman leaned out of a window and after listening for a moment said "silly bitch" and slammed the window.[15] Varley became the first woman member of the Bradford Trades Union and served on its executive committee. Later, she became an organizer for the Transport and General Workers Union. In 1904, disguising herself, she tramped from Leeds to Liverpool allegedly looking for her husband. She was investigating the living conditions in hostels for itinerant women. In 1917 she became a member of the Labour Advisory Board of the Ministry of Labour, and for many years (from 1924) of the General Council of the Trades Union Congress—the top decisionmaking body of the British national labor unions.

Another early fighter was Mary Macarthur (Anderson) who was Scottish-born. She worked in her father's drapery business and was so appalled at the shop employees' conditions that she joined the shop assistants union in 1901 and soon became an active organizer and speaker at trade union meetings. A witness reported seeing "a slip of a fair-haired girl, mounted on a chair," speaking to a crowd of employees of the Croony Clothing Factory "with great fire and persuasiveness."[16] The year after joining the union she went to its annual meeting in Manchester where she met a colleague with whom she was to work closely for many years—Margaret Grace Bondfield. Macarthur was described as "emotional, highly strung, given to tantrums, exuberant, sweeping colleagues and workers along."[17] She became general secretary of the Women's Trade Union League—and, while participating in trade union conferences, met her future husband, Will Anderson, one of the most beloved leaders of the British trade union movement. She was also one of the founders of the National Union of Women Workers in 1906, which grew to a membership of 80,000 before it merged in 1926 with a mixed general union.

Margaret Bondfield, whose working experience sparked a dynamic career, was considered the most outstanding woman in the trade union movement of her era. She was born in Somerset, England, in 1873 of a working-class family with many children and few assets; her father became unemployed while she was still in school. Forced to go to work, she was apprenticed as a "living in" shop assistant—a system widely used at that time to provide young women with chaperonage, food, and lodging as part of their wages—15 to 25 pounds (about $75 to $125) per annum for working sixty-five hours a week. A chance reading of a newspaper wrapping her fish and chips which had a letter from the secretary of the National Union of Shop Assistants, Warehousemen, and Clerks led Bondfield into the trade union movement.

"I would wait," she wrote, "until one or two of my roommates in the dormitory were asleep and write articles for joint action."[18] She joined a union and very shortly began her career as a union researcher, investigator of conditions of exploitation, organizer, secretary, and officer. She became the first British woman cabinet member when the Labour Party came into office in 1924.

Despite the early efforts of women such as these, progress in the improvement of working conditions in the United Kingdom—as well as in other industrializing countries—was still very slow. Two women in particular, born close to the end of the nineteenth century, experienced hardships all too similar to those of their predecessors. Florence Hancock, a native of Yorkshire, worked as a dishwasher in a cafe from seven in the morning until nine at night. For this she received the handsome salary of three shillings (about 75 cents) a week and board. When both her parents died she managed to keep herself, two brothers, and a sister on these wages. She became a trade unionist in 1913. She was the only girl among twenty workers to attend an organizing meeting of the workers union. Two of its leaders were fired but later reinstated. Within two weeks a strike was called over the issue of overtime pay. This achieved partial satisfaction, but, more importantly, it resulted in women receiving a minimum of twelve shillings a week.

Miss Hancock's career has been described as "a microcosm of the women's trade union movement" during the period 1914–51. Educated in trade union politics during the 1920s and 1930s, "she rose to prominence in the TUC establishment as a woman leader in Ernest Bevin's powerful Transport and General Workers Union."[19] She chaired the Women's Advisory Committee between 1941–44 and 1948–52. While the Labour Party was in power she presided as chairman of the TUC General Council. She received the Order of the British Empire (OBE) in 1943, Commander of the British Empire (CBE) three years later, and was made a Dame of the British Empire in 1951. Her positive participation in organizing women on an international basis and her role in the ILO will be discussed below.

Another contemporary of Hancock was Anne Loughlin, eldest daughter of an Irish boot and shoe worker. When she was twelve her mother died and she went to work in a garment factory. While looking after her family, still in her teens, she became a shop steward and, at the age of twenty-one, an organizer for the Tailors and Garment Workers Union. Described as "small, golden-haired and blue-eyed" she resolutely fought for and achieved acceptance of women by the union.[20] "She did it by faithfully carrying out union instructions to establish union rates and conditions, town by town." At the age of twenty-two, "a fiery speaker and tireless worker," she took part in the famous Hebden Bridge strike of 6,000 workers and, on becoming a national organizer in 1920, she traveled the country negotiating, organizing, and settling disputes. Nine years later she was elected to the TUC General Council. By 1948, when she became general secretary (the first woman head of a mixed union), the membership had risen to 100,000.[21] She was made a Dame of the British Empire and served as a member of royal commissions and government committees concerned with holidays, equal pay, safety, and unemployment insurance.

She developed a close relationship with many of her colleagues from the United States and other countries, forging a strong tool to assist her later in dealing with many issues at the ILO.

United States

Across the ocean, U.S. women trade union activists were also fighting their own battles. Many of them were immigrants or first generation citizens. It was they who provided the labor force for the sweatshops in factories or in their homes. One of the early women trade union leaders who was later to play a role in the ILO was Pauline Newman, born in a small village in Lithuania where her father sold fruit and taught the Talmud to well-to-do boys. When he died, her mother brought her three young daughters to the United States. Newman worked as a small child first in a brush factory, then in a cigarette factory, and, at about the age of eleven, at the infamous Triangle Shirtwaist factory which was soon to become the symbol of the oppression of young women in the U.S. garment trades. Horrified at the conditions she found, she joined the Socialist Party and two labor groups, the International Ladies' Garment Workers Union (ILGWU), an affiliate of the AFL and the National Women's Trade Union League (NWTUL), which played a major role in the establishment of international federations of like bodies and later in the work of the ILO. It was this experience that gave Pauline Newman her interest in global women's issues.

Newman left the Triangle Shirtwaist factory in November 1909. That month the first great garment strike took place in New York City—the "Uprising of the Twenty Thousand." Newman, who had never been out of the city, and had to borrow a suitcase, was sent upstate by the union while the strike was under way to address labor and women's groups and to raise money for the strikers who had no strike fund. On her return she became the first woman organizer for the ILGWU. She was jailed briefly in Cleveland while organizing the cloakmakers' strike, and in Kalamazoo she helped to direct the corsetmakers' strike. She became director of health education at the Union Health Center of the ILGWU. Years later she commented on the fact that the young generation had not "experienced the mental fatigue that comes from an unlimited working day and from a seven day week. They don't know what it means to work long hours in airless, filthy fire-traps; to come home and sleep in windowless bedrooms, without air, without light and without heat; with toilets in the yard and with sickening smells everywhere," and she added "if these wretched conditions are (by and large) a thing of the past it is due almost entirely to the labor movement."[22]

Another early immigrant who also became a leader in the NWTUL and later played a role at the ILO was Rose Schneiderman. She was brought from Poland in 1890. She was a four feet, six-inches redhead. In her autobiography she said, "I may not have been seen but I saw it all." She started as an employee in a department store at age thirteen, with a salary of $2.25 for a sixty-four-hour week—the family breadwinner after the death of her father during her mother's pregnancy. In an effort to improve her lot she became a machine operator in cap factories and joined the United Cloth and Cap Makers Union. She served as an organizer for a series of unions, including the ILGWU. Still in their teens, she and Pauline Newman led the shirtwaist makers' strike. Shortly thereafter on March 25, 1911, a fire broke out in the Triangle Shirtwaist factory, a wooden six-story building, trapping hundreds of young women who found the exits barred to keep them from taking a few minutes' break or stealing a few needles. Of the five hundred who worked in the factory, 143 died and many more were injured. Rose Schneiderman made a bitter speech at the memorial service held a week later: "This is not the first time girls have been burned alive in this city. . . . The life of men and women is so cheap and property is so sacred. There are so many of us for one job it matters little if 143 of us are burned to death."[23] Shortly before, Schneiderman had joined the New York Women's Trade Union League. She worked her way through the ranks, ultimately to become its president. Out of these activities she came to meet the women backers and leaders of the social reform movement—both in the United States and abroad.

Mary Anderson, a Swedish emigré who had come to the United States at the age of sixteen, worked for eighteen years as a machine operator in shoe factories. She became active in the Boot and Shoeworkers Union and had organized women workers for the NWTUL. In 1909 she and her guest, Margaret Bondfield, had been active in the New York garment workers' strike. In 1917 she was drafted by the National Defense Advisory Committee to serve as assistant to Mary Van Kleek, who had just been appointed chief of the newly organized Women in Industry Service of the Department of Labor. In 1919 Mary Van Kleek resigned and Mary Anderson took her place. Shortly after, as a result of the lobbying of the

NWTUL, the service became the Women's Bureau of the Department of Labor. Anderson was named as its first chief, a post she retained until 1944. She worked closely with Margaret Bondfield on women's wartime problems.

Women at the 1919 Peace Conference

In 1914 the outbreak of war began to change the position of women, at least temporarily, and reinvigorated their organizations. Shortages of man-power drew them into war plants, where they assumed new responsibilities and earned newfound respect. Thus women members of the trade union movement, feminists, suffragettes, and leaders of the peace move-ment expected to have a role in the forthcoming peace conference. They claimed this as payment for their wartime services—but only a few were to obtain a hearing.

As the war drew to a close, plans began to be made for a postwar world—a world that had seen the Russian revolution and the end of the tsarist monarchy—a world that echoed increasingly with the demands of labor. The voice of the latter had been heard in numerous wartime meet-ings and it was recognized that labor must have a place at the Peace Conference. The trade union movement had no intention of leaving to chance or to governments what its place at the Conference might be. An International Trade Union Conference was held in Berne in 1918 and the following spring a French Trade Union Congress was held in Paris.[24] Both had been convened to discuss labor's demands at the Peace Conference.

The channel that the Peace Conference provided for this purpose was the Commission for International Labor Legislation, chaired by Samuel Gompers, president of the American Federation of Labor. Many of the members of the commission had participated in the International Asso-ciation for Labor Legislation and drew on this experience in creating a new international body with a broader mandate than any of the existing intergovernmental organizations. Although the commission dealt with a number of issues that directly affected women, no woman was a member of it. However, many of the women leaders made their way to Paris and obtained interviews either with members of the Commission on Interna-tional Labor Legislation or with those drafting the Covenant of the League of Nations. The views they expressed were as diverse as the movements they supported, varying from the prohibitionists, to the suffragists, to those most concerned with the conditions faced by women wage earners. Their difficulty in obtaining recognition at the peace negotiations was a reflection of the situation of women nationally where the lack of broad organizational strength has been a handicap that has not been fully overcome up to the present time.[25]

The most effective woman negotiator was Margaret Bondfield, who, as a member of the TUC General Council, had represented her organization both at the 1918 Trade Union Conference in Berne and the French Trade Union Congress in Paris. At the latter she was accompanied by Mary Macarthur and Sophy Sanger, one of the founders of the British section of the International Association for Labor Legislation. Bondfield took advantage of being in the same city as the Peace Conference to call on the British delegation. She managed to convince George Barnes, a member of the British War Cabinet, representing the British government on the Commission on International Labor Legislation and long a colleague of Bondfield in the labor movement, to insist upon provisions concerning women in what was to become Part XIII of the Peace Treaties. Part XIII provided for the establishment of the International Labor Organization. As a result of this meeting, on March 11, 1919, Barnes proposed two amendments to the text of the future ILO Constitution: one to Article 3 to provide that when any question concerning women's labor was under discussion, one of the advisers to each delegate should be a woman; the other, to Article 9, requiring the director of the International Labor Office "to employ a certain number of women on his staff."[26] These changes were agreed to by the commission.

Margaret Bondfield was by no means the only woman's voice at the Peace Conference. Also converging on Paris were delegations of Belgian, French, American, and other British women, but unfortunately they arrived very late in the proceedings and submitted a disparate set of demands that lacked focus. The International Council of Women (ICW) demanded equality of opportunity for men and women, including equal pay for equal work; participation of women "on the same footing as men in the deliberations of all international commissions concerned with labor organization"; and limitation of the working week to forty-four hours and suppression of night work for women, where possible, *without creating a situation unfavorable to women*. These demands took the form of a resolution submitted by three ICW representatives, Mrs. Jules Siegfried,

Mrs. Avril de Sainte Croix of France, and Mrs. Tivoli of Italy, all leaders of feminist movements, deeply concerned with the welfare of working women. They were not, however, themselves wage earners.

The views of the Conference of Allied Women Suffragists were presented by Mme Brunschwig from France (who also spoke for the delegations as a whole) supported by Mrs. Borden Harriman, a wealthy socialite, who had been involved in both the woman suffrage and the settlement house movements, and Mrs. George Rublee, a fighter for women's economic rights (both from the United States), Margaret Corbett Ashby from Britain, and Mlle Van Den Ples of Belgium. These were all society leaders and social reformers rather than academicians or technicians. Mme Brunschwig submitted to the Commission a series of specific proposals and amendments, some dealing with the Preamble to the proposed ILO Constitution, others dealing with voting procedures and methods of naming delegates. With respect to the ILO's Governing Body it was proposed that there must be some women members. One of the resolutions urged that "a female labour committee should be set up in every country consisting of women alone (representatives of Governments, Trade Unions, Associations, scientific women, women doctors, etc.) to whom should be submitted for advice all exceptional legislative measures proposed concerning women." Mlle Van Den Ples discussed the agenda of the proposed first conference of the new organization and asked that it include the issue of half-time work for married women. She also asked for inclusion in the agenda of the item, "Equal Pay for equal work without distinction of sex."

Margaret Corbett Ashby asked that the agenda be amended to include payment to a woman during the period she was forbidden to work before and after childbirth. Mrs. Borden Harriman stressed the right of women to enter all professions and asked that the upcoming conference provide that girls have the same vocational training facilities as boys.

Other members of the delegation came from professionally oriented organizations and trade unions, such as the Office des Interets Feminines with Mme Duchene, an influential member of the Council of French Women and an ardent pacifist as spokeswoman; les Syndicats Professionals Independents (Beckman); and les Syndicats Ouvriers Confédérés, represented by Mlle Bouillot and Mme Jeanne Bouvier, a former factory worker, maid, dressmaker, labor union activist, and author. She had been a member of the Conseil Supérieur du Travail, the Comité des Salaires de la Seine, and of the Commission Paritaire du Chômage du dix-huitième

Arrondissment. Miss Bouillot called for a forty-four-hour week instead of the forty-eight-hour week included in the General Principles (or Labor Charter, of the ILO) and Mme Duchene stressed the need when dealing with minimum wages, to ensure equal pay for men and women. Jeanne Bouvier, speaking for the Federated Dressmakers Union, asked that social insurance for women include unemployment insurance.

Marie Verone, a French advocate known for her eloquence, was the newly elected chairman of la Ligue Française pour le Droit des Femmes. She regretted that the Commission on Labor Legislation was solely composed of men and called for recognition in the peace treaties of the need for minimum equal wages so as to avoid international economic competition. She then submitted a list of the demands of the Ligue, which did not in practice differ greatly from those of the other organizations represented.

Finally, Mme Brunschwig handed to the Commission a series of resolutions agreed upon by the women's delegation as a whole, which contained provisions relating to duration of work, unemployment, hygiene, and child labor.[27] Their long, and in some cases repetitive, statements detracted from their effectiveness, but the fact that they received a formal hearing from the commission lent support to the various amendments that Barnes had introduced following his talks with Margaret Bondfield, and provided a platform for many of the plans advocated by the various groups in the years ahead.[28] Mary Anderson and Rose Schneiderman arrived in Paris with the proposals of the NWTUL of the United States. These called for: compulsory education of children up to eighteen years of age; abolition of child labor; an eight-hour day and a forty-four-hour week; no night work for women; one day of rest in seven; equal pay for equal work; equal opportunities for men and women in trade and technical training; and social insurance and old-age benefits as well as pensions and maternity benefits.[29] They met with Barnes who showed them the commission's draft provisions, including the proposals of Margaret Bondfield. They agreed that the Bondfield provisions were the best that could be obtained and that they would permit U.S. women to support the conclusions of the commission, establishing the ILO and determining the agenda for its first Annual Conference.[30]

While one group of women were preoccupied with the ILO, another group—with some overlapping—were lobbying in connection with the Covenant of the League of Nations. Lady Aberdeen, then president of the ICW, was the leader of a joint delegation of the ICW and the Inter-Allied

Conference of Women Suffragists. They were accorded a hearing on April 10, 1919, before a plenary session of the Commission drafting the Covenant of the League of Nations. This was the result of repeated requests by Lady Aberdeen to the commission's chairman, President Wilson, who declared that the delegation represented "the mothers of the world."[31] The delegation asked that women be eligible to occupy posts in all bodies of the League, that members of the League agree to suppress traffic in women and children, create international bureaus for public health, control and reduce armaments, and recognize the principle of women suffrage. This last provision alarmed the Commission. Delegate after delegate protested their devotion to the cause of women but unanimously declared that the League Covenant was not the place to deal with women's political rights. However, the delegation was more successful in achieving a provision in Article 23 that members "will endeavor to secure and maintain fair and humane conditions of labor for men, women and children," a provision that became the responsibility of ILO.

Despite the efforts of Lady Aberdeen and the delegation she headed, as well as the provision in the Covenant that "all positions under or in connection with the League, including the Secretariat, shall be open equally to men and women," old attitudes continued to prevail. The participation of women "was delimited by a conception that women's special space was that of social and humanitarian issues, as well as international peace." Only one woman ever held the post as head of section in the Secretariat and that was the social section. When the Assembly met for the first time there were two women as substitute delegates. Nine years later there was only one woman delegate and eleven substitutes. The experience of an Austrian substitute delegate who sat as a full delegate in the absence of her male colleague on the committee that dealt with finance, budgets, and the codification of international law epitomizes the climate of opinion. When she took her seat, the chairman was said to have asked, "Have you lost your way Madam?"[32] This attitude continued to dominate its successor organization, the United Nations, where for many years most of the women participants were allocated to the Committee on Social and Humanitarian Affairs.

2. Women's Role During the
First Twenty Years

The participation of European and American women in the Peace Conference discussions gave new impetus to the desire for international action and the need for an organized approach by women advocates. One step in this direction was the first International Congress of Working Women, held in Washington, D.C., in 1919. Its purpose was to lay before the ILO "the well considered recommendations of the working women of the world."[1] The call for this congress had come from the veteran organization, the National Women's Trade Union League of America (NWTUL). Rose Schneiderman, vice president, and Mary Anderson, then chief of the Women in Industry Service, a federal wartime agency, had presented the views of NWTUL to the Paris Peace Conference.[2] While in Paris they had worked with a number of the European women to plan a meeting in Washington to develop a unified women's approach to the new international Organization's first Annual Conference. The NWTUL then agreed to organize and sponsor the International Congress of Working Women.[3]

The International Congress of Working Women

The Congress was attended by representatives of accredited trade unions from nineteen countries. Most of the women had attended the Paris Peace Conference and all were well known to each other through the growing network of women's organizations.[4] From the United Kingdom came Margaret Bondfield (British Trades Union Congress) and Mary Macarthur (the National Federation of Women Workers);[5] from France, Jeanne Bouvier (the National Women's Federation of France and the Colonies, as well as the French Federation of Clothing Workers); from Canada, Kathleen

Derry (member of the Boot and Shoe Workers Union and spokesman for the Dominion Trades and Labour Congress); from Italy came Mrs. Casartelli-Cabrini (the Women's National Association of Italy and the Central Committee of the Government Employment Bureau); and from Norway, Betzy Kjelsberg (factory inspector and representative of the Women's Telegraphers Union). All of these women, as well as most of the other participants in the congress, were to attend the first International Labor Conference as members of the delegations and were subsequently to play a substantial role in the work of the ILO.

The agenda of the congress was based on the items concerning women that had been allocated to the first International Labor Conference by the Peace Conference. These included employment of women before and after childbirth, at night, and in unhealthy processes; similar questions concerning children, including minimum age of employment; the principle of the eight-hour day; prevention of employment; and the application of the Berne Convention regarding prohibition of white phosphorous in matches.

The congress agenda, however, also included some items of a more broad-based and ideological nature. For example, the congress asked for international conventions for equal distribution of raw materials in the world.[6] It also sought to ensure far more women representatives at the forthcoming ILO Conference than were likely to be appointed to the official delegations of most countries. The two real successes of the congress were the establishment of an ongoing International Federation of Working Women (IFWW), and the thorough preparation of its participants for their role in the first Annual Conference of the International Labor Organization. The IFWW was the first international women's trade union body which united many of the efforts of the national organizations such as the NWTUL.[7]

At the close of the 1919 Congress its secretary wrote to the president of the International Labor Conference requesting changes in the proposals concerning hours of work and those dealing with the minimum age and conditions of work for young persons. The letter states:

> In behalf of the International Congress of Working Women, it is my privilege to ask you to lay before the International Labor Conference of the League of Nations for their consideration and, we hope, favorable action, this expression of the views of the delegated representatives of the working women of 13 of the nations signatory of the League of Nations Covenant.

The following is the Resolution:

The first International Congress of Working Women requests the first International Congress of Labor of the League of Nations that an international convention establish:

(1) For all workers a maximum 8 hour day and 44 hour work week.
(2) That the weekly rest period shall have an uninterrupted duration of at least one day and one half.
(3) That in continuous industries a minimum rest period of one half hour shall be accorded in each 8 hour shift.

The resolution referring to young persons called for a sixteen-year minimum age limit, with an eighteen-year minimum limit for work in mines and quarries, and stated that the legal workday for young persons between sixteen and eighteen years of age "shall be shorter than the legal workday for adults." With respect to night work, no minors shall work between 6 P.M. and 7 A.M., while work in unhealthy processes should be prohibited for young persons. Administrative provisions were included in the resolution, calling for work permits and inspection. It also called for compulsory continuation schools for minors up to the age of eighteen.[8]

The ILO Conference was duly respectful of the efforts of the Congress of Working Women (thus setting the precedent for later, more formal relations with nongovernmental organizations), and referred the first resolution to the committee dealing with hours of work, and the second to the committee dealing with the employment of young persons. However, neither committee fully accepted the proposals of the Women's Congress; the ILO Conference kept the working week at forty-eight hours, and the minimum age at fourteen for most purposes.[9] The question of weekly rest was dealt with at a subsequent conference.

The general thrust of ILO's standard setting was thus consonant with the goals of the Congress but it was far more conservative. This could only be expected in an organization concerned with legislation. Governments are seldom prepared to act on international agreements until similar provisions exist within their own legal framework. Furthermore, a big international organization has both divergencies among its member states as well as its constituent employers' and workers' bodies. If the organization is to achieve any form of consensus-making action possible, the standards must reflect their range of views. Accommodation has become increasingly difficult as the evolving membership incorporates differing cultures and economic needs.

Women at the 1919 International Labor Conference

The first International Labor Conference opened, in accordance with the plans agreed upon in the course of the Peace Conference, in Washington, D.C., in October 1919. These plans provided that the ILO's legislative organ would meet annually and would conduct its business both through plenary sessions and technical and standing committees.

The standing committees deal primarily with the way the Conference conducts its work. There is a Selection Committee responsible for the day-to-day operation of the Conference. A Credentials Committee has the delicate task of determining whether employer and worker delegates are truly chosen by the "most representative organization" in their respective countries. If the credentials of either an employer or worker are ruled invalid, both lose their votes. The Standing Orders Committee formulates and occasionally amends the rules of procedure of the conference, its committees, and subcommittees. While it is an essential tool of the conference, its responsibilities are largely procedural. Other committees have been added since the first conference. One is the Finance Committee, not foreseen at the Peace Conference, whose role is precisely what its title implies. It is the only committee which is composed exclusively of governments. The two remaining standing committees are concerned with the substantive activities of the ILO as a whole. The Resolutions Committee determines which proposals, other than those dealing with technical items on the agenda, are within the competence of the ILO and should be put to the Plenary to be voted upon. The Application of Standards Committee (previously entitled the Committee on the Application of Conventions and Recommendations) is the major tool for assessing the implementation by governments of the conventions and other instruments adopted by the Conference. This committee is part of the enforcement machinery of the ILO which later served as a model for a number of intergovernmental bodies.

When the first International Labor Conference opened in Washington, although the United States played host and its secretary of labor chaired the opening session, it could only participate as an observer since the United States was not a member of the ILO, having rejected membership both in the ILO and the League of Nations in the week just preceding the conference. Samuel Gompers, president of the American Federation of Labor, addressed the conference on several occasions and Florence Thorne, AFL director of research and an old friend of many women attending the meetings, "observed" many sessions. Moreover, Grace Abbott was named by the Secretary-General of the Conference to serve on the staff as secretary of the Commission on Employment of Children. There were twenty-three women from fifteen countries out of a total of 269 participants from forty countries.[10] The British delegation was the only one to have women advisers for all its four delegates. In addition to the two stalwarts from the Peace Conference and the Women's Congress, Margaret Bondfield and Mary Macarthur, there were also Mrs. B. Majoribanks, late chief of the Employment Bureau for Women in a business firm—adviser to the employers delegation—and Constance Smith, senior lady inspector of factories, government adviser. The latter had been an active participant in many of the prewar and wartime congresses and was a member of the British women's network. In that capacity she had spoken on women's rights in both Canada and the United States. Sophy Sanger of Great Britain, who had been the founder of the British Association for Labor Legislation, was appointed to the staff of the Conference and served as the secretary of the Commission on the Employment of Women.

Both Jeanne Bouvier of France and Margaret Bondfield of Britain served as workers' members on that commission, as did Miss Majerova of Czechoslovakia, municipal councillor in Prague, all of whom had also participated in the Women's Congress. Two other women who began a long association with the ILO were Mrs. Casartelli-Cabrini of Italy, the general secretary of the National Women's Association of Italy, and Mrs. Gabrielle Letellier of France, inspector of factories, both government advisers.

Constance Smith chaired the Commission on the Employment of Women which dealt with two conventions—one on employment before and after childbirth and the other on night work for women. The former covered a variety of provisions governing maternity benefits in industrial and commercial undertakings. The latter barred women from employment between 10 P.M. and 5 A.M. In speaking to the maternity convention Jeanne Bouvier was the protagonist for a provision that women were not to work for six weeks after the baby's birth and could leave six weeks beforehand if provided with a medical certificate.[11] Kerstin Hesselgren of Sweden opposed the six weeks' leave provisions which she thought should be decreased in order to encourage ratification. The Convention also provided that when absent from work a woman should be paid benefits "sufficient for the full and healthy maintenance of her child," and should be entitled to free attendance by a doctor or certified midwife.

Smith and Macarthur successfully opposed an effort to delete a provision which placed restrictions on the employer's right of dismissal because of absence. The British government vainly sought to exclude commercial enterprises from the scope of the Convention.

In a 1939 Report to the Conference, the Director declared that "The Convention concerning the employment of women before and after childbirth set up standards considerably in advance of current legislation at the time when it was adopted. . . . In 1919 not a single State was in a position to ratify it at once."[12] Twenty years later only sixteen states had ratified; evidence that Hesselgren's warning had some justification.

The provision in the night work Convention prohibiting the employment of women after 10 P.M. or before 5 A.M. was challenged by a number of the women participants. Casartelli-Cabrini strongly urged that women should not work after 9 P.M. in order to have eight hours of rest. She asked that this proposal constitute a recommendation and as such be submitted to the Governing Body for consideration at the next conference. Gabrielle Letellier pointed out that when a shift system was used, debarring women from too long a period of night work might force management to eliminate rest periods. The issue of protective legislation for women only as epitomized in this convention has never ceased to be the target of attack. One of the first voices raised in opposition came from Betzy Kjelsberg of Norway in 1919 who stated: "I am against special protective laws for women, except pregnant women and women nursing children under one year of age because I believe that we are furthering the cause of good labor laws most by working toward the prohibition of all absolutely unnecessary night work. It is hard to see old worn out men and young boys in the most critical period of development work during the night. Many accidents take place in the middle of the night when the workers are most tired." She went on to explain that she would work for the gradual elimination of night work as regards men as well as women; thus opening up the controversy between the protectionists and the equal righters at the first International Labor Conference.[13]

The Commission on Employment of Children also developed two conventions, one setting the minimum age for admission to industrial employment at fourteen and the other prohibiting night work for children under eighteen (with a number of exceptions). Mary Macarthur unsuccessfully sought to eliminate an article providing for exceptions to the minimum age where local conditions make it inapplicable or subject to modification. Margaret Bondfield was more successful in obtaining a revision of a clause relating to the application of the convention to India, over the objections of the Indian representative, limiting the exemption to children under twelve.

The conference also adopted a recommendation that women and children be prohibited from engaging in activities where there was a danger of lead poisoning. This was the first of a series of conventions and recommendations dealing with occupational safety, underground work, weight limitations, benzine, radiation, and the provision of health and welfare services—issues which have been gradually extended and updated to become a respected, applied, and enforced part of the International Labor Code, now in most countries applied equally to men and women.

When Mary Marcarthur returned home after the Conference, she was queried by reporters as to the contribution of women; she said, with a smile, "I think the women did very well."

In addition to its legislative business, the Conference, at this first session, had to elect the members of its administrative organ, the Governing Body, which in turn would elect the director. Albert Thomas was first named provisional Director until agreement was reached in the Governing Body a few months later. The two candidates were Thomas, a French political leader, and Harold Butler, a senior British civil servant, one of the designers of the ILO, and Secretary-General of the Conference. Thomas won and appointed Butler as deputy director.

The fiery and dynamic Albert Thomas had been a leader in the French socialist movement and minister of munitions in France during the war. He led the International Labor Office during its seminal years, until his premature death in 1932. Indefatigable—statesman, orator, and administrator—he traveled the world making and maintaining relations with governments, employer groups, and trade unions. His concepts shaped the unique role of the Office. He regarded the legislative and administrative organs of the conference and the governing body with the kind of benign neglect that Frenchmen often give to their parliaments. The professionals would do the job—the director, his cabinet and the staff—and then negotiate with the ILO constituencies. Implementation of this approach was facilitated by the tripartite structure which allowed considerable room for maneuver. But neither Thomas nor Harold Butler wanted women in policymaking positions. They relied on women as efficient clerical workers, researchers, editors, and technicians. One of the rare exceptions was Marguerite Thibert who joined the staff in 1926. Born in 1886 in Burgundy, she was the daughter of a wholesale hardware merchant. As a child she had witnessed the brutality of mounted policemen charging the strikers at a dockyard. This incident and the tutelage of a liberal uncle led her into the socialist party where she met Albert Thomas. As a militant socialist she had campaigned in local elections and also became the fourth woman in France to receive a doctorate in letters.

Thomas's concept of an international staff greatly affected the role of both women and men throughout the history of the ILO. Even before the ILO moved to its permanent quarters the Director had invited the staff to elect a committee with a mandate to ensure easier and more regular contacts between himself and the staff as a whole. This was the origin of the staff union whose role had to be developed within the framework of an international civil service.

One of Thomas's first acts was to establish the ILO headquarters in Geneva and to convene the third International Labor Conference there in 1921. (The second Conference, held in Genoa, dealt with maritime issues and the only woman participant was the daughter of the Netherlands workers' delegate, Jan Oudegueest, who occasionally replaced him in a session.)

Just prior to the 1921 Conference the International Congress of Working Women held its second session in Geneva—where the International Labor Conference was to meet—and transformed itself into an International Federation. One of its first acts was to establish relations with the ILO and to invite an observer to the congress. Martha Mundt, a staff member of German nationality, was sent as the observer. She had already organized a liaison service with women's groups. The formal objectives of the federation were: "to examine all projects for legislation proposed by the International Labour Conference of the League of Nations" and "to promote the appointment of working women on organizations affecting the welfare of the workers."[14] The congress at this second session did not limit itself to items on the agenda of the ILO. It took action on a wide range of issues: disarmament (an issue of deep concern at that time to many of the other women's organizations such as the Cause and Cure of War); famine in Russia; unemployment; employment of children and youths under eighteen on board ship; the use of lead in paint; anthrax; and conditions affecting agricultural workers.

Women in the ILO's Formative Years

While a number of women participated in the 1921 Conference, only two held any office; Mary Fitzgerald of South Africa, president of the Women's

Industrial League and a member of the workers delegation, and Margaret Bondfield. However, the women served not only on the one committee specifically dealing with women but also on two committees dealing with subjects equally applicable to men and women, and one on a key standing committee. Margaret Bondfield was the reporter of the second Agricultural Committee, composed largely of women, which led to one convention dealing with the age of admission of children to employment in agriculture, and three recommendations concerned with night work of women and young persons and maternity benefits. Mary Fitzgerald was elected vice chairman of the Committee on Anthrax. Gabrielle Letellier and Jeanne Bouvier sat on the Committee on Weekly Rest. Betzy Kjelsberg was a government member of the Selection Committee, the standing committee responsible for the conference proceedings. This committee determines the size and allocation of members to the various technical committees, and schedules the time between plenary sessions and committee meetings. The allocation is made in accord with the nominations of each of the three groups.

Conference action regarding agriculture was strenuously objected to by the French government. It insisted that conditions in industry and agriculture were totally dissimilar, that the peace treaty never mentioned agricultural workers, and that, given the devastation of war, it would be imprudent to add financial burdens to countries possibly resulting in diminished production. Eventually, such matters fell within the province of the International Institute of Agriculture in Rome. When the conference ignored the French protest, the latter took the matter to the Permanent International Court of Justice for an Advisory Opinion.[15] Unfortunately for France, the Court affirmed the competence of ILO, and by 1939 no less than seven conventions affecting agricultural workers had been adopted.

The British National Council of Women for its part objected to the ILO's inclusion of women in agriculture on the ground that protection "should be based not upon sex but upon the nature of the occupation." A member of the National Board declared "there is nothing logically to prevent it (protective legislation) being further extended to include brain workers." Feminists, she said, must combat "differential sex legislation."[16]

The next year passed with few women appearing at the conference and no woman officer. The situation improved slightly in 1923 with ten nations including women in their delegations, almost all of whom had been at one of the previous meetings—the Peace Conference, or in Washington,

D.C.—and many of whom were factory inspectors in their own countries. Three governments, Canada, Japan, and Norway sent women as full government delegates, two of whom were presidents of their national councils of women. The Canadian delegation included Miss C. E. Carmichael, president of the National Council of Women, and Violet Markham (Mrs. James Carrothers), a British authority on labor legislation, who knew Canada well, and was a friend of the Canadian prime minister. Violet Markham Carrothers also served on the Governing Body, substituting for the Canadian minister of labor where, as noted by Albert Thomas, "This was the first time a woman had participated in the work of the Governing Body and her able collaboration was much appreciated."[17]

The Conference had two committees dealing with labor inspection—one on the nature of the functions and powers of inspectors and the other on the organization of inspection. Not surprisingly, women played an active role in both since many of them were factory inspectors. The only woman worker representative on these committees was Margaret Bondfield who had recently been elected as the first woman chairman of the British Trades Union Congress. The balance were all government representatives.

A direct consequence of the participation of women factory inspectors was the adoption of a recommendation providing that the labor inspectorate should include women as well as men, that they should have the same powers and duties as the men, and equal opportunity for promotion. As Bondfield said, "good laws, of course, are important but the good and effective administration of those laws is equally important."

Shortly after the 1923 International Labor Conference the International Federation of Working Women held a key session in Vienna to discuss the problems of working women, to review the progress being made by the ILO, and to consider its own role within the international trade union movement.[18] Most of the participants had been active in the earlier women's movements as well as in the previous ILO sessions. From the United States came Margaret Drier Robins and her sister, Mary Drier, Mabel Swartz, Elizabeth Christman, and other leaders of the National Women's Trade Union League who had been at the helm since its inception; Mary Anderson, Rose Schneiderman, Pauline Newman, and Frieda Miller, all of whom were to play top-level roles in their own countries and in the ILO, as well as Agnes Nestor and Agnes Johnson, trade union organizers whose activities gave standing to U.S. women in the labor movement.[19]

The British delegation, led by Margaret Bondfield and Julia Varley, included several members of the British Women's Trade Union League, as well as leading labor organizers. The French delegation again was led by Jeanne Bouvier, supported by Jeanne Chevenard and Suzanne Lion—women who were to participate in ILO conferences for many years.

Much of the congress discussion—and resolutions—dealt with women's work for peace. The women condemned the military occupation of the Ruhr, and called for a world conference to deal with economic issues. Specific measures to organize women into trade unions were unanimously adopted. The congress then reviewed the progress of ratifications of the ILO conventions adopted between 1919 and 1923, and raised the issue as to whether standards should be applied by legislation or collective agreement. The ILO Constitution, it may be recalled, requires that governments must submit each convention adopted by the conference to its national authority with a view to ratification. If a government ratifies, it must implement the convention through legislation "or other action" and report to the ILO what actions it has taken. The U.S. women sought to have standards agreed to through collective bargaining, while the Europeans wanted them applied through legislation; a difference which reflected national practice in their respective countries. Another cause of disagreement was the concept of family allowances—endorsed by the Europeans but feared by the United States as being likely to keep wages down.

The major disagreement developed over the constitution of the federation itself. The European delegations were unanimous in their belief that, if the International Federation of Working Women was really to serve the best interests of the organized working women of Europe, there must be a women's department as an integral part of the International Federation of Trade Unions (the international union body that had organized the wartime labor meetings and the recognized nongovernmental trade union organization working with the ILO)—an organization officered and controlled by men. The U.S. delegates objected on the ground that a women's department in such an organization could not achieve the goals of the International Federation of Working Women. The issue was finally postponed until the following congress, when the United States lost and the federation became part of the larger body.[20]

For the next few years (1924 until 1928) very few women attended the International Labor Conference, but those who did vigorously espoused the women's point of view, although with little immediate impact. Some of the early leaders, such as Gabrielle Letellier of France, Betzy Kjelsberg of Norway, and Kerstin Hesselgren of Denmark did yeoman service. But the dominant woman throughout this period was Margaret Bondfield. In 1924 when she was elected to Parliament and became minister of labor, she served as British government member of the Governing Body, and attended the Annual Conference. (However, she only participated in the two opening sessions, with a male substitute replacing her for the balance of the meeting.) In 1926, after the fall of the Labour government, she returned to ILO as a member of the workers' group. She served as vice chairman in 1926 of the Committee on Simplification of Inspection of Migrants on Board Ship, and in 1927 and 1928 as chairman and vice chairman of the Committee on Article 408.[21] In 1930, with the Labour Party back in power, Margaret Bondfield was again minister of labor, and returned to the Conference as government delegate, serving as chairman of the Selection Committee.

During this period only a few items on the Conference agenda were of direct concern to women, namely utilization of spare time (Betzy Kjelsberg served as reporter for this item) and protection of females on board ship. Women migrants were often treated as slaves, forced into hard labor, beaten and sexually abused. In 1926 the Conference adopted a recommendation using a phrase that has a gently archaic flavor, which called for "a properly qualified woman who has no other duty to fulfil on board . . . to give such emigrants any material or moral assistance" as they might need.

During the late 1920s the major emphasis of the conference was on such items as sickness insurance, minimum wage-fixing machinery, and protection against accidents for dockers. In 1930 it again took up an item of long-term concern to women, namely the reduction of hours of work, which clearly affected the conditions of work of both sexes. It also for the first time dealt with forced labor, opening the ILO future debates on human rights. Most of the women who attended these sessions of the annual conference were those who had become perennial participants, by then equally concerned with the general issues being dealt with, and the work of the standing committees. Examples of these women were Kerstin Hesselgren, Gabrielle Letellier, Betzy Kjelsberg, and Gertrude Stemberg from the government side, and Anne Loughlin, Julia Varley, and Eugenia Wasniewska from the workers.

Meantime, the network of women's organizations moved in new directions. With women suffrage achieved in most Western nations and with no immediate drive to prevent mobilization for war, the new goals were centered on equality—in suffrage, in political positions, and in conditions of livelihood.[22] They also sought an increase in the proportion of women employees in League of Nations proceedings. These goals represented a sharp departure from those of the National Women's Trade Union League and the International Federation of Working Women, which increasingly concentrated their activities on influencing the ILO with respect to women's problems and on national and local trade union issues. There were, however, frequent issues on which both groups collaborated in their approach, especially with respect to conditions of work for working women; there was also frequent overlapping in membership among all the organizations.

As part of their interest in international affairs both the International Council of Women and the International Alliance of Women relocated their headquarters in Geneva. In 1920 the president of the Danish National Council of Women (NCW) spoke before the plenary session of the League of Nations Assembly on the subject of traffic in women and children. She was the first woman to speak in the assembly. In 1925 these organizations became part of a multi-organizational women's committee, the Joint Committee of Representative Organizations. The members of this group included the Women's International League for Peace and Freedom, the World's Women's Christian Temperance Union, the World's Young Women's Christian Association, the International Council of Nurses, the World's Union for International Concord, and the International Federation of University Women.

The aim of the joint committee was to use their combined strength to influence the League of Nations both on issues such as world peace, world health, the abolition of prostitution, and on programs such as child welfare, education, and the wages and working conditions of the working class—an issue which had been delegated to the ILO. The joint committee was recognized by the League as a strong pressure group, and their proposals were duly heard and acknowledged, but they never obtained their objective of having a higher proportion of women employees and women delegates participate in League proceedings. The Secretary-General called attention to the principle of equality set forth in Article 7 of the League Covenant and used it to justify his position that he could make no special provision for women.[23] Ultimately, in 1937, the Assembly approved the appointment of a Committee for the Study of the Legal Status of Women—thus paving the way for the Commission on the Status of Women established later by the United Nations.

One of the early acts of the League was to authorize the inclusion of representatives of private international organizations on some of the advisory committees of the Assembly. Avril de St. Croix, vice president of the ICW, served on several committees dealing with the prevention of traffic in women and children. Organization representatives also served on a number of other committees, both of the League and the ILO, dealing with such subjects as health, infant mortality, child welfare, forced labor, and mandates. ILO representatives also attended a number of League committees, served on occasion as expert advisers or participated in joint committees. One such committee, initiated by the health section of the League, included in its mandate industrial hygiene. Dr. Alice Hamilton was chosen as one of three "assessors" of the committee. She also served on the ILO Committee on Industrial Hygiene. She was the first woman to serve on the staff of the Harvard Medical School and had achieved an international reputation for her work in identifying and controlling diseases caused by industrial poisons.

In his report to the 1928 session of the International Labor Conference, the Director included a section entitled "Women's Organisations" which stated that "another of the great forces working for justice is the women's movement, which, if it sometimes seem disjointed or incoherent, is nevertheless making steady progress. It has again manifested itself in 1927 in its twofold aspect—the general feminist movement claiming absolute equality between women and men, and the working women's movement with its special claims, which sometimes coincide with working men's claims and sometimes are opposed to them particularly on organization problems." He noted that at the last meeting of the International Council of Women it was decided that "no steps should be taken in connection with women's protective legislation without previous consultation with the working women's organisations concerned."[24] This recognition by the director of the role of women's organizations was one facet of ILO's efforts to involve the international private sector. It was not until 1949, however, after the United Nations had provided for formal consultative status with its Economic and Social Council, that the ILO made similar arrangements for participation of nongovernmental organizations in the deliberations of the Conference.[25]

While the ILO continued to stress protective legislation, the international women's organizations in the 1920s and early 1930s put increasing emphasis on the issue of equality. The drive for equality, with all its ramifications, began to override the reformist concept that protection of women against exploitation through legislation must precede efforts for political and social opportunity.

In the United States the most militant and single-minded exponent of the drive for political equality was the National Women's Party (NWP),[26] headed by Alice Paul, who, as mentioned, had introduced the idea of amending the constitution to guarantee women complete equality with men. It became the leading proponent of the Equal Rights Amendment (ERA) and thus the active opponent of protective labor laws for women.[27] This position was naturally greatly resented by Mary Anderson, chief of the Department of Labor Women's Bureau, and all those women leaders who had brought about women's protective labor legislation in the United States and had worked to the same end with their colleagues in other countries.

Paul's approach to equality met with a warm reception from some colleagues in Great Britain who had also begun to rethink their goals for the women's movement. Suffrage in Britain in the 1920s and early 1930s was not equal. Single women under thirty as well as certain other categories could not vote. Thus one goal of the suffragists was to achieve universal suffrage. This battle was led by Ellen Wilkinson, the only woman Member of Parliament (after Margaret Bondfield had lost her seat in 1924) who came from a labor background. She also initiated a campaign to have protective legislation apply equally to men and women.[28]

While the ILO was later to act on the general issue of equal rights for women, it did so from the point of economic and social rights, their primary responsibility, and not such political rights as woman suffrage. Meanwhile, it continued its efforts to broaden international protective legislation. In 1931 two substantive items on the agenda, namely the age of admission to employment of children and revision of the night work convention, were of particular concern to women trade unionists who came in exceptionally large numbers. Eleven women sat as members or substitutes on the Committee on Age of Admission of Children to Employment in Non-Industrial Occupations, with Dora Schmidt of Switzerland as reporter. A member of the Swiss Federal Office of Industry, Arts and Crafts, and Labor, she was an intrepid war-horse for the rights of children and women over a twelve-year period in which she represented her government at the ILO. Another veteran, Gabrielle Letellier, was the reporter of the committee dealing with the proposed revision of the Convention on Employment of Women during the Night (the convention adopted in 1919), designed to give it greater flexibility. Eighteen women were members of this committee, but only eleven were workers. Gertrude Hanna, secretary of the Confederation of German Trade Unions, served as vice chairman of the committee. In speaking to this item in the plenary session of the Conference, both Kerstin Hesselgren of Sweden and Miss Martindale of the United Kingdom spoke on behalf of the revision. Eugenia Wasniewska, worker adviser from Poland, objected to the revision stating that the Office study was inadequate, and then asked that "the section of the Office which deals with Women's Work should be extended and an Advisory Committee set up composed of representatives of the professional women's organizations interested in the problem." The revision of the convention was approved by 54 to 43, but this did not provide the two-thirds needed for adoption.[29]

The following year the Conference completed action on the Convention on Minimum Age for Admission to Employment and Night Work for Young Persons, on the one hand extending the scope to new occupations, and on the other making some of its provisions more flexible. Thirteen women participated in the session, all veterans of previous meetings. Julia Varley served as vice chairman of the Workers' Group of the Conference, but there were no women committee officers. Betzy Kjelsberg, speaking to the inadequacy of the representation of women, pointed out: "Many countries have never appointed women as members of their delegations, in spite of the fact that questions of the most vital importance to women have been on the Agenda. Countries which formerly had women in their delegations now refer to financial difficulties. When sacrifices are to be made, women are always the first victims. . . . The interests of the great work for peace between the nations cannot but gain by the collaboration of women. Women represent the mothers and in a family the fathers and the mothers must cooperate if good results are to be obtained."[30]

Global Trends in the Women's Movement: The Interwar Period

One reason for the relatively poor showing of women during the 1930s was the economic situation at home. The depression cast its shadow over the whole decade. "The depression turned what had been the previous decade's joyous discovery of freedom to work into a bitter defense of the right to a job; it buried the options and choices for which women had struggled beneath the relentless pressure of family need."[31]

By 1933 nearly 13 million people in the United States alone were out of work. As jobs became scarce hostility to women wage earners grew. Increasingly, even in women's magazines stress was laid on the conviction that women's place was in the home, that healthy families required a traditional wife. The U.S. Federal Economy Act of 1932 decreed that if there were personnel reductions, married employees should be fired first if the spouse had a federal job. The Brotherhood of Railway and Steamship Clerks declared that no married woman was entitled to a job if a husband could support her. By 1939 legislators in twenty-one states were debating bills to bar married women from state jobs. While the National Industrial Recovery Act of 1933 resulted in a significant increase in women's wages, the differential between men's and women's wages persisted. This obtained even in the Works Progress Administration (WPA). Male workers received $5.00 a day while female workers received only $3.00.[32]

In Europe similar conditions prevailed. Belgium, France, the Netherlands, and the United Kingdom all introduced measures against double income families, especially in the civil service. French women also suffered from the inability to vote. The fact that they were granted suffrage so long after the other democratic countries (1944) has been attributed by Minister Edwige Avice, Ministry of Foreign Affairs, to the conjunction of two different political pressures—the conservatives imbued with the traditional view of women's role and the socialists who believed that women were inherently conservative. This climate was not limited to France and it fostered the growth of conservative parties. The women themselves, facing so many obstacles and burdened with the responsibilities of home and families were often filled with a nostalgic yearning for the past. "People spoke of the 'failure' of the women's movement."[33]

In Germany and Italy the picture was even bleaker. Nazi Germany first offered a carrot and then a stick to keep women at home. A 1933 Unemployment Act offered brides a generous loan on condition that they left their jobs and with every successive child the amount of the loan decreased. Total subservience to the Nazi state and devotion to its cause was a prerequisite for survival. Women's organizations were "purified" and either agreed to nazification or were dissolved. Nazi women became ardent supporters of the slogan "kinder, küche, kirche." Italy, under a fascist dictatorship, followed a similar course. A 1934 law permitted women to be replaced by men, even in occupations that were traditionally theirs.

In Latin America a different situation obtained and the forces affecting

women stemmed from other causes. Political and social evolution has
varied from country to country. In Brazil there was paternalism, in Chile
an intense sense of legalism, in Venezuela the lack of any aristocratic
tradition, and in Peru a substantial Indian population. In Bolivia, Cuba,
and Mexico revolutions had lessened the impact of traditionalism.[34] Since
the eighteenth century powerful individual women had left their homes
and imposed their imprint on society. The few women who have had a
political career nationally or participated in international forums came,
for the most part, from the top 10 or 15 percent who often had been
partially educated abroad. One of the rare exceptions, but not the only
one, was Evita Perón, wife of the dictator Juan Perón. By and large,
however, women did not seek political office and eschewed the fight for
equal rights. They were active in broad-based political activities rather
than in specific feminist causes. In Chile, for example, a federation of
feminine organizations fought for the right to vote but when it was granted
in 1934 the federation faded away. Tradition, the Church, and the macho
attitude of men kept the women home-based and subservient to their
husbands. The one exception to the man's domination was his mother,
who often dominated him. Brides were expected to be virgins, and once
married their way of life was rigidly circumscribed, while the husbands
spent their time in sexual activity as proof of their masculinity. The result
was that married women were alone most of the time and thus had a free
hand at home and in the rearing of their children. Many were reluctant
to jeopardize this security and the independence they had, however circumscribed, by any activity their husbands might frown on. Thus the
problem in Latin America was not, as in Europe, to overcome adverse
legislation but to overcome the weight of tradition and traditional attitudes.

Similar conditions obtained in China and Japan. Women remained influential in the household, but in the household they remained. Moreover,
for some fifteen years both countries had been living in a state of war as
a result of the Japanese invasion in 1931. No Chinese or Japanese women
attended ILO conferences from the late 1920s until after the Second World
War.

The ILO in the 1930s

Meantime, in the ILO major changes had taken place. Immediately following the 1932 Conference, Albert Thomas died and Harold Butler was

elected Director. This involved fundamental changes in the emphasis of the ILO and the methods of leadership. Clearly, Harold Butler knew the house well, but he approached his job more as a civil servant and economist than Thomas had done with his emphasis on political dynamism. Butler made the major emphasis of ILO the employment problems of the Depression with special studies in most of the industrial countries, resulting in conference action on such issues as unemployment insurance and pension rights.

Although the ILO did its best during this period to mitigate the effects of the Depression through its conventions and recommendations, it was powerless to prevent unemployment and to turn the tide of the Depression. At the 1933 London Economic Conference it proposed measures to stabilize international monetary conditions and to develop extensive public works. However, the conference itself was torpedoed by the United States which ended such efforts at international cooperation in the economic sphere. All that was left for the ILO to do in the monetary field was to "preach Keynesian economics to unheeding finance ministers."[35]

The 1933 session—the first after Butler became Director—adopted conventions dealing with fee-charging employment agencies, and old age and invalidity insurance. Letellier was the reporter of the Committee on Fee-Charging Employment Agencies. This Conference was noteworthy for the attendance of the first delegation of U.S. observers, headed by Mary Anderson. However, the total number of women attending, including Mary Anderson, was only twelve. The text provides for the ultimate abolition of profit-making employment agencies. The fees imposed by agencies for finding an applicant for a job had long been a sore point for both employers and workers.

While 1931 had seen the largest number of women participants during the prewar years, 1934 was the year in which women achieved positions on committees of the greatest importance; the total number of women attending went up to fifteen, including four women workers: Julia Varley of Great Britain, Marie Krausova of Czechoslovakia, Jeanne Chevenard of France, and Eugenia Wasniewska of Poland.

The 1934 Conference reverted to the questions of employment of women in underground work and at night. This time it was successful in revising the night work for women convention. Kerstin Hesselgren, a Swedish government delegate then and for many years after, was elected chairman of the Night Work Committee, with Julia Varley of Great Britain as labor vice chairman, and Milena Atanatskovitch, section chief, Yugoslav ministry of social affairs and public health, as reporter. At this session, in contrast to the situation in 1931, the only opposition to revision of the night work convention came from Atanatzkovitch who stated that she was opposed to any revision that constituted a weakening of the convention, calling it a retrograde step affecting protective legislation. The revisions were adopted by a vote of 120 to 1.

Gertrude Stemberg of the Netherlands chaired the Committee on Underground Work, and she chaired the same committee the following year when a convention on the subject was adopted. Stemberg, who joined the Ministry of Labor, Commerce, and Industry in 1916, served in one capacity or another in ILO meetings for almost thirty years—from 1925 to 1954. From 1946 to 1951 she was a government representative on the Governing Body. In 1946 she was also a member of the joint staff pension board, and served as its vice chairman until her death in 1962. In 1948 she was the first woman appointed to the Committee of Experts on the Application of Conventions, in which she participated for eight years. Even after Stemberg's official retirement she continued for several years to return to ILO meetings, accompanying the Netherlands or, when Belgium replaced the Netherlands as the Governing Body member, the Belgian government delegate to the Governing Body.

The other women officers of the 1934 Conference Committee on Underground Work were Jeanne Chevenard, workers vice chairman, a member of the executive of the French General Confederation of Labor (CGT) and Bala Subbarayan of India, reporter of the committee, both of whom had known the ILO from its early days and had also been active participants in the women's nongovernmental network. Presenting the report of the committee to the plenary session of the conference, Subbarayan stated "The Conference is aware, I think, that there are two views on this general question. One is held by a section—and it is evident that the majority belong to this section—which believes that protective legislation is necessary for women on the assumption that women are not yet in a position to decide on the suitability of the conditions of their employment. The other section has absolute faith in equality of rights for men and women and is consequently strongly opposed to any idea of discriminatory legislation. The Members of the Committee, which consisted of governments, employers and workers, [nevertheless] unanimously accepted the principle that women should not be employed on underground work in mines."[36]

In 1934 there were two major changes in ILO membership. Both the

USSR and the United States joined the ILO. The USSR entered the League of Nations in 1934, primarily to help organize collective security against Nazi Germany. This automatically entitled it to membership in the ILO. Membership, however, involved sending tripartite delegations to most meetings, and Russian employers were not accepted by those from capitalist countries. In spite of this issue, the USSR sent a delegation of observers (which did not include women) to the 1935 Conference. In the course of the discussion of the agenda item calling for a forty-hour week, the USSR changed the status of its delegation so as to be able to vote— and thus found itself voting with the United States to obtain adoption of the Convention.[37]

The entry of the United States came as a result of careful preparation, for which the major credit goes to a woman, Frances Perkins, then the first woman secretary of labor. In the early 1930s Butler, then ILO Deputy Director, had made a number of visits to the United States in connection with studies of employment, unemployment, and the effect of the Depression. He had worked closely with Frances Perkins, at that time the New York State industrial commissioner. Both Butler and Perkins had long hoped for U.S. membership. The auspicious moment to start the ball rolling came when Franklin Roosevelt was elected president and Frances Perkins was made secretary of labor. Her efforts to persuade Roosevelt that the United States should join the ILO were abetted by the chief of the Women's Bureau of the Department of Labor, Mary Anderson, who had headed a delegation of observers to the 1933 Conference. This was her second, and this time successful, attempt. Two years earlier, when Herbert Hoover was still president, an effort by the Department of Labor to send her as an observer to the Conference was vetoed at the last moment by the Department of State, and she "observed" the Conference from a French hotel in the mountains overlooking Geneva. The 1933 delegation of observers was selected in the belief that if the issue of membership came before the U.S. Congress, the participants would be strong spokesmen for U.S. entry. Their on-the-spot observation resulted in a favorable report on the work of the ILO. (One of Mary Anderson's activities, as head of the Women's Bureau, had been to build up a coalition of women's organizations to support protectionist legislation and fight the equality concepts of the National Women's Party. She had thus been a consistent supporter of the ILO approach.)

The next year a full tripartite observer delegation was sent to the Conference, on the eve of congressional consideration of U.S. membership in the ILO.[38] Just before the Conference ended Congress passed a joint resolution authorizing the president to accept membership in the ILO.

The United States Enters the ILO

In 1935 the United States took its seats at the Conference, with Grace Abbott, ILO staff member at the 1919 Conference and one of the early leaders of the National Women's Trade Union League, as one of the two U.S. government delegates. She was elected chairman of the Committee on Unemployment Among Young Persons and immediately took a leadership position in the Conference deliberations. Her committee adopted a wide-ranging recommendation covering unemployment among young persons. A convention prohibiting underground work for women in mines was also adopted. This convention was developed by a committee chaired by Gertrude Stemberg. A group of nongovernmental organizations, coordinated by the Catholic Union of International Studies, objected unsuccessfully to some of the exclusions, particularly one permitting females to spend a period of training in the underground parts of a mine, as being subject to abuse. They also asked for an investigation of the general working conditions of women in colonial territories and in other areas with analogous conditions.

A third committee dealt with holidays with pay, which, like the Committee on Employment of Young Persons, had the largest number of women participants. Only one woman, however, took part in the 1935 Committee on Reduction of Hours of Work, whose aim was to reduce the number of hours to forty per week, which was politically the most important item on the conference agenda.

There were only two women worker participants in the Conference, namely Eugenia Wasniewska of Poland, who served on the Committee on Underground Work in Mines, and Krausova of Czechoslovakia who served on the same committee—an indication of the limited role still allowed to women in trade unions.

In 1936 Frieda Miller served as a U.S. government delegate. She had done graduate work in economics, sociology, political science, and law and had close relations with the trade union movement. She was an able and experienced negotiator. At that time she was director of the Division

U.S. delegates to the 1936 Conference. Frieda S. Miller and John G. Winant are in the center.

of Women in Industry and Minimum Wage of the New York State Department of Labor.

Although there were no women officers at the 1936 Conference, seven women spoke in the plenary sessions. Amongst them were Isabel Oyarzabal de Palencia of Spain and Brighid Stafford of Ireland. De Palencia had a long history of work with the ILO, serving in some instances as government adviser and in others as workers' adviser—a change in position which has been possible for only a few women, including Margaret Bondfield. De Palencia was always a fighter for liberal provisions. Stafford, speaking to the Convention on Holidays with Pay declared that it was not the usual practice of her country to vote in favor of a convention unless its provisions had already been implemented. However, in the case of holidays with pay, since there were some laws already in effect and others under consideration, she said her country would vote for the Convention.

The total representation of women continued to be small. Out of 51 countries (with 153 delegates and 236 advisers) there were only 17 women from 14 countries. This situation led the Governing Body, partly on the initiative of the United States, to adopt a resolution at its November 1936 session calling attention to the provision in the ILO Constitution that all delegations should include women whenever a woman's issue was on the agenda, and pointing out that questions important to women would be dealt with at the 1937 session of the Conference. This was quietly ignored by governments and by worker and employer organizations. Only two more women were present in 1937 than in 1936—or for that matter at the very first conference in 1919.

At the 1937 session the spectrum of concern with women's issues widened sharply. From a preoccupation with the protection of women, primarily as childbearers, the Conference then directly entered the field of women's rights. It adopted a resolution which had been submitted by two U.S. government delegates—Grace Abbott and Edward O'Grady. The resolution called for a reexamination by all governments of the status of women with respect to their political rights and opportunities, economic conditions, and protection from economic exploitation. This resolution was precedent setting in calling attention for the first time in an international organization to the broad question of women's rights as citizens and workers. In introducing the resolution Grace Abbott noted that it "proposed a general statement by the Conference of the principles which should govern the legal, social and industrial position of women if they are to protect themselves against industrial exploitation and assist in carrying forward the general purposes of the International Labor Organization." She added, "Moreover, experience shows that working men suffer from the denial of equality of approach to working women, so the whole objective of the Organization is involved." She concluded, "There has been no recognition by the Conference that much protective legislation would be unnecessary if women enjoyed equal civil and political rights with men."[39] This appeal opened the door to the essential linkage in the ILO between protective legislation and equal opportunity.

The item on the conference agenda of most concern to women dealt with the extension of provisions contained in earlier conventions regulating the minimum age and the conditions of employment of young persons in nonindustrial employment. A liaison committee of major international associations sought to raise the age, wherever it was set at fourteen, to fifteen. This move was only partially successful.

The ILO in Crisis

By the time of the next Conference, in June 1938, the world was in crisis, which was reflected in the atmosphere of the session. Frances Perkins led the U.S. delegation, with Frieda Miller as her substitute. A new addition to the U.S. delegation at this session was Clara M. Beyer who was then assistant director of the Labor Department's Bureau of Labor Standards. The daughter of Danish immigrants, she became interested in the problems of the working classes because she, as well as her widowed mother, had been unskilled laborers. Later she received a college education. For the ILO she was a staunch trooper who missed only one annual conference in ten or fifteen years and served on various regional conferences and committees, including industrial committees and in the technical assistance activities of the ILO for almost twenty years. Her wide-ranging experience in the U.S. government and her drafting skills made her an invaluable asset to each of the meetings on which she served as U.S. spokesman.[40]

Ten women from other countries who participated in the session were particularly effective in obtaining compromises that would permit adoption of conventions and recommendations because of their knowledge of conference procedures and their technical competence. These included Florence Hancock, the only woman worker; Gertrude Stemberg, Netherlands government adviser; and Kirsten Gloerfelt-Tarp, Danish government adviser. Women also served on the delegations of France, Mexico, Norway, and Spain.

Women on the Staff

Throughout the early years of the ILO, only a few members of the staff were primarily concerned with women's issues. One of the most notable of these was Marguerite Thibert, who had been brought into the Office by Albert Thomas in 1926, worked initially on immigration problems and later on those dealing with women and children. Under her leadership a service for women and children was established, with a small staff of research assistants.[41] This enabled her to begin the publication of a number of special studies on women's issues, including a summary of the protective legislation for women in different countries throughout the world as it existed in 1931. This study had been stimulated by suggestions from a number of women's organizations. She subsequently brought this study up to date and expanded its scope under the title, *The Law and Women's Work*.[42] As the Director's representative she shaped the discussions relating not only to questions of women and children, but also to indigenous workers and migrants at annual conferences and at various special conferences. Nevertheless, in spite of her influential activities, she never became chief of division. Even after her retirement, until she died in 1982, she continued to be extremely active in promoting and defending women's interests in France.

Other staff members worked on research, preparation of conference reports, editing, translation, interpretation, supervision of clerical staff, and in clerical jobs, as well as in a number of administrative positions. While women were in a minority in the senior professional category, they constituted a majority of the junior professional and clerical positions.

Sophy Sanger, the first woman professional on the staff, was immediately named as chief of the service dealing with labor legislation. She was elected to the first Staff Committee in 1920 and was particularly concerned with the problems of new staff members. She had considerable private means, which enabled her to carry out informal liaison between the ILO and the League of Nations through her entertainment of delegates. Nevertheless, she never obtained the confidence of the director and she resigned in 1924 when, over her protests, he promoted a new German staff member ahead of a Swedish colleague whom she had recommended.[43]

Elna Palme Dutt was one of the most effective staff members both professionally and in her relations with other staff members. She joined the Office in 1921, retired in 1951, and died in 1982. She was an economist and linguist of Swedish/British/Indian parentage, a rather useful combination helping her to maintain personal relations with her Swedish, British, and Indian compatriots. In 1945 she received the *Illis Quorum* medal from the king of Sweden "for eminent services in humanitarian and social fields." She was educated at Cambridge University and started her professional career as statistical assistant at the London School of Economics. She began her ILO career in the statistical section but soon transferred to the translation service, in time becoming senior editor of many ILO publications.

Another early recruit was Miss Matthieu of Britain (later Lady Howard), who was first a member and later chief of the agricultural service. She was largely responsible for directing the attention of the ILO to the importance of women in agriculture and the need to provide agricultural workers with benefits roughly equivalent to those of industrial and commercial workers.

Two examples of women who are still remembered for their pioneering work in administration were Miss Hill and Genevieve Laverrière. The former, an Englishwoman living in Geneva, joined the staff as a "local" but ultimately became assistant registrar and organized the ILO registry as it operated for many years. Laverrière was a dynamic and sometimes overbearing French woman who headed the stenographic and clerical services and the reproduction of mimeographed materials. Like Sophy Sanger, Laverrière was elected to the first staff union committee and became a strong defender of the clerical workers in the Office.

The career of Katherine Natzio illustrates how the ILO's international civil service regulations could operate at their best.[44] A graduate of Oxford University, she joined the staff as an interpreter in 1931, after successfully winning an international competition announced in British universities. Of Greek/British nationality (her father was Greek consul in Manchester), she retained close personal relationships with the governments of both countries. In addition to serving as an interpreter, she also worked in various technical departments as researcher or editor and in the section dealing with the operation of the Governing Body. At the time of her retirement she had obtained the rank of Counsellor and frequently played an influential role in dealing with members of the Governing Body.

In the mid-1930s, following U.S. membership in the ILO, two young Americans joined the staff. One was Carol Riegelman, who had done a considerable amount of research and writing on the ILO. Her initial job at the ILO in 1935 was as assistant to John G. Winant, the first American assistant director. When Winant left the ILO (to return nearly three years later, in 1937, first as Assistant Director and then as Director in 1939), Riegelman became a member of the conditions of work section, preparing reports and servicing committees on hours of work. She also held a number of other assignments, including that of transfer agent in Lisbon in 1940, described below, and a mission to the United Kingdom in 1943. In later years she specialized in the study of international migration problems, and especially its financing. Her role was always somewhat ambivalent, since she had joined the staff when, as one of a very small group of American citizens, she was frequently used in a liaison position between the Office and senior U.S. representatives, an assignment which frequently gave an impression of greater influence than was the case.[45]

The other American woman was Elizabeth Mayer (who later married

Frieda S. Miller, industrial commissioner of New York
State and delegate to the International Labor
Conference, at the 1938 session.

Ainsworth Johnstone and became a Canadian citizen). Her father was the
organist of West Point; she went to Mt. Holyoke College, where she studied with Amy Hewes, one of the early supporters of both labor legislation
at home and of the ILO. Immediately after college Elizabeth Mayer spent
a period of internship at the Washington branch office of the ILO. She
joined the Geneva staff in 1937 and was placed initially in the nonprofessional category. Her first job was in the clipping service under Mlle Schap-
pler. Soon after she was transferred to the employment service, but did
not obtain professional classification until after the move of the Office
staff to Montreal. She soon became the expert on employment service
organization and problems of labor supply. In addition to her regular
activities, she wrote many of the speeches of the senior staff, including
the directorate (initially those of John Winant, and later speeches by both
Jef Rens and David Morse). She thus began an indirect, but truly influential, policymaking role.

Shortly after the 1938 Conference the impending threat of German occupation of Czechoslovakia led to a realization that the ILO would probably have to adapt to a world at war. In recognition of these developments Butler deemed it important to strengthen links with the United States. He sought to achieve this by increasing U.S. influence in the Governing Body, and by hiring additional U.S. staff members. As early as 1937 he had brought back John Winant as Assistant Director with the understanding that when Butler resigned he would make every effort to obtain Winant's election as his successor. Winant had been Assistant Director in 1935, and although he left after a few months to become chairman of the U.S. Social Security Board, his post had never been filled. Winant, prior to coming to the ILO in the first instance, had been governor of New Hampshire, and before that a New Hampshire legislator. He was a liberal Republican politician with a warm approach to people's problems. He served for only two years and then left to become U.S. ambassador to the Court of St. James. However, in that crucial period in the life of the ILO he lived up to Butler's expectations and left his mark upon the Organization.

3. The War and Immediate Postwar Years

The approaching outbreak of hostilities cast its shadow over all other preoccupations throughout Europe. The buildup of military forces, the construction of air-raid shelters and, somewhat later, the devising of escape routes for those in peril occupied the forefront of concern. For the ILO the problems were somewhat different. An organization devoted to meeting economic and social needs, what could it do in the middle of a war? The ILO director, John Winant, in his first and only report to an ILO Annual Conference—*The World of Industry and Labour*—made it abundantly clear that the ILO was firmly on the side of the democracies. He stressed "the determination of the member countries to protect themselves against aggression and to preserve those democratic institutions which are the hope of mankind." This involved first and foremost the ability to wage the war successfully and that, in turn, meant to strengthen the industrial backbone. But what contribution could the ILO make and from what base could it operate?

Meantime it was 1939. War had not yet broken out when the ILO held its Conference in June. Business had to go on as usual and as long as it could. The only woman delegate to the Conference was Gertrude Stemberg of the Netherlands but there were women government advisers from Brazil, Denmark, France, Ireland, Mexico, Norway, Switzerland, Yugoslavia, and the United States. The only woman workers' adviser was Florence Hancock from the United Kingdom.

Two actions taken by the Conference were of direct concern to women. The first was the adoption of a resolution, introduced by Leon Jouhaux, workers' delegate of France and Evert Kupers, workers' delegate of the Netherlands, that the Conference, "considering that it cannot yet be said that a satisfactory solution has been found for the problems of equality of women in industrial and public life . . . recognizes that one of the tasks

Delegations and staff at the ILO Havana Regional Conference, 1939.

of the ILO is to raise the position of women workers throughout the world." The resolution concluded that the "Conference recognizes the importance of the principle of equality of pay and asks that the ILO should complete the inquiry into present practice as quickly as possible." Dora Schmidt of Switzerland, discussing the resolution, noted that action rather than further studies was needed. The other Conference action was the ratification of a Governing Body decision to hold a second conference of American states in Havana, at the end of the year, in order to meet the expressed desire of many Latin American countries for greater flexibility in ILO conventions dealing with women's employment so as to facilitate their ratification. This was duly held in November 1939, despite the outbreak of war, and it adopted a declaration reaffirming support for ILO's wartime role (see chapter 6).

The regular Conference held in May also adopted two conventions. One dealt with vocational training and apprenticeship. Clara Beyer served as reporter of the committee responsible for this item. The second convention formulated regulations concerning migration and settlement of migrants and their families, which clearly affected women either as workers or as family members. The only women participants in the committee dealing with this item were Aase Lionaes, an economist from Norway, and Florence Hancock. Had the war not intervened, these actions might have been landmarks, defining new roles for women; in fact, however, they were of little significance until after the Second World War.

Shortly after this conference ended, the burning question became: where and how could an international organization composed of nations from both belligerent and neutral countries continue to function? One thing had been agreed upon by the Governing Body and the Director. ILO had no intention of going into deep freeze. It was going to function somehow, somewhere. A list was drawn up of the staff requirements for the continued operation of the ILO, wherever that might be, and members of the staff were selected on this basis, subject to possible visa problems or national service demands. The remaining staff was divided into those put on special leave, subject to recall, those with suspended contracts or eligible for retirement, and those to remain in the Geneva office.[1]

With the invasion of Denmark and Norway in April 1940, it was recognized that it might soon be necessary to implement the plan, made even before the actual outbreak of war, to move major activities out of Switzerland to Vichy, France, the site of an organizing center which might become a temporary headquarters. Office documentation and personal baggage for those staff members to be transferred to the temporary headquarters were sent to a hotel in Vichy and staff was ordered to have knapsacks ready in case of a sudden move. Then came the fall of France. Personal suitcases were returned. Cases of documentation—unopened—provided seats for Germans in Vichy, after its occupation. They were all recouped after the war.

The Move to Montreal

The noose around Geneva began to tighten after the invasion of Belgium and Holland. Within days cables were sent out canceling meetings, including the Annual Conference. Some of these meetings were to have dealt with such issues as treatment of families of migrants—an issue of particular concern to women. With Vichy untenable, where should—or could—the ILO go? The Director, with the support of Frances Perkins, the secretary of labor, as well as the president of the AFL, and those members of the ILO Governing Body with whom contact could still be made, sought to get permission to settle the ILO, for the time being, in the United States. This was refused by the secretary of state, Cordell Hull. The basic reason was fear that the U.S. isolationists might object—and make even more difficult acceptance of the lend-lease program. After the fall of Paris, when it became clear that further delays might make it difficult, if not impossible, to leave Geneva, the United States agreed, as a compromise, to authorize the U.S. embassy in Berne, Switzerland, to issue transit visas and permits for designated ILO staff and their families, and for materials to be sent to the United States, in transit to a still undesignated country. This, in turn, meant that similar transit visas could be obtained to permit travel through unoccupied France, Spain, and Portugal.

While these negotiations were taking place, Winant proceeded to London to discuss what areas would be suitable for the wartime headquarters. Suggestions varied from London to the Azores, to Brazil, and finally to Canada. (One not very serious proposal was St. Michael's Island—a remote spot near the Azores.) There was still no final decision as to location when the transfer of staff from Geneva began. Meanwhile, Winant had gone to North America to negotiate on the future site.

Some of the staff went by car, more by buses organized for both ILO and League of Nations staff, and then by train. A few made their way to Madrid and then flew to Lisbon. Staff with large families and those from occupied countries were clearly in the most difficult situation, especially when they did not even know their next destination. Carol Riegelman (Lubin) drove to Lisbon with the chairman of the Governing Body, and then, as a U.S. citizen having no passport or family problems (and eager to remain in Europe) was assigned as transfer agent in Lisbon. This involved finding lodging for staff, meeting planes and trains when arrivals were known, and then attempting to obtain space on the few ships or planes available from Lisbon to Americas. When she met the first group—in the middle of the night—she was asked where the staff could meet the next day. The only place that came to mind was the café bar where those of the Geneva staff already in Lisbon frequently spent evenings! Thus meetings were held in a central bar at 11 A.M. every day—and even the Jesuit priest who was a member of the staff became accustomed to watching the "girls" come to work.

Prior to the staff meeting, each morning Riegelman would have breakfast with the representatives of the American Export Line, Pan American

Airways, and sometimes the Greek line in order to report upon available or potential bookings. The meetings also gave the staff an opportunity to share problems, such as their lodgings in Lisbon or the basis of allocation of places on ships or planes; the criteria used included size of family, nationality (priority for those who might face difficulties if Portugal acceded to any of the German demands), and the urgency of their work in the new working center. They also enabled the staff to develop joint demands that Winant come to Lisbon to consult with them. At the end of each meeting Riegelman would meet with the Deputy Director, Edward J. Phelan (who had arrived in Lisbon shortly after the first staff busload), to report on what the staff concerns were and to receive instructions for the next day.

During this period Winant had obtained the permission of the Canadian government to establish a working center in Canada, and an invitation had been received from McGill University to locate on its campus in Montreal. The next step was to announce the decision to the nation members of the ILO, as well as to the Governing Body, and to install the staff in its new working center.

By the end of October 1940 the ILO working center in Montreal was in full operation. When the last of the staff arrived from Lisbon, they found the earlier arrivals ensconced in an old chapel—with pews piled up in the center aisle—and the only private office that of the director, in the area behind the former altar, where the desks of his assistant and secretary were installed. Although at that point neither rank nor sex played a role, a few months later when the staff was moved into its permanent wartime offices, bureaucracy as well as discrimination took over once more. Women tended not to be given private offices, and new women recruits were often hired at lower salaries and in lower classifications than men. Thus Isabel Craig of Canada joined the staff at a level below her technical qualifications. She became one of the outstanding experts in the field of social security. Another recruit during this period was Joan Riley, a Chilean national, trilingual in French, English, and Spanish. She was brought in for research in the social security section, and subsequently became a member of the editorial section.[2]

Meanwhile, the ILO began full wartime services to its members and early planning for the postwar world. The move to Montreal gave the ILO an allied nations role, and saved it as a viable institution for the future. With the ILO safely established in Montreal, Winant accepted the invitation of the U.S. president to become ambassador to the Court of St. James,

View of the ILO's first wartime working center, McGill University, Montreal. To the rear of the picture is the chapel altar, and on either side of it are two doors leading to the offices of the Director and Deputy Director, the only private offices.

and the Deputy Director, Edward Phelan, an Irish citizen, became the Acting Director. Phelan, like Butler, had been Deputy Director and an ILO leader from its conception. Of all the directors, he was, perhaps, the most adroit in his use of language and his manipulation of people to further the aims of ILO. Phelan had always been a universalist and was more concerned with the future survival of the ILO as a model, worldwide, international organization than with its role of providing direct service to the allied nations. He had initially been reluctant to leave Geneva, fearing this would compromise its postwar international status. This attitude resulted in doubts by some of the allied leaders, including many of the U.S. representatives, as to the role he would assume as Acting Director. With respect to women's issues, he was a strong advocate of "protective legislation" and standard setting in general, but was not as much concerned with women's rights to equality. From a personnel point of view, like so many of the national and international civil servants of the period, he showed little concern for the status of women on the staff.

The First Wartime Conference: 1941

Although the war was in its early stages (with the United States still neutral) and with the outcome still uncertain, there was a clearly felt need among the allied and neutral nations, as well as the workers' and employers' representatives who had managed to maintain contact with the ILO, that the Organization reach beyond the immediate exigencies of battle to declare its faith in the future and stake out a role for itself in the postwar world. How this should be done became the focus of debate in ILO circles.

Recognizing that any ILO meeting dealing with postwar problems should include neutral as well as allied members and to this end should be held in a neutral country and preferably in a nongovernmental setting, the U.S. government, and in particular Frances Perkins, and Carter Goodrich as chairman of the Governing Body,[3] prevailed on Nicholas Murray Butler, president of Columbia University, to invite the ILO to hold an international labor conference at Columbia. This conference was not a regular session because the Governing Body had been unable to meet and fulfill its constitutional obligations with respect to fixing time, place, and agenda.[4]

The initiative for this first conference on U.S. soil had come from Jef Rens, the representative of the Belgian workers-in-exile, who had attended a number of prewar ILO conferences. The Acting Director set the tone of the meeting in his report, *The ILO and Reconstruction*. The report called for the adoption of a new Social Mandate for the ILO and included in its main "points and principles" a series of such items of concern to women as the elimination of unemployment, improvement and extension of social insurance to all classes of workers, and particularly, "a minimum living wage for those too weak to secure it for themselves," and "greater equality of occupational opportunity." It is worth noting that the report called for greater equality not full equality.

The conference formally adopted the Social Mandate along with a strong resolution calling on the ILO to take the lead in planning reconstruction—thus setting the stage for its continuing efforts to become part of the allied postwar planning. The conference also adopted a resolution submitted by the workers' delegate from Australia which declared that "the male occupational standard rates or the rates for the job irrespective of the sex of the worker should be recognized as the basic principle of war and post-war industry" and urged that "steps should be taken immediately to secure the elimination of sex differentials in wage standards." The conference requested the Office "to resume its investigation of women's work, and, through the Governing Body, to formulate plans to combat the exploitation of the pool of efficient and underpaid labor."

The adoption of the Social Mandate was inspired by more than a desire for justice. It was an effort to provide a bulwark for democratic ideals in the face of the Nazi juggernaut. Placing itself squarely on the side of the Allies, the conference adopted one resolution endorsing the Atlantic Charter and another expressing "its warmest admiration and profound gratitude to the brave people who are fighting against the most savage barbarians that history has every known, and thus saving mankind from complete defeat; by their heroic resistance these free men and women have not only saved the world from defeat but have also laid the foundations for the victory of democracy which can alone guarantee social progress and freedom."

That the conference was viewed as a contribution to the war effort was evident from the attendance of officials already fully occupied with the prosecution of the war. There were fifteen cabinet members, including those from the United Kingdom, almost all the governments-in-exile, Mexico, New Zealand, Canada, and the United States. The attendance of these cabinet members at an ILO meeting across the Atlantic during the war may well have been a key factor in the continued existence of the organization in the war years and postwar years.[5]

The conference included a number of individuals who would play extraordinarily important roles in the future development of the ILO. One example was Henri Hauck, minister of labor and social welfare of the Free France movement. Hauck spoke to the conference as an observer, since the position of the government of unoccupied France was still anomalous, and the Vichy government was represented at the conference by its Washington minister, M. Panafieu. There was also J. H. Oldenbroeck, chairman of the contact committee of organizations of employees of the Netherlands merchant navy, and Dirk Valstar, chairman of the union of employers of Dutch merchant shipping lines, both of whom had been active in keeping Dutch ships from falling into the hands of the occupying powers. All in all, there were 117 representatives from thirty-five countries (including two observers—Costa Rica and Free France). But only five included women in their delegations. They came from Argentina, Chile, Luxembourg, New Zealand, and the United States, and served both on the committee discussing collaboration among employers, workers, and governments, and on the committees preparing resolutions on postwar reconstruction. Graciela Mandujano, government adviser of Chile, speaking at one of the last plenary sessions, deplored the fact that there was only one resolution relating to women and she called upon the ILO to promote national bureaus to deal with the problems of women in industry, peasant women, and children. She drew attention to the problems faced by peasant women "who have borne a double burden from the economic situation, from their lack of education, from the exploitation of which they are the constant victims."

The most significant role played by a woman was that of Frances Perkins, who served as president of the conference—the first time a woman had occupied the position and the last until 1984, when Anna-Greta Leijon, minister of labor of Sweden, was elected to the post. Perkins, in practice, determined the agenda and directed the day-to-day operations of the conference. She played a key role in the ILO both at the conference and throughout the war years, influencing the subjects to be investigated and suggesting appointments of senior U.S. staff, such as an assistant director from the United States in 1942.

It may be noted that the ILO staff hardly benefited from the increased wartime role played by women, either in government or private employment. Some of the most effective women in the ILO left to join national services—particularly where their own countries were at war. Many of those who returned after such service, while they did not lose seniority, found promotion no more likely than before. Some new recruits—such as Mildred Fairchild—ultimately obtained higher rank than their predecessors but this was the result of other factors, such as nationality or recognition of the significance of their jobs, and not of their wartime services. Similarly, while women's groups during the war often mobilized in support of wartime or postwar women's issues, they expressed little concern for the role of women on the staff of international organizations.

ILO's Wartime Contributions

In addition to providing an allied meeting ground for governments, workers, and employers, the ILO in Montreal undertook renewed services to its constituents. One of these was a series of Canadian-American meetings, convened at the request of the two governments and hosted sequentially by the Canadian minister of labor and the New York State Department of Labor, under the leadership of Frieda Miller. These sessions provided opportunities for exchange of experience and technical assistance in wartime labor supply and production issues and led to such publications as those on women's wartime problems and their role in the defense industries. By coincidence rather than design the major staffing of the Canadian-American meetings, including the preparation of the reports submitted by the Office, was carried out by two women staff members, Elizabeth Mayer (Johnstone) who was responsible for several reports on labor supply and national defense, and Carol Riegelman (Lubin) who made the studies on joint production committees. Both of these women, in order to obtain the necessary documentation, undertook missions in the United Kingdom.

During this same period a Canadian-American Women's Committee on International Relations made up of the Women's Committee on International Relations of Canada and the U.S. National Committee on the Cause and Cure of War had been established to examine problems of joint concern to women. It held a conference in Montreal in April 1943 which was attended by seventy delegates. Frances Perkins, Margaret Bondfield, Rose Schneiderman, and several senior members of the ILO staff (including the Acting Director and Assistant Director) addressed the conference and discussed the wartime activities of the ILO. A round table session, at which Elizabeth Mayer Johnstone reviewed the wide gains of women during the war, gave special attention to the problems of domestic workers. The session was attended by women-in-exile from Czechoslovakia, Free France, Poland, Luxembourg, Belgium, and the Ukraine. This group, like the ILO's Canadian-American meetings, indicated the usefulness of international cooperative machinery in the social and economic fields. Another meeting held in London in October 1943 of the women members of the Transport and General Workers Union and addressed by Ernest Bevin, then minister of labour and national service, and by Florence Hancock, then the national woman officer of the TGWU, adopted a series of resolutions aimed at bringing more women into the war effort and into the trade union movement as members, officers, and inspectors. Much of the discussion dealt with equality of pay, and, particularly with the equality in pay rates that would allow women to stay in the labor force in the postwar world. One resolution greeted the women of the Soviet Union (a Soviet delegation attended some of the sessions), and one sent "to the women of the United Nations its [the Conference of British Trade Unionists] congratulations on their splendid courage and the example they have set to the whole world, in their fight against the common enemy. We pledge ourselves to do all in our power to increase production for a speedy victory and a closer cooperation between the women of the United Nations."[6]

As a result of a number of missions by ILO to Latin America, the Peruvian government in 1939 had convened a conference on social insurance in which the ILO Director participated. This conference led to the establishment of the International Committee on Social Security, under the auspices of the ILO. The Office also published a report, *Approaches to Social Security,* which it had prepared in response to a request by the British government to assist a committee set up under the chairmanship of the noted economist Sir William Beveridge. One further area in which ILO paved the way for future action concerned the non-self-governing countries and territories. Perhaps there was a touch of prescience of the headlong, postwar rush to independence.

Meanwhile, the Emergency Committee of the Governing Body met, in 1942 and 1943, in London where several of its members were based, to supervise the work of the ILO, to ensure that it provided maximum service to the allied members, and also that it did not ignore the concerns of neutral members. At its first meeting after the New York conference (in April 1942) it reviewed each of the resolutions adopted by the conference and authorized the acting director to take all responsible actions to implement them. One specific action was to appoint an Advisory Committee on the Economics of Postwar Reconstruction to work with him in developing appropriate ILO plans and to facilitate the participation of the ILO in whatever meetings were held to shape the postwar world organization. The Emergency Committee also took particular note of a communication from the Liaison Committee of Women's Organizations asking the Office to bear in mind the special needs of women workers when, as requested in another conference resolution, it undertook a new study of wage standards.

The participation of women during this period was obviously limited to those from unoccupied countries or to those associated with the governments-in-exile. Those in the occupied countries could only act within resistance movements. In the USSR, women were mobilized almost totally: many served in the armed forces, many in heavy industry. By 1945 women composed 56 percent of the labor force, often working fourteen to eighteen hours a day. As for women in the enemy countries, dominated by the kinder, küche, and kirche philosophy, they were incorporated into the state apparatus. In Germany, for example, girls learned to "Be brave! Be pure! Be German."[7]

During this period Frieda Miller was serving as an assistant to Ambassador Winant in London, providing liaison with British working women. She frequently took part in the Emergency Committee meetings, representing the United States, when Carter Goodrich, the chairman of the Governing Body, chaired the meeting. She was sometimes the only woman. Also at this time the Office staff was strengthened by the appointment of an Assistant Director from the United States, Lindsay Rogers, a distinguished lawyer occupying a chair of public law at Columbia University, whose major role was to provide the liaison with the United States that had been somewhat weakened after Winant's resignation.

The Philadelphia Conference: Preparing for Peace

As the war drew nearer to a close and the prospects of an Allied victory were virtually assured, the ILO placed greater emphasis on its role in a world at peace and its future relations with the intergovernmental organizations already in existence or about to be created. In 1944 a key policymaking conference (the first formal session since the outbreak of war) was held at Temple University in Philadelphia. The most significant report submitted to the conference, *Future Policy, Programme and Status of the International Labour Organisation* concluded with a draft declaration designed to restate the ILO's goals, principles, and competence in the years ahead. This Declaration, as amended by the Conference, became the new "Charter." It was made an annex to the original Constitution. It clearly affirmed that "all human beings, irrespective of race, creed or sex, have the right to pursue both their material well-being and their spiritual development." These rights should be the center of national and international policy. To this end, it affirmed the competence of the ILO to deal with the economic and financial aspects of social policy and sought to give ILO wide "watchdog" responsibilities for ensuring that national and international policies were directed to the achievement of social justice. The Conference also discussed the social and labor clauses that should be included in the peace treaties and changes that would have to be made in the ILO Constitution to provide for formal separation from the League of Nations and association with its successor.

A total of sixteen women from ten countries as diverse as Czechoslovakia, Egypt, Liberia, Mexico, and the United Kingdom managed to arrive in Philadelphia, despite enemy action and transportation problems. Bertha Lutz, government adviser from Brazil, president of the Brazilian Federation for the Advancement of Women, founder and permanent delegate to the Inter-American Commission of Women, participated in the Conference for the first but not the last time and served on the Committee for Dependent Territories. Trained as a biologist, she had won a post in the national museum in Rio de Janeiro, thus opening government service to women. Frances Perkins did not, as at the previous New York Conference, preside over the Conference (its president was Walter Nash, minister from New Zealand) but instead chaired the committee dealing with constitutional issues on the one hand, and on the other the proposed social clauses that the ILO hoped would be included in the peace treaties. Frieda Miller was chairman of the Subcommittee on Constitutional Issues, including the separation of the ILO from the League of Nations. Muriel Retson, controller of health insurance and pensions of the Department of Health for Scotland, a British government adviser, provided expertise in the discussions of the insurance problems to be faced in the transition from war to peace. The veteran Florence Hancock and Dame Anne Loughlin, chief woman officer of the British National Union of Tailor and Garment Workers, were spokeswomen in both the committee and plenary sessions dealing with postwar problems.

The relatively prominent role taken by women at the Philadelphia Conference was primarily the result of their wartime role in their own countries. As was the case in the First World War, women at all levels had taken over many jobs usually classified as "for men only"; they had demonstrated leadership capacity not only in industry but in government service and often in the planning field; and their participation in the defense and military establishments had been recognized. All these factors were recognized, at least in a limited way, in their nomination to delegations and election as officers at Philadelphia.

The Philadelphia Conference adopted two recommendations of particular concern to women, one dealing with employment organization in the transition from war to peace (number 71) and one concerning employment services (number 73). The former stressed (1) "the principle of complete equality of opportunity for men and women" in the redistribution of women workers in the transition from war to peace; (2) encouragement of "the establishment of wage rates based on job content without regard to sex"; and (3) raising "the relative status of those industries and occupations" that traditionally employ women. The second recommendation outlined a series of measures to enable the public employment services to implement the above principles. The thrust of these recommendations foreshadowed the increasing emphasis in future years by the ILO on principles of equality. Eight women sat on the committee which developed these recommendations. These women had been deeply concerned with the same issues in their own countries, where, as noted earlier, women's conferences had been adopting resolutions on equality of women in the war and postwar worlds.

A third recommendation (number 67) on Income Security contained a section dealing with women. It repeated the provisions of the 1919 Convention regarding women's work before and after childbirth and required that benefits must be extended for "longer periods or on other occasions" as might be indicated on medical grounds. Still another provision covered the payment of survivors' benefits for the widow of an insured man and their children, and authorized women, when they reached the age of sixty, to claim old age benefits. Six women sat on the relevant committee.

Establishing the UN: The ILO's Role

Just a year after the Philadelphia Conference, the UN Conference on International Organization met in San Francisco to design a successor to the League of Nations. For the ILO the major preoccupation in this period was to maintain its jurisdiction in the social and economic fields. Only thus could it implement the goals and principles enunciated in the Declaration which had been so enthusiastically endorsed by the participating delegates at Philadelphia. An immediate problem for the ILO was to define its relationships in the new constellation of international organizations. This became a frustrating and, in many respects, impossible task. The era in which the ILO had been virtually alone in its chosen field had come to an end. In the future it would be part of a network of intergovernmental organizations, often with overlapping jurisdictions that were to have their impact on women's programs. Its initial hopes were fated to be only partially fulfilled. Despite the role the Philadelphia Conference had envisaged for the ILO, the Organization had very limited success in getting a foothold in the top-level negotiations to draft the instruments for postwar cooperation. These were being carried out by the foreign policy planners, while the ILO had its base, in the United Kingdom and the United States, respectively, in the Ministry of Labor and the Department of Labor, neither of which was in a position to control the decisionmakers. Nor was the ILO much more successful either at Bretton Woods, which established the parameters of what were to become the International Bank for Reconstruction and Development and the International Monetary Fund, or at Dumbarton Oaks, where agreement was reached on the basic structure of the United Nations, including its organ for economic and social affairs. By the time the UN Conference on International Organization convened in San Francisco in 1945 to write the charter of the new body, the pattern had been established.

The ILO sought vainly to have a tripartite delegation accepted as a full participant in the San Francisco Conference. This was rejected on several grounds. The tripartite formula was unique and appeared to add further complexity to already complex negotiations. Then, it was pointed out, as far as full participation was concerned, the ILO was only one of a growing number of intergovernmental organizations. To seat it would open a Pandora's box. Moreover, the fact that the USSR had refused to participate in the Philadelphia Conference was used as a further argument against expanding the role of the ILO. Thus the Organization and other intergovernmental bodies were invited to San Francisco merely as "consultative delegations."

However, the ILO did make its voice heard in regard to future relations with the UN. On May 15 Carter Goodrich, as chairman of the Governing Body, was invited to speak to Committee II/3 (the committee dealing with the structure of the UN in economic and social fields) to present the views of the ILO. He stressed the desire of the Organization to be inside and not outside the framework of the United Nations, to have access to the General Assembly, and generally to be in a position to make an effective contribution, even though it was recognized that there was no chance of explicit reference in the UN Charter to the ILO's Social Mandate. Goodrich also stated that the ILO would maintain its tripartite structure and its direct relations with governments. As finally drafted, the UN Charter authorized the Economic and Social Council to "enter into agreements" with specialized agencies, subject to approval by the General Assembly.

Two issues that arose during the drafting of the UN Charter were of particular concern to women. A number of women's organizations, including most of the major groups which had worked with the League as well as the ILO during the prewar years, and some governments had called for the inclusion in the UN Charter of provisions for equal rights and opportunities for women. The spokeswoman for this demand was Virginia Gildersleeve, dean of Barnard College of Columbia University from 1911 and president of the Association to Aid Scientific Research for Women, the only woman member of the U.S. delegation. While no specific provision was included, there were scattered statements throughout the Charter that the objectives of the United Nations were to be achieved "without distinction as to race, *sex*" (italics added).

A more contentious proposal, which divided the women as well as the men, was whether the UN Charter should provide for a special commission on the status of women. This was proposed by Bertha Lutz of Brazil and supported by a number of her colleagues. Her vehement espousal of a woman's commission at San Francisco led to the nickname, in some quarters, of "Lutzwaffe." Virginia Gildersleeve, among others, was opposed on the ground that this would only exacerbate the segregation of women rather than promoting their integration into the body politic, a debate that was to echo far into the future.[8] Although Lutz lost initially, the UN General Assembly, at its first session in 1946, established a Sub-Commission on the Status of Women under the aegis of the Commission on Human Rights. A few months later, the Economic and Social Council elevated the sub-commission into a full commission reporting directly to it. The Commission attributed to itself a sweeping mandate. It considered itself responsible for all women's issues, with authority to coordinate international efforts involving women's equality. At its first session the Commission asserted that it intended to "raise the status of women, irrespective of nationality, race, language or religion, to equality with men in all fields of human enterprise," and added "women should be given equal rights with men with respect to labor, wages, holidays and other economic and social rights." This last claim clearly raised jurisdictional problems with the ILO.

The First Postwar Conference: The Role of Women

The postwar world was a very different one from that which had obtained in the 1920s and 1930s. The tumultuous world was revolutionizing interstate relations. The previous dispersion of power among a number of relatively equal nations was substantially modified by the appearance of two superpowers. Colonial empires began to crumble with unforeseen alacrity and in the years ahead new nations came onto the scene in ever increasing numbers. The Western nations that had run the world for so long found themselves in a minority among vociferous states claiming their place in the sun. The rule of law which had obtained for centuries in Europe was challenged by countries which had had no role in its making.

Inevitably, women too were affected by these changes. Increasingly, women challenged the taboos of centuries regarding their place in society. Many had earned their spurs while the men went to war. Many had themselves joined the services and their voices were to be heard with growing clarity. The influx of new states into the comity of nations also changed the geographic mix of women in the ILO and the type of services the ILO was called upon to perform.

This was the background of the first ILO Conference in the wake of San Francisco. It met in a Paris that was just beginning to recover from wartime shortages. The euphoria of liberation had passed and the material problems of daily life weighed heavily, not only on the population of the city but on the living conditions—both physical and moral—that surrounded the participants in the meeting.[9]

The Conference, however, had other preoccupations than the state of the world or conditions in Paris. It dealt primarily with such questions as the effect of the new UN jurisdiction as defined at San Francisco and the changes required in the ILO Constitution to bring it into line with the reconstituted world organization. The Conference action was based on a preliminary report, prepared by the ILO Committee on Constitutional Change, established immediately after the San Francisco Conference, under the chairmanship of Frieda Miller.[10] It set the tone for the Conference analysis of the specific steps the ILO would have to take to carry out its role in reconstruction and to adapt its Constitution to the new intergovernmental arrangements. These included subject matter responsibility, financial relationships, and such staff issues as salaries, classification, and pension funds.

Frances Perkins, no longer U.S. secretary of labor, was chairman of the government group and spoke on the Director's Report in the Plenary.[10] She called attention to the place of women in industrial life, stressing the need "to prevent their competition for jobs from undercutting wages and lowering general standards of living." She urged particular attention to the establishment of a general "rate of wages for the job regardless of sex." She concluded with a pointed statement of support for a broad mandate for the ILO which, through its cooperation with the United Nations, "would itself gain strength for the accomplishment of the purposes of the Declaration of Philadelphia."[11]

At this Conference the substantive decisions followed traditional lines with one exception, an item on employment issues. Florence Hancock of the United Kingdom served as workers' vice chairman of the Conference Committee on the Protection of Children and Young Workers on which eighteen women served. Katherine Lenroot, chief of the Children's Bureau of the United States, and Alva Myrdal of Sweden were the rapporteurs of this committee. Myrdal, at the time director of the Stockholm Training College for Preschool Teachers, became a leading diplomat, sociologist, and writer, serving as ambassador to India, and as her government's representative to the ILO (including the Governing Body), the United Nations, and UNESCO, and for a period on the staff of the last two bodies.

The Conference Committee on the Protection of Children and Young Workers was charged with the formulation of "general principles on the protection of children in relation to the preparation of the child for his future role as a worker, and the protection of non-adult workers as a step towards fulfilment of the Declaration of Philadelphia." The committee was also asked to deal with two special questions: medical examinations for fitness of young workers for employment; and regulation of night work for children and young persons in nonindustrial employment. As a result, these questions were placed on the agenda of the 1946 Conference, which adopted two conventions and recommendations on the subject. The debate on the general principles that should govern the welfare of young persons (including the relation of employment to education, social welfare,

71

and health) focused on the age of admission to employment, school leaving age, and prohibition of work during school hours as well as night work. It was agreed that the age should be set at sixteen—instead of the prevailing fourteen—but that this would have to be achieved gradually. It was also agreed that hours of work for all under eighteen should be fixed at forty per week. Emilie Arnould, Belgian worker member and general secretary of the Young Christian Women Workers' Organization, submitted a memorandum on the protection of young workers prepared by a group of leaders of Christian Working Youth and of the Socialist Youth Movement. The memorandum asked the ILO to try to devise means which would permit groups of young workers to be associated with the work of the ILO.

The item on employment issues arising as the world returned to a peacetime economy had been placed on the Conference agenda for the purpose of a general discussion. A Conference committee was appointed to consider the item. This was the first time that a committee had been allocated an item that was not designed to lead to formal action such as the adoption of a convention or recommendation. The report submitted by the Office as a basis for this discussion was entitled, *Report on the Maintenance of High Levels of Employment during the Period of Industrial Rehabilitation and Reconversion.* The committee changed both the title of the item and the resolution it adopted from "High Levels of Employment" to "Full Employment," and recommended "the establishment of appropriate minimum wage standards for satisfying reasonable human needs."[12] Among the methods suggested were increased public works, changed taxation, and similar measures to be taken by national governments. Much of the discussion turned on whether the ILO should deal with such economic issues or if these matters should be referred to other international bodies considered more competent in these fields, thus again narrowing the scope of ILO jurisdiction. Karin Koch, professor of economics at Stockholm University, served as reporter of the committee and submitted its report to the plenary. The only woman officer, her influence was clearly as a world renowned economist and not as a woman—in fact, there was little if any concern with the direct effect of these measures on women.

In addition to Sweden, six other countries, all but one European, included women in their delegations—France, Eire, Italy, the Netherlands, New Zealand, and Switzerland. They were to leave their mark on ILO deliberations for many years. Olga Raffalovich, assistant director and later deputy director in the French ministry of labor and social security, attended conferences for some fifteen years. At the 1945 session she served as government member of the Conference Drafting Committee. A determined, self-contained woman, she was commonly known in France as "le Sphinx." Another woman who served almost as long was Marguerite Schwarz-Gagg, member of the Swiss Federal Factories' Commission. Two others were also factory inspectors. Brighid Stafford, chief inspector of factories in the Irish Department of Industry and Commerce, and Ruby Skyring, inspector of factories, New Zealand Department of Labor. The fifth woman who only attended two conferences was Laura Riva Sanseverina, professor of labor law at the University of Pisa, the first Italian woman to serve on the first Italian delegation after the war.

When the Paris Conference held its first postwar election of new members of the Governing Body, Gertrude Stemberg became a full member, as the appointee of the Netherlands government. She had previously served as a substitute member. The chairmanship passed from Carter Goodrich of the United States to Sir Guildhaume Myrddin Evans of the United Kingdom, resulting in lessened U.S. influence for a number of years. These changes marked the end of a decade in which the role of women primarily from the West had gradually increased within the ILO structure as a whole, partly at least as a result of the influence of Frances Perkins and Frieda Miller.

At its first meeting after the Conference, the Governing Body took a number of actions that determined the immediate work program of the organization. One of these was to agree to a meeting of a limited number of members of the Correspondence Committee on Women's Work to set priorities for an ILO women's program. This committee had been set up in 1932 in response to the Polish representative's request that an advisory committee be established to assist the ILO's service for women. When the Governing Body initially agreed to the establishment of a correspondence committee of over one hundred experts on women's issues, it was made clear that the committee would not meet, but that the Office might "from time to time call a meeting of a certain number of its members who were qualified to advise it on any question it was studying." The Governing Body also insisted that it should not necessarily be limited to women, and that its membership should be representative of "all points of view." (This specification was in response to expressions, particularly by the labor and British government representatives, that the appointments should not be based on organizational pressure from women's groups, nor on the basis of governmental designation.) The members appointed were primarily women experts who were known to the Office from their participation in conferences and other ILO meetings and, in fact, included one early member of the ILO staff, Martha Mundt, a German citizen who had effectively provided liaison with the many women's organizations in the 1920s. The initial membership, in conformity with the wish of the Governing Body, had also included three men! Members served a three-year term but were reappointed regularly, and new appointments were made whenever a member died or resigned. The Office made extensive use of the membership by correspondence—sending drafts of studies, proposals, or activities to elicit reactions.

Eight women (ten were invited), all in government service, attended a meeting of a panel of the Correspondence Committee in July 1946 in Montreal.[13] Kerstin Hesselgren served as chairman and Frieda Miller as reporter. Although the group was small, all members of the Correspondence Committee had been asked beforehand to provide information relevant to the agenda of the meeting. Its purpose was to consider resettlement and readjustment problems in the period of transition to peace and to assist the Office in implementing the resolutions adopted at both Philadelphia and Paris. The meeting called on the Office to make special studies of home aid social services, and of the new aspects of industrial homework, particularly in regard to measures to regulate its abuses. The panel also asked that the status of domestic workers be placed on the agenda of the conference at a forthcoming session in order to adopt a recommendation on the subject. (This issue, originally raised in 1936, has still to be dealt with.) The 1946 meeting was considered so useful that it led to the holding of another one in Geneva in 1951. The latter assisted in the planning of research needed to implement the equality of remuneration convention adopted by the Conference. The Correspondence Committee remained a useful tool for bringing greater expertise to the Office and a wider knowledge of women's issues throughout the world.

One of the most important actions taken by the Governing Body at its 1945 Paris meeting was to name the members of the ILO negotiating team with the United Nations. The membership included the United States and the latter appointed as its representative Frieda Miller, the only woman member of the team, who, it will be remembered, had chaired the Committee on Constitutional Change.

The following year the Conference met in Montreal. This was the first and only one held at the seat of the ILO's wartime headquarters. It was primarily concerned with the ratification of the agreement with the UN Economic and Social Council and with making the changes required in the ILO Constitution to enable it to become a specialized agency. Miller submitted to the Conference the report of the negotiating team.

The 1946 Conference also completed the action initiated in Paris by adopting a series of conventions dealing with protection of children and young workers. Eleven women sat on the committee responsible for these items; Florence Hancock served as vice chairman and Olga Raffalovich as reporter. Two conventions and a recommendation dealt with medical examinations for fitness for employment of children and young persons, one in industrial and one in nonindustrial enterprises. The latter aroused the antagonism of a number of the employers. Thus, for example, a Belgian employer sought to turn the convention into a recommendation on the grounds that this would facilitate legislation by a government instead of forcing it to "conform with the text of a too rigid Convention." The women participants in the committee reacted angrily. Beatrice McConnell, assistant director of the division of labor standards in charge of child labor and youth employment, U.S. Department of Labor, strongly urged the adoption of a convention "as one step in the meeting of our obligation to safeguard the health and the general welfare of the children of the world." These sentiments were echoed by Jennie Matyas, vice president of the International Ladies Garment Workers Union, U.S. worker member, Olga Raffalovich, French government, and Marie Couette, secretary of the General Confederation of French Trade Unions. Hancock expressed regret that the convention was not as progressive as many people would have liked but, nevertheless, she deemed it "a great step forward." The proposal of the Belgian employer to turn the convention into a recommendation was lost by a vote of 18 to 62. A third convention and a recommendation dealt with restriction of night work of children and young persons in nonindustrial employment, setting limitations upon the age of admission.

A significant addition to the ILO staff, Mildred Fairchild, joined the ranks in the last days of the Montreal operations as the successor to Marguerite Thibert. She was the first woman to achieve the title of chief of division. She had been professor of social economy and social research at Bryn Mawr College. She was a strong fighter for the position of women on the staff. Soon after she became a staff member she married Robert Woodbury, chief of the statistical division (a collector of miniature owls and owl portraits), becoming the first senior staff member who was not handicapped by being the wife of an official with equal rank—because she held the position before marriage. (See chapter 4 for her role with respect to equal pay for women, as well as with the UN Status of Women Commission.)

A first step in determining the ultimate headquarters of the ILO was the decision of the Governing Body to hold the 1947 Conference in Geneva. This led, of necessity, to the dispatch of the requisite staff and this, in turn, influenced the subsequent decision to make Geneva the permanent headquarters.

The formal legislative actions of the 1947 Conference were the adoption of conventions and recommendations dealing with two items discussed previously: labor inspection and social policy in nonmetropolitan territories. Two additional items received initial discussion and were formally acted upon in the following year: employment services organization and freedom of association.

This was the first time the conference had adopted a convention dealing with labor inspection. It provided that "both men and women shall be eligible for appointment to the inspection staff; when necessary, special duties may be assigned to men and women inspectors." This was a somewhat belated step in view of the fact that from the 1890s on Western governments had been appointing women inspectors and the ILO itself had already adopted a recommendation to the same effect in 1921. The impetus in 1937 reflected the influence of women inspectors at ILO conferences. One of these was Brighid Stafford, from Ireland, who chaired the committee that dealt with this item. Other active participants in the framing of the texts were Clara Beyer of the U.S. Bureau of Labor Standards, Ms. Marit Aarum of Norway, state and factory inspectorate, and Mrs. Kolabinska, Polish labor inspector.

One of the articles in the Convention on Social Policy in Non-Metropolitan Territories called for appropriate steps to improve the status of women, and another article asserted the "aim of policy" to be the abolition of all discrimination among workers on grounds of race, color, and sex. Sharita Mukherjee, an Indian worker, took an active role in the committee, insisting on the inclusion of the word "sex" in the definition of discrimination. (This was also one of two committees on which Mildred Fairchild served at her first ILO Conference.)

The item on employment services organization stemmed from the 1944 recommendations concerning employment in the transition from war to peace. The Convention on Employment Service Organization, as adopted the following year (1948), called upon all countries to "maintain or ensure the maintenance of a free public employment service." Provision should be made for cooperation with representatives of employers and workers regarding organization, operation, and policy of the employment service. Assistance should be given to workers in finding suitable employment and information should be circulated concerning the labor market. The convention was applicable to all persons. The only specific references to women came in the recommendation which provided for "adequate arrangements for the placement of women on the basis of their occupational skill and physical capacity." Another provision required referrals to be made without regard to "race, color, sex or belief." The reporter of the committee dealing with the Employment Service Convention in 1948 was Mary Smieton, under secretary, Ministry of Labour and National Service of the United Kingdom. The drafting of the texts was primarily the work of Elizabeth Mayer Johnstone, and she and Mildred Fairchild were the ILO experts serving the committee.

An item on freedom of association and protection of the right to organize was an important example of a new phase in the ILO's approach to industrial relations and human rights. Even though women were not referred to specifically, the provisions, initially discussed in 1947 and incorporated in a convention the following year, ensured that "workers and employers, without distinction whatsoever, shall have the right to establish and, subject only to the rules of the organization concerned, to join organizations of their own choosing without previous authorization." This was supplemented in 1949 by the Convention on the Application of the Principles of the Right to Organize and Bargain Collectively. As far as women were concerned, these rights encouraged them to join trade unions, as will be seen in chapter 5. (However, reflecting their situation at the time, there were no women on the relevant Conference committee in 1947.)

At this session the Conference also adopted a resolution concerning the need for greater equality in employment between men and women, especially with respect to stabilization of wages. The resolution was introduced by the United States as a "statement of homage to women worker's contributions." Speaking to the resolution, Sharita Mukherjee, assistant secretary, All India Trade Union Congress, declared that "to place women workers on a basis of equality with men workers, which is the declared objective of the ILO, it is essential that the Conventions on women's employment should be ratified and applied. . . . It must be realized however with great regret that the policy of implementing these principles has not been pursued as actively as it should have been." She urged that the ILO send out missions to find out the real conditions of women's employment.

Marie Couette of France reported that the principle of equality of wages had now been legalized in France. However, she sought more than that. "To women must be given complete freedom, freedom to choose either industrial work, production work, or household work, where she can carry out her work as housekeeper and mother of a family and at the same time fulfill her role as citizen and worker." Apparently uneasy lest the emphasis on equality lead to a downgrading of the traditional role of women and to the protection afforded them in that role she demanded that the ILO make a study with particular reference to the protection which should be given to women in society. She added "even though we ask for equality it would not be right to have equality in all things." While there was no disagreement as to the desirability of women obtaining equal rights, there was at that time considerable fear that the drive for political equality—such as that advocated by the Equal Rights Amendment (ERA) in the United States and similar groups elsewhere—could undermine some of the benefits obtained by women in the social and industrial fields. The problem was basically one of strategy and timing in the struggle to eliminate discrimination and obtain equal opportunities for men and women.

In the United States many legislators, as well as private citizens, lined up behind ERA and in 1946 the amendment had won a majority but lost the requisite two-thirds. Lobbying on the other side had been the National Committee to Defeat the Unequal Rights Amendment. With the support of the Women's Bureau, forty-three national organizations, including the American Civil Liberties Union, had fought the ERA. Men seeking to recapture their prewar jobs, unions and employers, and even the majority of women still under the slogan—women's place is in the home—remained in substantial opposition.[14]

The 1948 Conference, which took place in San Francisco, was the last one to be held in North America. It was also the last session at which Edward Phelan served as secretary-general. Its agenda included, in addition to the adoption of the Freedom of Association and Employment Service Organization conventions, revision of both the Night Work for Women Convention and the Night Work for Young Persons Convention, a first discussion of a vocational guidance recommendation and of a protection of wages recommendation. The number of women participating in the Conference was a little less than the previous year but there were a number of newcomers of interest. Thus, the United States included a woman employer, L. E. Ebeling, director of personnel of Sherwin Williams Paint Company, who was to remain active for several years. At the 1948 session she worked with the committee dealing both with employment service organization and vocational guidance (a committee run, from the Office level, by Elizabeth Mayer Johnstone). Mrs. Noel de Matteris de Lorenzi, a former senator from Uruguay, who served on the committee responsible for the revision of the Night Work for Women Convention, noted that in her country there was an absolute prohibition of night work for women in all forms of industrial employment. Gertrude Stemberg was reporter of this committee—which was staffed primarily by women, under the leadership of Mildred Fairchild.

The Conference, in addition to its legislative actions, adopted two resolutions of particular importance to women: one dealing with the conditions of employment of domestic workers, and the other with equal remuneration for work of equal value, both of which set the stage for future ILO activities. The Resolution on Domestic Workers asked that the subject be placed on the agenda of a future session of the Conference, hopefully in 1950. The Resolution on Wages took account of the March 1948 resolution of the UN Economic and Social Council and a memorandum of the World Federation of Trade Unions urging that the item be placed on the agenda of an early session.

The most far-reaching action taken by the ILO in San Francisco was the naming of David A. Morse as Director-General. At the time he was undersecretary of labor, chief of the U.S. delegation to the ILO Conference, and U.S. member of the Governing Body. The Governing Body, meeting during the first days of the Conference, accepted the retirement of Phelan (to take effect a few months later when he became sixty) and elected Morse as his successor.

In 1949 the participation of women was rather low-keyed. At least one woman sat on most of the committees—Mrs. Pless of Brazil on Standing Orders, Williams of the U.S. on Resolutions, and Gertrude Stemberg on Finance. The only woman officer on any committee was Stemberg, who served as vice chairman of the Committee on Industrial Relations. No woman spoke in Plenary. The one convention adopted that was of special interest to women dealt with the revision of a Convention on Migration for Employment. Five women sat on the committee dealing with this item. As revised, the Convention provides that each member "undertakes to apply without discrimination in respect of nationality, race, religion or

Eleanor Roosevelt holding a poster of the Declaration of Human Rights, 1949
(courtesy of United Nations).

sex to immigrants lawfully within its territory, treatment no less favorable than that which it applies to its own nationals." Provision is made to include family allowances for migrant workers and to cover women under social security. The Recommendation and its attached model agreement adds members of their families to the migrant workers protected by its provisions.[15] These texts were supplemented in 1975 when provisions were included for facilitating family reunification.

Meanwhile, the last act of Edward Phelan as Director-General was to arrange for the closing of the Montreal working center and the transfer of the ILO back to its Geneva headquarters. One phenomenon of the period was the beginning of second generation staff. At the 1947 Conference Françoise Thomas, daughter of Albert Thomas, the first ILO Director, was secretary of the Committee on Non-Metropolitan Territories. She served on the staff for many years as both research worker and liaison officer.

Elizabeth Miller, the daughter of Frieda Miller (who had just been appointed as a research assistant), served in the press section at the Conference. Margaret Mortished, daughter of one of the former senior chiefs of section, served as an interpreter, although she too was on the research staff where she worked for many years. Antoinette Waelbroeck Beguin was a third generation staffer, since both her father and her mother's father had preceded her in the Office. She too joined the staff as a research assistant just before the Office returned to Geneva, but on a number of occasions she also served as an interpreter. Her exceptional career (she ultimately became Assistant Director-General) is described in chapter 7. Mary Erulkar, daughter of an Indian employer who had attended many conferences and governing body sessions, also joined the staff at this time as research assistant. She married James Burtle, another young (U.S.) member of the staff; they remained into the mid-1950s when they returned to the United States.

Some other new members of the staff, recruited in Montreal during the final years there, were transferred not to Geneva, but to the newly established Liaison Office to the United Nations, which also served to retain links outside of Europe. Finally, the reintegration of the staff in Geneva also brought a number of promotions for women members—such as the naming of Elizabeth Mayer Johnstone as assistant director of the enlarged manpower division, where she became responsible for much of the work in the field of employment policy and later served as coordinator for women and children's affairs.

The transfer of the Office back to Geneva marked the end of the era of survival and rejuvenation of the ILO. Its changed mission will be discussed in the chapters that follow.

4. The Ongoing Agenda:
Setting International Standards

The present chapter brings together the elements of the International Labor Code that affect women. During roughly its first thirty years ILO instruments applying specifically to women had dealt primarily with maternity protection and the safeguarding of women against onerous or unhealthy occupations. In the 1950s and early 1960s the focus shifted to basic human rights—equality of opportunity and treatment with men, equal remuneration, social security coverage, and health services in places of employment. While most of the ILO instruments obviously apply to women as well as to men, growing sensitivity to problems of discrimination resulted in explicit prohibition of discrimination based on sex. From the mid-1960s, attention centered on practical methods of enabling women to achieve their full potential in the field of economic development. Included were such issues as freedom of association, training for new technological jobs, measures to provide women with access to all positions within the society, and recognition of the joint responsibility for the family of both men and women.

Protective Legislation

Instruments relating to women fall into two general categories—those covering both men and women, and those affecting women exclusively. The legislative standards within the latter category primarily deal with maternity protection, night work, and underground work. With the exception of the underground work provisions, all stemmed from the decision of the 1919 Peace Conference to put these subjects on the agenda of the first ILO Conference.

The major protective legislative instruments, applicable to men as well as women, which contain special provisions affecting women only are: work in unhealthy processes; industries involving physical or mental strain; social security; and reduction of hours of work. Women are restricted from employment in industries involving dangerous substances such as white phosphorous, white lead in paint, anthrax, radiation, and benzine. The elimination of white phosphorous in matches dates back to the pre-World War I Berne Conference and was incorporated in a Recommendation adopted in 1919. All females are prohibited, by a Convention adopted in 1921, from working in industries involving the use of white lead paint. A 1919 Anthrax Recommendation calls for the disinfection of wool infected with anthrax spores. The Radiation Protection Recommendation, adopted in 1960, requires that "every care should be taken to ensure" that women of childbearing age are not exposed to high radiation work.

The 1967 Maximum Weight Convention prohibits any worker from transporting a load so heavy that it might jeopardize his health or safety. It specifies that women must carry loads substantially less than those for men. A recommendation goes further and prohibits a pregnant woman from being assigned to manual transport during the ten weeks after confinement if a qualified physician so stipulates.

The Benzene Convention (1971) provides a number of safeguards to protect workers from exposure to benzene but flatly bars the employment of pregnant women and nursing mothers in any processes involving exposure to benzene or products containing benzene. This and other protective measures singling out women and leaving men to face hazards led Seija Karkinen, visiting minister from Finland to declare, at the 1973 Conference, that "when working for the improvement of the status of women, the aim should of course be equality between the sexes, not the placing of women in a special position. . . . If some types of work are considered hazardous, all workers should be equally protected. Frankly discrimination should not be practised against men because of women and should not be practised against women because of men."

Only a small number of women participated in the committees dealing with such issues by contrast with the number serving on the committees concerned with social security and maternity benefits—indicating the greater concern of women with the latter.[1] The committee dealing with the maternity provisions in the Convention on Minimum Standards of Social Security (1952) was attended by eighteen women with Hancock as vice chairman and Stemberg as reporter. Two women members of the social security section of the Office, Miss Bodmer and Miss Craig, served as the staff. Both had participated in the preparation of the report that was the basis of the discussion. The convention is divided into nine parts, covering medical care, cash benefits, old age benefits, family benefits, maternity benefits, invalidity benefits, and survivors benefits. The provisions include medical care "in respect of pregnancy and confinement and their consequences." It also provides for both prenatal confinement and post-natal care by either doctors or midwives.

At this same session of the Conference, another committee was dealing with revision of the convention concerning maternity benefits. In order to prevent any contradiction occurring in the drafting of the two texts, the officers of the two committees met. They ascertained that the texts provisionally adopted by the two committees were mutually compatible in the sense that no member ratifying the social security instrument would be prevented thereby from ratifying that of the revised Convention concerning maternity protection.

The committee dealing with the revision of the Maternity Convention included twenty women, among whom were Florence Hancock, vice chairman, and Gertrude Stemberg, the reporter. The latter, reporting on the work of the committee, stated: "the revision has had as its aim to make the Convention more flexible and to bring it into harmony with the idea now prevailing on the subject." It would widen the scope, she said, from industrial undertakings to bring in all kinds of nonindustrial undertakings, including domestic workers and homeworkers, though "temporary exceptions" would be permitted in respect of domestic workers and women wage earners working at home. The revision specified that there should be no distinction with regard to age, nationality, race, or creed. In addition, the twelve weeks leave, already provided, was more precisely defined. Hancock, speaking for the workers group, objected to a proposal that employers should be required to pay for maternity benefits on the ground that it could be discriminatory, while Inga Thorsson noted that the Swedish government was against a provision calling for payment for interruption of work for purposes of nursing. The Danish government proposed an amendment to the text, stating the principle that the employer should not be individually liable for the costs of cash and medical benefits due to the women employed by him since a requirement of this kind would be detrimental to women's employment opportunities. This proposal was accepted (by a vote of 47 to 4 with 33 abstentions) and was coupled with

Frances Perkins, U.S. Secretary of Labor, with her commissioner of labor statistics, Isador Lubin, frequently a U.S. member of the ILO Governing Body.

a provision that such benefits should be provided either by means of compulsory social insurance or by benefits from public assistance funds. Another new provision was the requirement that no woman could be given a notice of dismissal while on maternity leave.

Another 1952 committee dealt with workers' health and, although only four women served on this committee, one, Frances Perkins, then U.S. civil service commissioner, was its chairman. In 1980 and again in 1981 the Conference dealt with safety, health, and the working environment. Mrs. Koradecka of Poland was the chairman, and in discussing the report of the committee in the Plenary gave particular thanks to the ILO for its actions to improve conditions of work and the working environment. Mrs. Leonitcheva, worker adviser from the USSR, stressed the importance of preventing industrial accidents and dealing with industrial diseases.

Regulation and reduction of hours of work was a primary concern of the ILO from the outset—the 1919 Conference having adopted a convention setting hours at forty-eight per week with an eight-hour day (a figure, it will be recalled, protested by the women's organizations, discussed earlier). The general principle of a forty-hour week had been the major issue of the 1935 Conference, and a number of conventions reducing hours in particular industries were adopted—and some defeated—in later years. In none of these texts were any provisions included dealing specifically with women. It was not until 1962 that a recommendation concerning the progressive reduction of hours of work was adopted which contains a number of provisions specifically applying to women and older workers.[2] It noted that priority in application should be given to industries which involve particularly heavy physical or mental strain and where the workers consist mainly of women and young persons. Another provision states that in arranging for overtime work, due consideration should be given to the special circumstances of young persons under eighteen, of pregnant women and nursing mothers, and of handicapped persons.

Two Swedish women government advisers successively sat on the committees dealing with hours of work in 1961 and 1962. The first was Signe Holst, chief of the social section, Workers' Protection Board. At one time she had been personnel director of a chain of thirty-one restaurants. During her years at ILO conferences she also served twice on the Committee on Health Services and, in an intervention in Plenary, she said it had become evident to her that something must be done for the women in Africa or Asia or "everywhere where they were oppressed. We had," she said, "to make people wake up to see this." Her expression of concern was symptomatic of a growing awareness that the ILO needed to give more attention to the very different needs of the developing countries— an awareness soon to be heightened by the presence of so many independent countries. The second Swedish speaker was Ingrid Hilding, legal adviser to the ministry of social affairs. She sat on a number of committees between 1962 and 1972, first as an adviser and later as a full delegate. She sat on such committees as those dealing with social security and guarding of machinery. She started her career as a law clerk in the Stockholm magistrates' court, eventually became permanent under secretary in the ministry and in the last year of her ILO service was a justice of the Supreme Administrative Court.

The 1962 Recommendation was taken up again in 1967 when the Advisory Committee on Salaried Employees and Professional Workers drew attention to the particular problems facing women and young workers in the distributive trades, where hardship conditions frequently prevailed.

Protective legislation specifically for women has come under attack from a number of women's groups. The major targets have been those instruments dealing with women's work at night or underground. The exclusion of women from certain types of work has been viewed as discriminatory, one argument being that it restricts the right of women to employment. Another argument is that it may prevent women from working hours that are more convenient for family life—especially where young children are concerned—than the traditional daytime hours. However, many women workers are reluctant to accept the removal of a safeguard until similar protection is provided by other means. Women, particularly in developing countries, where employers are more unfettered and trade unions relatively weak, fear that employers might, if these safeguards were removed, be free to put women onto the night shift where they foresee the danger of harassment and sexual exploitation.

Meantime, a number of governments have denounced the conventions dealing with night and underground work for women. The Committee on the Application of Conventions and Recommendations in 1988 reported that the "Employers' members and several Government members stressed the contradiction existing between special standards of protection and the principle of equality between women and men and considered that certain employment prohibitions had to be re-examined in the light of technical and medical progress." The growing chorus of discontent with these provisions led the Governing Body to place on the 1989 agenda of the conference the question of revising the night work convention. The Office report, the basis for the discussion, suggested the adoption of a protocol to give more flexibility to the revised 1948 Night Work Convention and the adoption of new standards in the form of a convention supplemented by a recommendation. Such new instruments would cover wage earners of both sexes and apply to all branches of activity except agriculture, animal production, fishery, sea transport, and inland water transport.

An initial discussion of the way in which the Conference should deal with these issues illustrated the conceptual differences among the three groups concerning the role of the ILO in setting standards for issues such as night work. The Office had proposed that the discussion of the protocol should precede the discussion of the new standards. The workers' group objected to this order, indicating that they wished to know what new standards were to be adopted before considering how the existing convention should be weakened. The employers strongly approved the Office's suggested order of action, starting with the protocol and leaving to a subsequent stage the question of new standards. They wanted to obtain maximum flexibility to use women on night work with the fewest possible restrictions. Although the governments were divided on this issue, the proposal of the workers was adopted by a substantial vote (with a large number of abstentions) and the committee immediately took up the proposed content of the new standards.

The views expressed in the Conference indicated a high degree of consensus with widely varying motivations. It was clear that the employers generally were seeking the right to use women on night work as they pleased but using the argument of equal opportunity to sweeten their position. The workers, on the other hand, while seeking to maintain adequate protective features, wanted enough flexibility so that women were not unnecessarily debarred from working schedules that could be adjusted to family needs. Representatives from developing countries wanted enough flexibility to allow their governments to implement the proposals in accord with their own legal and administrative practices. Canada, the United States, and a number of other developed countries frequently agreed with the employers, but on very different grounds. They emphasized that women had begun to work increasingly in occupations previously dominated by men.

One of the central issues was the question of whether the new standards could be implemented by collective bargaining rather than by legislation. The employers took the view that whatever new standards were adopted they should be implemented by collective agreements, while the workers feared that recourse to collective agreements rather than by legislation might weaken national enforcement. Governments of the industrialized countries—particularly members of the European community—urged the wider reliance on collective agreements while the developing countries stressed the value of minimum standards, legislatively enforced.[3]

The concerns discussed in the Committee on Night Work for Women highlighted the dichotomy of protecting the special needs of women and achieving equality of employment between men and women. The committee comprised seventy-eight government members, fifty-four employer representatives, fifty-six worker representatives, balanced fairly equally with respect to sex.[4] The chairman was the government member from Indonesia, P. K. Suma'mur, its vice chairpersons were the employers member from Australia, B. Noakes, and the workers' member from Switzerland, Ruth Dreifuss, secretary of the Swiss trade unions and deputy member of the Governing Body; its reporter was the member from Belgium, Jo Walgrave, assistant mediator for collective bargaining in the ministry of employment and labor. The Drafting Committee was composed of two men and two women.

The Conference adopted the committee's report which included, in addition to the proposed new standards, the proposed protocol to revise the 1948 Convention. In regard to the new standards—although many details, especially those dealing with the definitions of night work, health provisions, and enforcement issues, were left to be worked out before final action in 1990—the basic issues of revision, flexibility, and equality were agreed on. The committee declared that its conclusions would provide new guideposts for standard setting in the future.[5]

In the United States, as in the ILO, the issue of legislation applying exclusively to women in one form or another continued to divide the feminists. In 1987 the U.S. Supreme Court upheld the right of states to provide pregnancy disability leave for women with no comparable time off for men. Feminists on one side deplored this provision, equating it with discredited protective laws. According to this group such special treatment distorted the labor market, encouraged employers to discriminate against women and contributed to their occupational segregation. Feminists on the other side rejected the comparison with protective legislation, maintaining that the provision merely focused on "how women's unique reproductive role affects them in the workplace."[6]

Although the ILO Conference had asked in 1975 and again ten years later for a review of ILO's protective legislation, it was not until 1989 that an expert committee was convened to consider the issue. One inference that emerged clearly from the discussion was the difficulty of making any firm recommendations. There was general agreement that, in an ideal world, protection should be extended equally to men and women without distinction except for such special measures as might be indicated during "pregnancy, nursing and early maternity." There was also general agreement that protective measures addressed solely to women could be a barrier to employment and career advancement. Beyond that the problem became more difficult. In many developing countries measures to protect the health of workers were either very limited or nonexistent, while at the same time women were moving into an increasingly wide range of jobs, many potentially hazardous.

Aside from geographical variations, there was everywhere limited knowledge of the precise effects of different kinds of hazards. Even in the Nordic countries which had abolished protective legislation, it was found that, because women "still carried the primary responsibility for household duties and care of the family" there was a decline in their health and increase of absenteeism. The committee concluded that national and international efforts to study the problem should be intensified. Further research and study was needed on "dangerous substances and agents . . . to assess the risks which may be specific to women's and men's biological condition" and their progeny in order to determine requisite adaptation of technology and job design. It was also recognized that a major effort needed to be undertaken to change some basic attitudes and practices which frequently negated existing legislation. Toward this end the ILO was urged "to strengthen the capacity of member states to deal with the safety and health needs of women workers and their quality of life" through training, technical advisory services, and technical cooperation.[7]

Instruments Relating to Equality

The era following the Second World War brought the issue of equality and nondiscrimination to the forefront, and since then it has been a constant thread in ILO standard setting. Conventions and recommendations dealing specifically with this subject include those on equal remuneration, equality of employment, vocational guidance and training, and workers with family responsibilities.

While the problem of equal remuneration for women with men has been a predominant issue for women from the early days of the industrial revolution, it was not generally accepted as a realistic goal until the Second World War—and even then the concept of equal pay for work of equal value was seldom practiced in either the public or private sectors. However, valiant efforts to obtain this objective were made as early as the First

World War, as evidenced in a report issued in 1916/17 by the Standing Joint Committee of Industrial Women's Organizations of the United Kingdom. The report, entitled "The Position of Women after the War," was signed by ten outstanding women trade union leaders, speaking for the Women's Trade Union League, the Women's Cooperative Guild, the Women's Labour League, the National Federation of Women Workers and the Railway Women's Guild.[8]

In discussing the effect of the war on women's wages, the committee notes that "in trades *where the organisations concerned have been sufficiently strong* war conditions have produced a marked rise in the wages of women, whether engaged on women's work or in substitution for men; that some small rise in wages has been paid in many other trades. . . . [T]here [is no] evidence to lead us to believe that women engaged in substitution for men have, unless in exceptional cases, obtained the men's full rate." The report concludes with recommendations concerning reconstruction policy stating "The problem before women workers is, how are they to keep the improved industrial position they have won without the effect of their employment being the reduction of the wages of men? The fundamental need to carry out the principle of equal pay for equal work, for the employment of women will always have a depressing effect on the wages of men as long as there is any economic sex distinction."[9]

This British women's initiative was more articulate than most of those formulated during the First World War but it was typical of the experience in many countries, and directly contributed to the atmosphere that led, as discussed in an earlier chapter, to the establishment of the ILO at the Peace Conference and the recognition in its charter of the need for a living wage along with reduced hours of work. There was, however, no specific call for equality in wage rates and, as experience soon proved, the gap between women's and men's wages in the interwar years tended to widen as depression and unemployment took over.[10]

In 1943 a National Delegate Conference of Women Members of the TGWU echoed many of the same concerns. However, there was evidently greater determination and more sophistication. The conference itemized a long list of demands regarding health, welfare, and safety provisions, including the need for nurseries and nursery schools. Women were urged to campaign for greater participation by women in unions, and the union was called on to employ more full-time women officers. In his address to the conference the acting general secretary declared that "women must take their part, the world over, in demanding the raising of the international standard of life, for it is only by the international raising of standards that we can maintain our own standards."[11]

The Second World War had brought back recognition of the need for higher wages and for substantial improvement of working conditions and provision of child care if women were to be attracted in sufficient numbers to meet the labor demands of the nation's manpower reserves. In many instances the same or closely similar organizations, and many of the same individuals, who led the women in the First World War worked for fairer pay scales in war industries and began to plan for the needs of women in the transition from war to peace.

In the United States the most notable feature of the early postwar period was the militancy of black women's organizations. Much of the leadership was assumed by the National Council of Negro Women which had been founded in 1935 by Mary McLeod Bethune and later led by Dorothy I. Height. Their primary concern was the fight against racism, and they were also opposed to the adoption of an Equal Rights Amendment. Many other political activists turned their attention to civil rights legislation. In 1962 discrimination in the federal civil service was outlawed by the Kennedy administration, and the following year it pushed through Congress an equal pay act, appended to the Fair Labor Standards Act, which prohibited wage discrimination on the basis of sex. Another example of the response to pressure by women's lobbies was the increase in posts requiring Senate confirmation and the appointment of Oveta Culp Hobby as secretary of the Department of Health, Education, and Welfare and Esther Peterson as assistant secretary of labor. Peterson prevailed on the president to establish a U.S. Commission on the Status of Women in 1961, and to name Eleanor Roosevelt as its first chairman.

Developments in the United Kingdom were influenced by those in the United States, although emphases and directions were often different. The fight for equal pay was led by militant labor women, like the sewing machinists in a Ford Motor factory who went on strike in 1968 demanding upgrading from unskilled to semiskilled. Although only partially successful, the strike stimulated the creation of the trade unionist National Joint Action Campaign for Women's Equal Rights (NJACWER). In 1970 NJACWER, together with various new left groups and suffrage organizations, participated in the first national Women's Liberation Conference. This in turn led to the establishment of a National Women's Coordinating Committee. Their four basic demands were: equal pay now; equal education and job opportunities; free contraceptives and abortion; and free twenty-four-hour nurseries. Later, three other demands were added: financial and legal independence; a woman's right to define her own sexuality; and an end to all laws, assumptions, and institutions perpetuating male violence and aggression toward women.[12]

In France mediocre education and the dominant influence of the Roman Catholic church perpetuated the image of a patriarchal society. Militant women became increasingly active early in the 1970s both in their unions and in the number of women's groups that had sprung up. By 1980 women in the salaried labor force had increased by 39 percent. A new dynamism, however, had already begun to be felt in 1974–75. Large numbers of young women entered the teaching profession and became elected to political jobs, although they have remained under-represented and tend to be assigned to local issues. The old slogan "be beautiful and be silent" has been changed to "be beautiful, intelligent, young, a performer and be silent."[13]

A regional development in Europe affecting women was the establishment of the European Community (EC) by the Treaty of Rome in 1957 which declared that each member state must ensure and maintain the principle that men and women should receive equal pay for equal work. The law created by the European Community institutions comprises regulations, decisions, and directives. This legislation superseded all the national laws of the members of the EC. In 1976 a directive was issued banning discrimination at work on the grounds of sex. Two years later another directive dealt with equal treatment in matters of social security. In 1984 the Council of Ministers addressed a recommendation to the member states urging them to adopt a policy of positive action to eliminate de facto discrimination against women at work.[14] The effect of the EC's emphasis on equality for women led it, as mentioned previously, to urge that the ILO abolish protective provisions in conventions that limited equality for women.

Equal Pay for Equal Work

Although the ILO had considered the problem of equal remuneration from the moment of its establishment, the specific issue of wages had been primarily dealt with as a protective measure designed to fix minimum wages for women. However, it took thirty years before equal remuneration was placed on the agenda of the Conference for legislative action. The

Commission on the Status of Women of the United Nations deserves some credit for this measure. In 1948 it adopted a resolution calling for action by the ILO with respect to equal pay for equal work. The following year it asked the ILO to include the rate for the job irrespective of sex, as well as calling for technical training and guidance, equal access with men for jobs and promotion, and abolition of legal or customary restrictions on the pay of women workers. In consequence of a study by the ILO, the commission in 1950 decided that no specific further resolution on the subject was necessary. Partly in response to the concern of the commission and partly in preparation for conference consideration of the issue, Mildred Fairchild was authorized by the ILO Governing Body to convene in Geneva a special conference of women worker experts which was attended by women from many countries and included both Frieda Miller and Pauline Newman, who, it will be recalled, had long been deeply concerned with wage regulation and sex discrimination. One of the issues resolved by this meeting dealt with British and U.S. government differences in concept between "equal pay for equal work" and "equal pay for work of equal value." The compromise reached made clear that equal value meant, for example, that certain domestic occupations were equivalent to those of gardeners or chauffeurs and should be paid accordingly.

When the 1950 session of the Conference met sixteen women sat on the committee discussing equal remuneration, with Frieda Miller as reporter. At this session the Scandinavians appeared in force. From Finland came Tyne Leivo-Larsson, director of the Social Museum and member of the Chamber of Deputies. She served as a government delegate in 1950, 1951, and 1971. In 1955 she attended as visiting minister of social affairs. Like most of the Scandinavians, she was a vigorous proponent of women's rights. Addressing the 1950 session, she declared that "the most important factors in the life of human beings are their salary and the conditions in which they perform their work and live." It was, she continued, "most unfortunate for women to know that they are considered as an inferior class of citizens in the employment market simply because they are women." She expressed the hope that the conference would complete a convention the following year.

Another Scandinavian newcomer was Inga Thorsson of Sweden who also served on the committee. She, like Alva Myrdal, was a graduate of the Training College of Teachers. She was a political activist and, at the age of forty-three, the first female city commissioner of Stockholm. Upon her appointment the press described her as an "obstinate, fiery spirit" as "indomitable as quitch grass" who "speaks like a rattling machine gun." In later years she succeeded Alva Myrdal as chairman of the Swedish delegation to the Disarmament Conference, a subject which became her predominant interest.

The differing perspectives with respect to equal pay of workers and of employers were reflected in the speeches of Anne Godwin, British worker, and L. E. Ebeling, U.S. employer. Godwin, noting that endorsement of the principle of equal remuneration had been included in the 1919 ILO Constitution, even if never acknowledged in practice, stated, "Now, after 31 years we are asking you to take the next step. We are not here as suppliants; we are a constituted part of this Assembly. We are citizens and workers in our own countries, and we bring this claim before you, not as women but as workers, asking for justice for a section of workers. We leave the claim with you with complete confidence."

Ebeling proclaimed employer adherence to the principle of equal remuneration, pointing out that there was no differential price in the market based on sex—a loaf of bread or pair of shoes cost the same for both men and women. However, while prepared to accept a recommendation, she would have to vote against a convention because she was convinced that the world was not ready for a convention on equal remuneration. She also objected to various provisions in the proposed text concerning methods of determining job classifications, analysis of job content, as well as a provision for welfare and social services that meet the needs of women workers, particularly those with family responsibilities, such services to be financed from public funds or from industrial welfare funds covering all workers.

The following year, when the Conference took final action on a convention and a recommendation, women once more played a prominent role. There were old-timers like Frieda Miller who again served as the reporter of the committee, Stemberg, Hancock (now Dame Florence Hancock), and Godwin. There were also voices from non-Western countries which underlined the worldwide concern with this problem and demonstrated that the conference provided an international platform for those who might otherwise be voiceless. Thus, for example, Indra W. Bose, a young member of the Indian National Trade Union Congress, declared in plenary, with some bitterness, "Some of the representatives of so-called progressive governments, including my own, have thought it fit to oppose a Convention for men and women getting equal remuneration for work of equal value. It is not necessary to point out the simple justice of such a Convention."[15] The importance of the Convention was emphasized by two other women workers, Florence Hancock of the United Kingdom and Simone Troisgros of France, assistant secretary-general of the Women's Committee of the Confederation of Christian Workers. Hancock regretted that "certain employers have either not understood, or more probably, not accepted the principle of equal pay." Troigros declared that, after years of discussion, "a solemn decision had been made regarding the imperious necessity of abolishing the inequality of women's wages in comparison with men's." She said, "women throughout the world have their eyes turned towards this Organization because they hold it in high esteem. Do not disappoint their hopes." Despite the attitude of some of the employers, such as Ebeling, the world seemed to be ready for a convention.

The Convention dealt with the general principle that "equal remuneration for men and women workers for work of equal value refers to rates of remuneration established without discrimination based on sex." It concluded that measures should be taken "to promote objective appraisal of jobs on the basis of the work to be performed." The Recommendation further specified actions to be taken "after consultation with the employers' and workers' organizations concerned" such as "equal or equivalent facilities for vocational guidance or employment counselling," with appropriate measures to encourage women to use these facilities. The Recommendation also provides for "welfare and social services which meet the needs of women workers, particularly those with family responsibilities."

The Commission on the Status of Women endorsed the actions of the ILO and urged member governments to adopt legislation or other measures in compliance with the Convention.

The Convention has now been ratified by 107 countries (almost the largest number of ratifications) and has had a significant effect on equality of remuneration in many countries.[16] The convention succeeded because it recognized the fact that at the time there was virtually no national legislation on equal pay. Hence governments were merely asked to "promote" and to ensure by "appropriate methods" implementation of the Convention. Furthermore, a number of the more controversial items, such as methods of financing special facilities for women were included in the Recommendation rather than in the Convention. The difficulty of monitoring a convention with such vague obligations was successfully met by a continuing dialogue between ILO experts and ratifying countries.

A subsequent convention (in 1962) reiterated the necessity to abolish all discrimination, including that based on grounds of sex, and called attention to the plight of lower-paid workers, most of whom are women. One provision called for all practicable measures "to lessen by raising the rates applicable to the lower-paid workers any existing differences in wage rates due to discrimination" by reason of sex.

Equal Employment Opportunities

In 1957 the ILO had already taken a further step in reducing discrimination against women. The committee concerned with this issue prepared the ground for the adoption of a convention and recommendation the following year. Eight women sat on the relevant committees in 1957 and in 1958, including a number of newcomers. The presence of Felina T. Reyes, labor attaché in the Philippine mission in Geneva, foreshadowed the growing role of Third World countries. Three distinguished East Europeans also made their influence felt at this time and were to do so for a number of years. One member of the committee was Mileva Srnska, from the Czechoslovak Ministry of Labor and Social Affairs. She brought to bear on ILO issues a well-trained legal mind and wide-ranging experience. She was a member of the faculty of law, Charles University, Prague, the National Human Rights Commission, and the national branch of the World Federation of United Nations Association. In addition to the Committee on Discrimination she sat on committees ranging from radiation to credentials to workers' housing and social security. She was a regular spokesman for her country in plenaries, stressing the importance of removing discrimination in employment and occupation. She called the issue "one of the most important questions ever dealt with by the ILO."

Another newcomer was Ekaterina Korchounova, senior research assistant at the USSR Institute of State and Law, who was a government adviser in 1957. She later became the first chief of the ILO's Office for Women Workers. Another East European was Hanna Bokor-Szego, head of the International Law Department of the Institute for Legal Administrative Sciences, Hungarian Academy of Science, professor of international law, University of Economics, Budapest, and secretary of the Hungarian branch of the International Law Association. Between 1968 and 1974 she served a number of times as vice chairman of the UN Commission on the Status of Women. She sat on various committees of ILO conferences, including two on forced labor and three on the application of conventions. This last was one of her areas of specialization and from 1979–81 she

---

served as a member of the ILO Committee of Experts set up to examine reports on the application of conventions, and she proved to be one of the most effective members of this committee. (She had been preceded in this position from 1955–78 by the Begum Liaguet Ali Kahn of Pakistan, one of the most distinguished women to serve on the committee from a developing country, who was later the founder and president of the Council of Women of Pakistan.)

Only three women workers served on the Committee on Equal Employment Opportunities. Florence Hancock, Mirjam Nordahl, and a newcomer, Maria Weber. Nordahl was secretary of the General Confederation of Norwegian Trade Unions. Beginning in 1950 she sat on a wide range of technical committees for some twenty years. Weber, member of the managing executive board of the German Confederation of Trade Unions, served at later conferences also for some twenty years, participating both in committees dealing with women's issues and on a number of standing committees.

The Convention on Equal Opportunity and Treatment in Employment (111) as adopted by the 1958 Conference calls for a "national policy designed to promote, by methods appropriate to national conditions and practice, equality of opportunity and treatment in respect of employment and occupation, with a view to eliminating any discrimination in respect thereof." Discrimination is defined as "any distinction, exclusion or preference made on the basis of race, color, sex." One provision specifically deals with protective legislation, stating that measures in other conventions and recommendations dealing with particular requirements of special groups or categories shall not be considered discrimination.

The Convention is supplemented by a recommendation which specifies the need for coordination by national authorities of antidiscrimination measures in other fields. It also makes special reference to the Migration for Employment Convention and Recommendations (as revised in 1949) relating to the lifting of restrictions on employment of immigrant workers of foreign nationality and members of their families.

As of 1989 the Convention had been ratified by 109 governments. Ratification had been facilitated by its flexible wording and it has proved useful in influencing governments to include equality of treatment in their employment policies.

In 1973 these provisions were amplified by a recommendation which prohibits termination of employment without a valid reason, specifically stating that termination because of race, color, sex, marital status, religion, political opinion, national extraction, or social origin are not valid reasons. Aside from Ljubinka Popović, chief, conditions of work section, Central Council, Confederation of Yugoslav Trade Unions, the only other woman on the committee was Alison Mary Stephen of Australia. In 1982 the Conference adopted a Convention on Termination of Employment. At this session one of the participants was a relative newcomer, Angela Smith of Grenada, president of the Employers Federation, who was employer delegate from 1980–85.

Employment Policy

In 1964 the Conference took another step toward linking employment to economic growth. It adopted Convention 122 and a recommendation setting forth specific employment goals. The Convention states that in order to stimulate economic growth and development, raise levels of living, meet manpower requirements, and overcome unemployment and underemployment, each member shall "aim at ensuring" work for all seeking and able to work. Such work should be "as productive as possible" and freedom of choice should permit opportunity for each worker to use his skills irrespective of religion, race, color, and sex. In addition to outlining measures to implement the policy, the Recommendation urges employers and workers in public and private sectors to apply the principles of the 1958 antidiscrimination text.

Only five women served on the Committee on Employment Policy, one of whom was a worker delegate from Malagasy (now Madagascar), Dorothee Raharison, member of the Confederated Bureau of Malagasy Trade Unions, and another was Nina Ivanova Pilipchuk of the USSR. The latter falls into a special category. She had come to the Conference in 1954 as a worker adviser, an expert in the All-Union Central Committee of the Agricultural and Food Workers Union. In 1961 she moved to a new job as senior economist, International Relations Section, State Labor and Wages Committee, Council of Ministers, and then came to Geneva as a government representative. She participated in a wide variety of technical committees as well as the Standing Orders Committee. In addition, she accompanied—and occasionally substituted for—the USSR government member of the Governing Body.

Equality in Vocational Training

The early instruments regarding vocational training in 1939 and 1952 made no reference to particular needs of women nor to special problems facing developing countries. In 1962 the Conference adopted a recommendation designed to give through vocational training reality to the employment goals for women. In 1961 Anne Godwin served as workers' vice chairman of the Committee preparing the text. The new text contained a provision covering all human beings (except for managers and supervisory personnel and seafarers who were covered by a 1946 text, and agricultural workers covered by a 1956 text). It stated that all training should be designed to prepare or retrain any person for initial or later employment or promotion in any branch of economic activity, including such general vocational and technical education as may be necessary.

In 1968 the Conference adopted a resolution reaffirming the principle of equality of rights and opportunities without discrimination based on sex. It commended the Director-General on his report, "The ILO and Human Rights," which drew attention to the resolution concerning women workers in a changing world (see below) and noted the Office's continuing research with respect to vocational guidance and training. The resolution emphasized the need for equality in vocational preparation as a precondition for improving women's place in the labor market. It called for specific guidelines for the vocational training and preparation of girls and women with a view to supplementing the 1962 Recommendation. It also asked the Governing Body to put the question on an early session of the Conference agenda for a supplementary recommendation "to promote equal treatment between men and female workers." No specific Conference action was taken on this resolution until 1975 when its objectives were included in the general text prepared for the Decade for Women.

Women Workers in a Changing World

Closely related both to the issues of employment policy and equal rights was a resolution adopted by the Conference in 1964 concerning women workers in a changing world. The Resolution was the consequence of sustained efforts by a number of women, led by Esther Peterson, then U.S. assistant secretary of labor, to bring the problems of women in developing countries to the attention of the Conference. She was born in

Utah of Danish immigrant parents and educated at Brigham Young University and Teachers College, Columbia University. From the beginning of her career she was involved in labor questions, first with the Amalgamated Clothing Workers and then with the AFL/CIO. Prior to her appointment as assistant secretary of labor, she had served as the director of the women's bureau of the Department of Labor, and subsequently consumer adviser to President Johnson.

Her efforts to have the problems of women workers dealt with at the conference were facilitated by the strong support of the IFCTU (International Federation of Christian Trade Unions), which in 1961 had reestablished a joint workers consultative committee on women workers' questions. Further support for a more active women's program came from the Second International Trade Union Conference on the Problems of Working Women, which met in Bucharest, May 1964, under the auspices of the World Federation of Trade Unions and sent a "Preliminary Memorandum" to the Director-General calling for a charter of economic and social rights of working women. An argument raised by Esther Peterson (in correspondence with David Morse, then Director-General), was that if the ILO did not undertake an active program in this area it might be preempted by the UN Status of Women Commission. The commission at its meetings in 1962 and 1963 had asked for ILO material concerning its program and documentation relating to the special problems facing women workers.

To obtain the agreement of the Governing Body to place an appropriate item on the Conference agenda a report was prepared by Elizabeth Johnstone, as the staff member responsible for women's issues, entitled, "Women Workers in a Changing World." In November 1962 the Governing Body placed the item on the 1964 agenda.

The resolution subsequently adopted by the Conference, after noting the increasingly important role played by women in modern society both in developed and developing countries, urged all member states to ratify the Equal Remuneration Convention (1951), and the Discrimination (Employment and Occupation) Convention (1958). It also urged that the 1962 recommendation on vocational training be implemented. It asked, inter alia, that governments consider the usefulness of establishing central units for coordinating research, planning, and programming for women workers' opportunities, needs, and problems, and encourage the dissemination of information on these subjects. Finally, it asked the ILO to expand and strengthen its activities in the field of women's work.

Both in 1964 and 1965 there was a Committee on Women Workers. In the former year women outnumbered men on the conference committee (70–23). The chairman, one vice chairman, and the reporter were all women. Mrs. Dackey of Togo, a social worker, was the chairman. She laid particular stress on the need to inform and educate public opinion on the problems that must be faced by women with family responsibilities and on the necessity for adequate services and facilities for the care of children. The vice chairman was Rosa Weber of Austria, counselor of the Austrian Federation of Trade Unions, who deplored the limited number of ratifications of conventions dealing with discrimination. She also said that inequality in pay threatened the earnings of male workers as well as being unjust to female workers. The reporter was Mrs. Gatti Caporaso of Italy. In 1965 she assumed the chairmanship. At that time the vice chairman was again Rosa Weber and the reporter was Souad Jedidi of Tunisia, attaché, Secretariat of State for Youth Sport and Social Affairs.

Raissa Mikhailovna Smirnova, scientific adviser, African Institute, USSR Academy of Science represented the USSR on the committee both in 1964 and 1965. She also served on the committee dealing with equality of treatment of women in 1975, at which time she was editor-in-chief of the Russian version of the Review, "Femmes du Monde." She stated, in 1965, in the plenary session that the right to work should not only be guaranteed by legislation but given effect in practice. A convention was needed. She subsequently became a member of the ILO staff.

The Canadian government's spokesman in plenary was Miss M. V. Royce, director of the women's bureau of the Department of Labor. She had obtained an M.A. from the University of Toronto at a time when few women sought an advanced degree. She started her career as a high school teacher and then joined the staff of the Young Women's Christian Association, first in Montreal, because she spoke French, and later with the World YWCA in Geneva, working on status of women questions. A woman who knew her own mind, she decided on the course of action to be taken and informed the deputy minister of her intentions. A number of the women participants at conferences during that period, she said, met regularly in caucus to discuss tactics, and she frequently served as their spokesman in committee.

Interest in ILO's renewed concentration on women led to growing participation by women's international, nongovernmental organizations. For example, among those attending in 1965 were Gertrude Baehr of the Women's International League for Peace and Freedom, Marguerite Amstus, International Council of Nurses, Lady Chatterjee, International Federation of Women Lawyers, and Agnes de Kahbeematten, of the Union of Catholic Women's Organizations.

The actions of the conferences in 1964 and 1965 led to the extension of ILO's concerns with women workers into the mainstream of ILO programs. Elizabeth Johnstone, newly appointed coordinator for women and young workers, was charged with ensuring that women's issues were taken into account by the various substantive divisions of the ILO. She was particularly concerned with helping women in developing countries and organizing seminars on women's issues as part of the technical assistance program. In a letter to Esther Peterson she had stressed the urgency of bringing women in newly developing countries "into the labor force with adequate opportunities for training and employment so they can contribute effectively to the economic and industrial development of their countries."[17]

Elizabeth Johnstone was the representative of the ILO at many sessions of the UN Commission on the Status of Women, and she made available to the commission her report, "Women Workers in a Changing World." Her predecessors were Mildred Fairchild (Woodbury) and Ana Figueroa, a Chilean diplomat. Fairchild had attended virtually every session of the commission and had vigorously espoused the views of the ILO. Figueroa had been a member of the UN commission and in 1952 had served as its vice chairman. When she joined the ILO in 1954 she became its representative on the commission and maintained her close ties with that body. She left the ILO in 1959, returning a year later as the first women Assistant Director-General. Her broader responsibilities meant that she had less time to devote to women's programs in the ILO, and this left a gap which was only filled when Johnstone took over responsibility for women's issues.

Workers with Family Responsibilities

In 1965 the first rather timid step was taken in the ILO to relieve women of some of the obstacles to working outside the home. The Conference adopted a recommendation dealing with the employment of women with family responsibilities. It stressed the need for an appropriate policy to enable such women "who work outside their homes to exercise their right to do so without being subject to discrimination." The competent authorities, in cooperation with the public and private organizations concerned, should encourage such consideration of the problems of women workers "as may be necessary to help these workers to become effectively integrated in the labor force on the basis of equal rights." Appropriate steps should be taken to ensure that child-care services and facilities are adequate for their special needs. The Recommendation also called for measures to facilitate their entry into employment or their reentry after a comparatively long period of absence, including vocational guidance and training, which should be available to women without distinction as regards age.

Among the speakers in the plenary at this session was a French worker as well as a British and a U.S. government representative. Simone Troisgros stressed the need for additional guarantees for women with dual responsibilities in their role as workers and in their reentry into employment. Mary Dublin Keyserling of the United States was an economist educated at Barnard College, London School of Economics, and Columbia University.[18] In 1961 she became the first director of the U.S. Commission on the Status of Women, established by President Kennedy to satisfy the demands of many articulate women and women's organizations in the United States, and initially chaired by Eleanor Roosevelt. Later Keyserling became the director of the U.S. Women's Bureau. Although she attended only one session of the conference, she had participated in the special conference of experts the previous year and she played an important role behind the scenes both in influencing U.S. policy and in her collaboration with the ILO Office in framing the documents that served for the Conference discussion on women workers. In supporting the Recommendation on Family Responsibilities, she declared "we are challenged, . . . to adopt new attitudes, new policies, to rise to new situations."

A more restrained view was voiced by Barbara Green of the United Kingdom, assistant secretary, Department of Employment and Productivity. She welcomed the flexibility of the Recommendation, explaining that the United Kingdom was not currently able to increase child-care provisions because of its already extensive public health and welfare coverage. She served for many years at ILO conferences, first as government adviser and then as delegate. Her length of service and the position she held in her own government made her one of the most influential British women. She sat on such technical committees as women workers, minimum wages, and holidays with pay, and also on a number of standing committees such as standing orders, application of conventions, resolutions, and structure. Her interventions were basically an appeal for slow and circumspect programs.[19] She accompanied the United Kingdom delegate on the Governing Body from 1967–69 and again in 1974 and 1980. From this date until 1985 she was the substitute member of the Governing Body.

From the beginning, this Recommendation was strongly criticized, particularly by the United States and Scandinavian countries, as implying that family responsibilities were only the business of women. A review was demanded within ten years—in fact, it took sixteen.

In 1981 the 1965 Recommendation was superseded by a Convention and a Recommendation. The new Convention prescribed "equal opportunities and equal treatment for men and women workers with family responsibilities," both in regard to dependent children and to "other members of their immediate family who clearly need their care or support." The Recommendation recognizes the need to create effective equality of opportunity and treatment as between men and women workers. It provides for maternity leave and extended child-rearing leave, as well as leave of absence in case of illness of the child or other member of the family, for either parent and for the development or promotion of child care and family services and facilities, as well as for social security. A provision relating specifically to women calls for measures to facilitate the entry or reentry of women into employment after a period of absence. These provisions, based on Scandinavian models, were revolutionary in the international field. Previously, as in the 1965 Recommendation, family responsibilities had been assumed to be solely the domain of women.

Some sixty women sat on the 1981 committee, and one of the vice chairmen was Elka Ter Veld, a Netherlands workers' representative. She was one of the most important new participants in ILO meetings in the 1980s. She came up through the ranks the hard way. She never finished high school, went to work as a saleswoman, and promptly joined the union. She became a union organizer and later headed up the women's department of the Confederation of Trade Unions. In addition to her influence in the trade union movement, she reached out to a wider audience as a broadcaster with a weekly program. Speaking on behalf of the workers' group, she warned of "the long-term danger in continuing to keep instruments dealing with women workers only." This, she said, might create barriers to their entering the market. She deplored the fact that the ILO had not taken heretofore "any action to promote more active participation by men in family life." She stressed the importance of arrangements that would allow women to participate fully, including the regulation of hours of work and provision of day-care centers. Her participation in ILO conferences ceased in 1985 when she became a labor member of the Netherlands Parliament.

Special Categories of Women Workers

In addition to instruments dealing with women workers in general, the conference has adopted a number of texts dealing with the specific problems of certain groups of women.

Migrant Workers

Migrant workers were one group to which the ILO had early addressed itself. The 1939 Convention made no specific reference to women nor to the problems of families. This was revised in 1949, calling upon all member states "to apply without discrimination in respect of nationality, race, religion or sex to immigrants lawfully within its territory, treatment no less favorable than that which it applies to its own nationals." Provision is made to include family allowances for migrant workers, and to cover women under social security. The Recommendation and its attached model agreement adds members of their families to the migrant workers protected by its provisions. These texts were supplemented in 1975 when provisions concerning equality of opportunity and treatment were adopted concerning migrant workers and members of their families, and special provisions were included for facilitating family reunification.

In 1949 five women had sat on the committee dealing with the migration item. One of these was Clara Beyer of the United States who bore primary responsibility for the inclusion of women in the Convention.[20] In 1975 there were six women on the committee, including one Norwegian worker, Liv Buck, secretary of the General Confederation of Trade Unions, and one of the most vigorous and determined women to leave her mark on ILO conferences.

Part-time Workers

Women workers employed on a part-time basis have proved to be one of the most troublesome categories with which the ILO has tried to deal. In 1952 the Commission on the Status of Women asked the ILO to prepare a report on part-time employment. Three years later, in a very cautious approach to the subject, a conference resolution urged continuing study of the subject and its possible inclusion on the agenda of regional conferences and "if appropriate" on that of the Annual Conference. In 1964 the Conference adopted a resolution calling for a precise definition of "part-time work" and a study of the number and nature of part-time employment opportunities and characteristics of persons who seek part-time employment. Esther Peterson, U.S. assistant secretary of labor, deplored the fact that the Resolution reflected old ways of thinking and did little more than call attention to the subject and request further study.

The problem was again raised in the 1965 discussion of the special problems of women workers in a changing world but was excluded, contrary to the draft proposed by the Office. The issue is controversial because of possible competition of part-time workers with unemployed full-time workers. For example, a number of groups, including workers groups, fear that the provision of full social benefits for part-time workers may undercut full-time employment. The proposal to put the item on the Conference agenda has come before the Governing Body on a number of occasions—1976, 1977, 1979, 1984, 1985, and 1986—in 1986 it was raised as a possible agenda item for the 1988 Conference by the Working Party on International Labor Standards. The Office prepared a law and practice report in 1979—which concluded that new ILO standards on part-time employment would be useful both for advanced and developing countries—proposed that these take the form of a recommendation, and "because of the controversy and doubts which mark the debate on the subject in some countries," the standards should "reflect a neutral attitude." Therefore, the proposals should not advocate part-time employment but should prescribe for such workers a number of benefits including (a) opportunities for access to employment without distinction as to sex, age, or level of occupation; (b) equality of treatment with full-time workers in respect to conditions of remuneration and holidays; (c) appropriate guarantees on work schedules and employment protection against unfair dismissal; (d) safety and health protection in the work place and access to social welfare services; (e) freedom of association and access to benefits gained for full-time workers; (f) coverage of social security legislation; (g) and opportunities to resume full-time employment by those workers who desire it. The 1986 law and practice report updates the 1979 report but leaves the controversy up to the Governing Body to deal with. By 1990 no final action had been taken.

Domestic Workers

Women working in household employment are another category where progress has been abysmally slow. Repeatedly over the years Florence Hancock deplored the lack of any protective coverage for these women and tried to get the Conference to deal with the matter. Although some countries have included domestic workers in their legislation, this low-income group is unorganized and frequently deemed unorganizable. On several occasions the Governing Body has considered putting the subject on the Conference agenda, looking toward the adoption of a recommendation or a convention, but no action has been taken. The only move in this direction was the 1965 Resolution on the Conditions of Employment of Domestic Workers that called attention to the urgent need "to provide for domestic workers in all member countries the basic elements of protection which would assure to them a minimum standard of living, compatible with the self-respect and human dignity which are essential to social justice." It urged states to "make all practicable efforts" to adopt protective measures for domestic workers, such as limitations on hours of work and provision of training. Efforts in the United States have fared little better. In 1938 a group of civil rights' and women's organizations lobbied to have domestic workers included under the maximum hours and minimum wage provisions of the Fair Labor Standards Act. This was rejected by the government on the ground that domestic employment did not impinge on interstate commerce and therefore the federal government had no mandate. Housewives, "faced with the choice of either meeting the demands of their families or regularizing the hours of their servants, opted for the former and resisted attempts to limit their claims on their employee's time."[21]

Older Workers

In 1979 and 1980 the Conferences considered issues of older workers, adopting (in 1980) the Recommendation on Older Workers: Work and Retirement (162). The vice chairman of the committee was Ursula Engelen-Kefer, vice president of the Confederation of Trade Unions. One of the most dynamic women who served at the ILO for many years, she was born in Prague in 1943 and was married with two sons. Trained as a political scientist and as a lawyer, she was sent to the United States in 1967 by the publication *Zeit und Handelsblatt* to study economic and social problems. In 1970 she joined the Institute of German Trade Unions, dealing with labor market analysis, and from 1974 on she served as senior legal counsel on the domestic policy of the Confederation of Trade Unions. In 1980 she became director of a new division on labor market policy and was also a member of the Social Fund of the European Community. She attended ILO conferences from 1974–84, almost always serving as vice chairman of some committee. Both in 1976 and in 1983 she participated in the Governing Body, accompanying the German worker member. Speaking about the Recommendation on Older Workers in the plenary conference in 1980 she deplored the present state of unemployment, particularly among older workers, stating, "at the beginning of the 1970s it was specifically the employers who made considerable efforts to mobilize the still existing reservoirs of labor to be found among older workers by improving protective measures and collective agreements." Now, she declared, in the face of serious unemployment, all this seems to have been forgotten. She urged the industrial countries, now unwilling to discuss the matter, to reconsider their attitude.

The Recommendation applies to all workers who are liable to encounter difficulties in employment and occupation because of age. It calls for measures to prevent discrimination because of age in the provision of vocational training, equality of treatment, protection against firing on the basis of age, special provisions for part-time workers, and flexible hours to meet the needs of older workers—whether men or women.

Teachers

Women teachers are another category of workers who have received special attention. Their problems were first considered in 1966 at a special intergovernmental conference held in Paris. The conference declared as a guiding principle that "all aspects of the preparation and employment of teachers should be free from any form of discrimination on grounds of race, colour, sex, religion, political opinion, national or social origin or economic condition." It established guidelines for the employment of women teachers with family responsibilities and urged that "marriage should not be considered a bar to the appointment or to the continued employment of women teachers, nor should it affect remuneration or other conditions of work." The guidelines added that employers should be prohibited from terminating contracts of service for reasons of pregnancy and maternity leave, that child care should be provided "where desirable" for children of teachers with family responsibilities and efforts made to ensure that where married couples are both teachers they should be able to teach in the same general neighborhood or in the same school. Finally, the guidelines urged that ILO provisions for maternity protection be applied to teachers.

Nursing Personnel

The situation of nursing personnel became a matter of considerable concern worldwide because of the low wages and inadequate standards that prevailed throughout. In many developing countries there was often little differentiation between nursing personnel and domestic workers. Inclusion of the item on the agenda was partly the consequence of a lobby by the trade unions which had organized many of the nurses and related professionals in industrialized countries. In 1976 the Conference held a preparatory discussion and a year later adopted a convention, a recommendation, and a resolution.

In both years women attended the Conference in large numbers, many coming from the specialized fields of nursing services, hospital administration, and departments of government dealing with health and social security services. The chairman of the relevant committee in 1976 was Rajendra Kumari Bajpal, minister of state for labor, Upper Pradesh, India, and the reporter was Joan Patricia Nash of the United Kingdom, chief nursing officer, Department of Health and Social Security. The latter was again the reporter the following year. One woman with a rather different background and range of interests from most of the other participants was Marie-Joseph de Font Reaulx, a French woman trade unionist who is chief of the international service of the Confédération Française du Personnel d'Encadrement. She attended ILO conferences every year from 1976 until 1986. She sat on the Nursing Committee in both 1976 and 1977. She also served on a number of other technical committees including labor administration, older workers, occupational health, equal opportunity, protection of dockers, social security, workers with family responsibilities, and equal employment opportunities. In addition, she participated in two of the European regional meetings.

She always insisted, when deciding on which committee she preferred to serve, to participate on those where she would be a full member, able to speak for the workers. This was one of the reasons she served on the Dockers Committee in 1979. She has been very aware of the fact that almost all the women came to the Conference as advisers and not delegates which, therefore, has meant few women in top positions. She is of Chinese extraction, comes from a family of jurists, and is herself a lawyer with a doctorate in political science. She frequently has used this training at the ILO by serving on various drafting committees. She considers that one of the major problems encountered by women is not that of discrimination but of their own lack of confidence in other women and, therefore, frequent unwillingness to vote for or serve under other women. The situation in France, she believes, has changed in favor of women since mixed schools have been accepted both in the public and parochial systems and young people have learned to take each other's skills and training for granted. There are, however, still relatively small numbers of women in top jobs in the unions and very few in the elected positions.

The 1977 Convention on Nursing Personnel sought to establish professional standards and to ensure that employment and conditions of work and life were adequate. It urged steps to promote the participation of nursing personnel in the planning of nursing services. It also provided that there should be equivalence with other workers as regards such matters as weekly rest, paid annual holidays, educational leave, maternity and sick leaves, and social security. This Convention, and an accompanying Recommendation, were designed to raise the status of nursing personnel in order to overcome the serious shortage in many parts of the world. As of 1989, only twenty-seven countries had ratified it.

Women in the Maritime Industry

The ILO held a series of regular conferences dealing with maritime issues. The first of these was held in 1921, the first session after the ILO was established. The position of women was not considered at any of the early sessions—probably because the shipping industry paid little attention to them and they were not employed in large numbers. In the early maritime conferences almost no women attended—but there were larger numbers at the first postwar session, mostly representing governments from Europe and China. At the 1976 session there were women representatives from twenty-two countries, including one each from South America, New Zealand, the Philippines, Thailand, and the Middle East, and three from Africa. Three of the women were employers. There were no workers. In 1977 thirty countries included women; of these six were employers and three were workers. They came from every continent; none were officers but several were influential old-timers.

The 1976 session of the conference adopted a resolution concerning conditions of employment. The resolution noted "that the current growing tendency towards the engagement of women on board ship, both as officers and ratings, is generally compatible with the requirements of employment and standards of living in modern vessels and therefore that for these and other reasons this is likely to continue in the future." It also recognized that "discrimination in recruitment, certain types of work in relation to manning, accommodation facilities and special social problems may adversely affect opportunities for employment of women on board ship." It consequently requested a comprehensive study to be made and submitted to the ILO's Joint Maritime Commission so that it could determine "what action may be necessary." At the most recent (1987) maritime session of the Conference, a resolution was introduced but given little attention, despite the efforts of several influential women at the Conference—including a British government delegate (Jennifer Dimond) and an employer substitute delegate from the Netherlands (Cornelie Hak).

Plantation and Rural Workers

The problems of plantation workers were dealt with by a series of ILO bodies including the Conference and the Committee on Work on Plantations. A convention adopted by the Conference in 1958 developed a code of labor standards, applying both to men and women in "any agricultural undertaking employing hired workers which is situated in the tropical and sub-tropical world." Among the provisions of the code are maternity clauses similar to those in the 1984 Convention. An accompanying recommendation provides for equal remuneration and social security without discrimination.

In recent years rural workers per se have been given special attention, particularly in the developing countries. Since a large proportion of these are women, they have become the subject of a number of technical meetings, and are the focus of the program on rural women, within the rural employment policies branch, discussed in chapter 5. However, to date there have not been formal conventions or recommendations or resolutions adopted by the conference applying specifically to women in this category.

General Instruments Relating to the Work
Environment Affecting Women

Instruments under this heading apply to both sexes but have special relevance to women. The 1964 Convention on Hygiene in Commerce and Offices specifies "sufficient and suitable" ventilation, lighting, washing facilities, sanitary conveniences, and seats. Other provisions cover temperature "as comfortable and steady ... as circumstances permit," a "sufficient supply of wholesome drinking water," suitable facilities for changing, leaving, and drying clothes not worn to work, protection against harmful substances, noise, and vibration, and a dispensary or first-aid post. A recommendation adopted the same year, 1964, spells out the implementation of the provisions of the above convention and also stipulates that "restrooms should be provided to meet the needs of women workers." As of 1989 the Convention had been ratified by forty-two nations.

Salaried workers have also received special treatment. In 1974 an Advisory Committee on Salaried and Professional Workers of the ILO concluded that flexible working hours could meet the needs of workers, in particular workers with family responsibilities. Such hours should be worked out by employers with "the participation of workers and/or their representatives." Temporary work may also be a method of obtaining flexibility, but temporary employment should not deprive workers of their normal benefits, which would be provided for full-time employment.

Other examples of this kind of instrument include those concerning paid educational leave, as set forth in the 1974 Convention which states that "paid educational leave shall not be denied to workers on the grounds of race, colour, sex, religion, political opinion, national extraction or social origin" and the 1960 Recommendation promoting effective consultation "at the industrial and national levels between public authorities and employers' and workers' organisations" which also stress that such consultations should be carried out "without discrimination."

The UN Decade for Women

The most significant actions of the ILO taken in recent years are those developed in connection with the UN Decade for Women designed to further the concept of equality, not only with respect to employment and training but to society as a whole. The Decade began in 1975 with a meeting in Mexico City which gave voluble expression to the demands of women throughout the world for equality with men and for recognition of their rightful place in all spheres of activity. As part of the preparation for this meeting, the 1975 session of the Conference adopted a convention and recommendation on human resources development, a declaration on equality of opportunity and treatment for women workers, and a resolution defining a plan of action to promote the objectives of the declaration.

Human Resources Development Instruments

In 1975 the Conference took a further step, with the adoption of both a convention and recommendation, toward extending the concept of equality, not only with respect to employment and training but of society as a whole. The Convention stated as its goal that both sexes should play an equal part in society. To achieve this goal the Recommendation states that there should be vocational guidance for women on a par with men. Access to all streams of education and to vocational training should be promoted. Further training for girls and women should also be encouraged "to ensure their personal development and advancement to skilled employment and posts of responsibility."

A large and distinguished group of women sat on the committee preparing these texts. Eight were workers and six were employers. Two of these were particularly important; first, a relative newcomer, was Cornelie Hak, an employer representative from the Netherlands, and second, another employer representative, was Diana Mahabir, of Trinidad and Tobago.

In 1982 and 1983 the subject of vocational training with particular attention to disabled persons was dealt with by the Conference. A convention and recommendation were prepared by a committee in 1982 and completed in 1983. The vice chairman of the latter committee was May-Britt Carlsson, ombudsman, Swedish Central Organization of Salaried Employees. Carlsson had also sat on a number of other committees including Occupational Health, Selection, and Resolutions.

Declaration on Equality of Opportunity and Treatment

The Declaration and Resolution Concerning a Plan of Action with a view to promoting equality of opportunity and treatment for women workers

---

were also adopted by the Conference and submitted to the Mexico City World Conference on Women as a contribution of the ILO to the International Year of Women which was being celebrated by the Conference.

The provisions dealing with vocational guidance, training, and equality appearing in the Convention and Recommendation on Human Resources are identical with those in the Declaration and Resolution submitted to the Mexico City Conference.[22] The Declaration and the Plan of Action have a much wider scope than the texts dealing with human resources and discuss the rights of women, and especially working women, in society as a whole. In the discussion of the preamble to the Declaration two paragraphs—dealing with the New Economic Order as a precondition for women in the developing countries obtaining economic and social justice, and the problems of women in occupied areas or facing apartheid—were strongly contested by the U.S. government and the employers' group. An attempted compromise to water down the paragraphs was defeated in the plenary, and the original text survived over rather bitter reservations. The Plan of Action lays down a full program at international, regional, and national levels, proposes new conventions to safeguard the rights of women, and calls for a series of measures—to be taken by the UN system as a whole—including the allocation by ILO of more staff to deal with women's issues.

Some seventy-five women participated in the committee drafting the Declaration on equality of opportunity and treatment and the Plan of Action. The vice chairman was Ethel Chipchase, M.B.E., the last of the old-time British labor leaders. Chipchase was the secretary of the Women's Advisory Committee of the Trades Union Congress. Although she attended only one session of the Conference her influence was pervasive over a number of years both in the national and international trade union movements and she played a major role in determining British labor policy in the ILO. She came out of one of the poorest British families that had been badly hit by the Depression. Her father never had a full week's work during those years and her mother helped to make ends meet as a dressmaker. Ethel Chipchase held various clerical jobs, joined her union, and worked her way up to become in 1962 the women's officer of the TUC. She became a member of her government's Equal Opportunities Commission and, at one time, shared the chairmanship of the Women's National Commission with the then government representative, Margaret Thatcher. The reporter was Tamara Toure Diallo, of Senegal, chief of the social security division in the office of the prime minister and technical adviser to the prime minister. As her government's delegate during three different periods—1969–73, 1975–77, and 1979–82—she played a major role. In 1979 and 1980 she chaired the Committee on Structure, the only woman to do so.

Among the Conference participants who also provided a link between the ILO and the United Nations—the UN Commission on the Status of Women, the Third Committee of the UN General Assembly, as well as the Decade for Women—was Dagmar Molkova of Czechoslovakia, vice minister of labor. Another link between the ILO and the United Nations was Aida Gonzalez Martinez of Mexico who served as coordinator of the Mexico City Conference, and also served on the Third Committee of the UN General Assembly. (See chapter 7 for a summary of the contributions of both Molkova and Martinez.)

At this same session Marguerite Thibert, formerly head of the women's service at the ILO, was a French government representative, although she was listed as coming from the Comité du Travail Femmes, as well as representing the nongovernmental organization, the Women's International League for Peace and Freedom.

The secretary-general of the UN World Conference on Women, Helga Sipila, assistant secretary-general of the United Nations, addressed the conference en route to Mexico City. She thanked the Office for the reports prepared for Mexico City and "for its continuous and most important cooperation with the UN Commission on the Status of Women and the respective unit at UN headquarters ever since the inception of the UN." She called for a review of the family responsibility and maternity instruments. She noted the needs of women whose problems are still formidable and not known, adding, "therefore their situation may have been worsening instead of improving, notwithstanding all the efforts of the UN and its specialized agencies." Thus the International Year of Women offered a real challenge "to all of us."

A large number of members of women's nongovernmental organizations embracing a varied political spectrum participated in the session, including the International Alliance of Women, the World YWCA, the International Catholic Girl's Society, the International Council of Women, the International Council of Social Democratic Women, the Women's International Democratic Federation, the International Federation of Business and Professional Women, the International Federation of University Women, the World Federation of Teachers, the World Union of Catholic

Antoinette Waellbroeck Béguin of Belgium, Assistant
Director-General *(courtesy of* ILO, *Geneva)*.

Women's Organizations, the International Federation of Women Lawyers,
and the Women's International League for Peace and Freedom.

Antoinette Béguin, then chief of the Employment and Non-Discrimi-
nation Department, represented the International Labor Office at the
meeting. Her contribution and that of her staff, both in the preparation
of the meeting and the tenor of the discussions, received high commen-
dation from several speakers, including the chairman of the committee.

The Mid-Decade Copenhagen Conference

For the Mid-Decade UN Conference, which was held in Copenhagen in
1980, the Office prepared a statement on its activities between 1919 and
1975 of special interest to women. This included the full texts of provisions concerning women as they related to basic human rights, employ-

ment policy and human resources development, conditions of work and social policy, social security, industrial relations, specific categories of workers, and labor administration.

The Copenhagen Mid-Decade Conference adopted a plan of action for the balance of the decade. It included recommendations concerning "women living in conditions of extreme poverty" both rural and urban, refugees, displaced persons, and migrants. In addressing the conference the ILO representative warned that it would be difficult to "shape the basic principles and values unless fundamental policies of our society toward women" were altered and modified. Their work should not be ignored; their labor should be adequately rewarded and they should be integrated with full equality in such areas as social security schemes and taxation. In the conference's aftermath, the ILO declared that a basis for strengthening and reorienting both ongoing and future activities had been provided. Implementation of the plan of action was discussed by the Governing Body both in 1980 and 1981.

Nairobi: The End of the Decade

In preparation for the Nairobi Conference which concluded the UN Decade for Women in 1985, the ILO Annual Conference adopted an omnibus Resolution on Equal Opportunities and Equal Treatment for Men and Women in Employment. The Conference requested that the conclusions of the Resolution should be brought to the attention of the Nairobi Conference (which was done).

The chairman of the committee that drafted the Resolution was Mamoleta Pitso of Lesotho. The vice chairman was Harriet Andreassen of Norway, secretary of the General Confederation of Trade Unions and a veteran participant in a number of ILO committees concerned with women. Speaking in Plenary she declared that women are "still to be found largely in a narrow range of unskilled occupations or where their skills are grossly undervalued." She said the recession had cut social services and those programs which enabled women to combine work with family responsibilities. The hardest hit of all were the rural areas where women were not prepared to deal with new technologies. It was "a rather bleak situation."

The Resolution summarized ILO's legislative policy in favor of women workers during the preceding ten years, appraised the progress achieved and outlined the measures to be intensified to achieve the objectives on both national and international levels. The Conference declared that there has been "undeniable progress." Increasing numbers of women in both developing and industrialized countries have joined the labor force and more women are now found in "highly skilled, technical, managerial and decision-making positions." Nevertheless, the Resolution asserted, "the pace of progress is uneven." Most women workers are concentrated in occupations requiring low skills or earning low remuneration. The world-wide recession, the introduction of new technologies, and political and social disturbances have all had a negative impact on women. Rural women are "severely affected by increasing poverty and deteriorating living standards"; unemployment weighs much more heavily on women; and the number of people in refugee camps, largely women and children, is growing steadily.

The Resolution concluded with a ten-point action program for the ILO. It included strengthening the organizational capacity of ILO to deal with questions relating to women workers, encouraging more women to apply as technical cooperation experts, and ensuring that the ILO "sets an example in all its services and structures in the implementation of equality of opportunity and treatment between men and women." Implementation of this action program was referred to the Governing Body, which in 1986 and 1987 examined its implications. (The action by the Governing Body is discussed in chapter 7.)

5. New Directions in Postwar Activities

When the Second World War ended in 1945, after almost six years of fighting over the length and breadth of Europe, the economies of most of its countries were in shambles and industrial production had come to a virtual standstill. Under the leadership of the United States, the European Recovery Program (known as the Marshall Plan after the U.S. secretary of state) was launched to put Europe back on its feet. The United States provided the money, and Europeans collectively decided how to spend it. Even while the program was in its early stages, however, it was recognized that there were other devastated areas of the world and many where dire poverty existed quite apart from the direct impact of the war. In January 1949 President Truman proposed that the members of the United Nations make available to these countries not only funds but the combined store of their technical knowledge "in order to help them realize their aspirations for a better life." Thus was born Point Four. In the United Nations this led to the creation of a Technical Assistance Program, later transformed into the UN Development Program (UNDP).

The new ILO Director-General, David Morse, had been involved in the Marshall Plan and both his interest and sympathies led him to embrace this new development with enthusiasm. Immediately after his election he consulted a number of members of the Governing Body as well as members of the UN General Assembly, meeting in Paris, to obtain support for a new operational approach. He sought to "start this change in policy by a program in the field of manpower, migration and technical training."[1] Although the ILO was to develop a vigorous program of technical assistance in the years to come, its first incursions into clearly operational activities related to migration. It sought to become the first international body to take responsibility for the transport and resettlement of migrants, displaced persons, and refugees, but it was frustrated for reasons which

120

had to do primarily with the McCarthy anti-Communist drive in the United States. A conference was convened in the autumn of 1951 in Naples, and while it was still in session the U.S. House Foreign Affairs Committee attached a rider to the Mutual Aid Bill prohibiting the granting of funds for migration to any organization with Communist membership. Although the USSR was not a member at that time, several East European countries, such as Czechoslovakia and Poland, were members. Consequently, having lost the U.S. financial support for the migration program, the ILO was limited in its activities and had to postpone for several years the implementation of special measures designed to protect migrants, including women and their families.

Meanwhile, a number of other aspects of the operational program had been going forward. While standard setting remained as an objective, the emphasis shifted to technical operations.

Industrial Committees and Related Activities

One of the first of such programs which had its gestation period during the war—especially in the various meetings of the Governing Body held in London—was the establishment of industrial committees designed to provide a forum for discussion of the special needs and problems of major sectors of industry, and industry related agriculture such as food processing, which contributed to overall economic growth and trade. In accord with the Governing Body decision, the first two committees (coal mines and inland transport) met in London late in 1945. Coal mines had been badly damaged during the war. Most needed repairs and some were not even functioning. Inland transport too was in a parlous state. Rolling stock had been scattered all over Europe and much of it had been destroyed. At the first meetings of these committees only one government, Poland, sent a woman—Anna Fidler, who later joined the ILO staff as a research worker. These committees, like the others that were created, dealt with subjects of varying concern to women—manpower and human resources problems, including such questions as vocational training, conditions of work, and labor management relations.

Industrial committees rarely consider problems of particular categories of workers except where they constitute the majority of the labor force. Most of the reports contain only a few references to women workers. This may explain why not many women have participated although the number has increased in those sectors where women make up a substantial proportion of the employees, such as in the textile industry. Hence women have always participated in the Textile Industrial Committee which had been expected to be the first industry committee to be established. It had been proposed at the 1937 Washington Textile Conference, but before it could be set up by decision of the Governing Body the war intervened and it was not until 1946 that it actually came into being. The European textile industry had long been in trouble because of growing competition from Asia, and obsolete machinery added to its problems. The women were the first to suffer from this situation, with lower salaries, poor working conditions, and often job loss. Five women participated in the first session of this committee. They came from Belgium, Denmark, France, India, and Sweden. The French woman was an employer delegate and served as vice chairman of its subcommittee on production and related questions. The Belgian government delegate was the secretary of the government group, while the Danish delegate served as the reporter of the Subcommittee on Social Security. At a recent session of the committee (the eleventh), held in 1984, one of its three employer vice chairmen was Miss A. Perez from Colombia, while one of the four worker vice chairmen was Mrs. M. G. Dolzhenkoven of the USSR. Since its establishment the committee has adopted several resolutions relating to women. In 1953 they included one calling for the financing of welfare and social services, as well as measures to safeguard the health and welfare of women workers; in 1978 another resolution emphasized the need for adequate inspection services, while still another drew special attention to the needs of working mothers in the industry. At a recent session emphasis was on prevention of exposure to occupational hazards and on other methods of improving the working environment—with six women speaking on the need for such improvement as a health measure.

Similar resolutions, adopted by the Leather and Footwear Committee and by the Food-Processing and Drink Industries Committee, dealt with the need for special training facilities designed to upgrade traditional small-scale and village level technologies used mainly by women in developing countries. Tripartite technical meetings were set up for this purpose, and in 1987 a research project was developed on conditions of women workers in these industries.

The Clothing Industry Committee is concerned with the "traditional distinction between men's and women's jobs" and the differences in wage rates in a "fairly large number of countries," and it has called for implementation of the principles of the Discrimination (Employment and Occupation) Convention. In the past the Committee on Forestry and Wood Industries was mainly concerned with questions of occupational safety and vocational training of loggers. This is being extended to deal with the specific problems of female employment in these industries, particularly in the developing countries. Another area to which the ILO is now directing special attention to women is the building sector since a surprisingly large percentage of women are being employed in construction and related activities. One project deals with low-cost housing and shelter in developing countries. The problems of these women figured prominently in the ILO contribution to a policy paper prepared for the UN International Year of Shelter for the Homeless.

The Committee on Work on Plantations has initiated a study on the impact of primary processing of plantation projects on employment and incomes of plantation workers, with emphasis on women workers as a first step in organizing a technical cooperation project aimed at improving the employment and living conditions of such women. At its first meeting Clara Beyer of the United States served as chairman of the committee. The concerns of women with the plantations industry has increased steadily, partly as a result of the growing recognition of their role in rural agriculture throughout the world. Eighteen countries are members of the committee, almost all coming from the Third World (five from Latin America, six from Asia, five from Africa, and one from the Middle East). In preparation for the ninth session of the committee (April 12–20, 1989) a questionnaire was addressed to all governments with plantations, focusing on training and retraining of workers and managers on plantations. Governments were asked specifically "what measures were taken and what progress has been made in the training of working women on plantations?" Typical of the replies was that of Cameroon which stated, "because women play a predominant role in the agricultural sector, seminars and training courses have been held to enable women to improve their skills and harmonize their family responsibilities with their working life." The Central African Republic indicated that "women are assigned tasks consonant with their physical capabilities; for example the gathering and packing of crops." The Comoros government stated that within its federal Center for the Promotion of Research there is an office for the advancement of women workers which includes training.

Another committee which has dealt with a number of problems relating directly to women is that concerned with the metal trades. In a resolution dealing with the social and labor problems of the industry in developing countries it stated, "In its activities relating to employment policy the ILO should pay special attention to the possibilities of productive employment offered by metal trades not only to men but also to women and young persons in rural areas as well as in town, and the job prospects which development of these trades can open up in other sections of industry." Cornelie Hak, long the Dutch employer representative at both the Governing Body and the International Labor Conference, served on the Metal Industry Committee as the employer member. More recently Lucille Caron, Canadian government member of the Governing Body and government delegate to the Conference, was elected chairman of the same committee.

In general, the structure set up for dealing with the special problems of individual industries has been a positive measure, increasing the involvement of women in ILO activities. The concept of industry committees goes back to the long history of the ILO maritime activities, including a series of maritime conferences (which adopted conventions and recommendations) and a Joint Maritime Commission of employers' and workers' organizations, responsible for determining the role of the ILO in the industry.[2] While the role of women had been limited in the prewar period, the war had involved women seafarers and at the first postwar Maritime Conference, held in Seattle in 1946, some of the problems facing women on board ship were examined and, for the first time, a number of women participated in the Conference.[3] Much of the new focus was concerned with helping women, as a vulnerable group, to improve their conditions of work and their standards of living in the particular industries or occupations, such as seafaring, in which they were employed or seeking employment.[4]

In a report to the 1988 Conference the Director-General (Francis Blanchard) indicated that the industrial committees as presently constituted might no longer serve a useful purpose. Because the committees deal with entire industries, wherever located, there was a growing tendency to engage in repetitive generalities. Blanchard has suggested that some more relevant forum might be devised to deal with conditions specific to the wide diversity of regions or countries.[5]

Technical Cooperation

The growing importance assigned by the ILO to its technical cooperation program was manifest in the same 1988 report by the Director-General.

Technical cooperation was termed "a major means of action for achieving the objectives of the Organization" and "a substantial component of the total ILO program complementing and reinforcing its other components: standard setting, research and dissemination of information." The program has also provided, the report continues, "a prompt, relevant and flexible response to the changing development needs and priorities" of its tripartite constituency.

While the ILO's contribution to technical cooperation from its regular budget has perforce been limited, two major sources of financing have made possible an extensive program. The largest of these has been the UN Development Program, discussed more fully in chapter 9. While percentages fluctuate, this has accounted for almost one-half of its technical assistance budget. The other source comes from the bilateral and multilateral donations from governments for specific projects. The proportion of the funds so far allocated to women under this program have been modest in the extreme—not more than 4.5 percent. Women have, however, benefited indirectly from programs not specifically targeted to their needs. Some concern both sexes, without specifically identifying the role of women, although in certain sectors, such as hotels and tourism, substantial numbers of women are involved. A number of technical cooperation projects on employment and self-employment in these areas have been proposed. Others may indirectly affect women as, for example, migration projects, involving primarily men, which may have a profound impact on women if they live in a society where farm work is normally shared by both sexes. Thus the migration of the men increases the burden of the agricultural work on the women left behind. There are also projects specifically addressed to women, or with a clearly identifiable women's component. These have concentrated primarily on the development of income-earning activities, vocational training (particularly in rural areas), and the development of cooperatives and other forms of organization particularly appropriate to groups of poor, rural women. In addition, a substantial number of projects have almost from the outset of the program dealt with family planning, with emphasis on its relationship to education, employment, and women. ILO's activities have been both responsive to local conditions and have served as a spur to local programs. As discussed in chapter 6, this approach has necessitated a whole regional structure designed to accommodate the diversity of the developing world. In Africa the educational level of women is still far behind that of men. Women work primarily in agriculture where technological innovations have tended to diminish their role and influence or in low-paying jobs in the service sector. While women's organizations are becoming increasingly common in Africa, they "tend to stake claims that reflect the position of compromise and insecurity of African women." The need "to control women has always been an important part of male success in most African societies." Women are necessary to help men get wealth and status. The fear that men have about women changing their role reacts on the women, who then begin to doubt the desirability of change.[6]

To begin to give African women the self-confidence to emerge from poverty and fear, the ILO's programs have emphasized training in the most basic skills. These include cooking, pottery, rug making and other handicrafts, cottage industries, and the development of cooperatives, including farm marketing. There have been several projects particularly designed for refugees, of which Africa has vast numbers, as well as a few on institution-building and on problems of technological change and its effect on rural women. In Ghana, for example, in 1985 a project was launched to train women in new technologies. It was possible to identify the most appropriate one on the basis of prior ILO studies. The focus was on women processing food and home-based industrial products, particularly fish, soap, palm oil, gari, and coconut oil. Improved fish-smoking equipment was introduced in five villages, and 135 women were trained in its use. A similar project dealt with palm processing and improved soap making. The objective was to make women's work less arduous and to achieve an impact in terms of incomes and working time. Another program concerns drought affected countries such as Ethiopia, the Sudan, and Mali. The program sought to identify specific income-generating activities and provide appropriate training.

In Asia the enormous diversity of stages of development that exists has called for a widespread spectrum of activities by the ILO. Many of these reflect the level of participation by women in both the social and economic sectors. Many projects have dealt with aspects of family planning, including in-plant clinics and rural fertility. There have also been a substantial number of handicraft projects. In West Bengal in 1981 a project on employment opportunities for rural women was initiated. The project started with thirty-four women workers who after eighteen months organized themselves into three groups comprising more than eight hundred women. They obtained $60,000 from their government, matching the ILO contribution. The project provided training in silk growing, maintenance and repair of sal leaf plate machines, basic management concepts and the care of poultry, goats, and pigs. One result was the transformation of wasteland into silk plantations to rear silk cocoons. The success of this approach convinced the state government to encourage the development of organizations for poor, rural women as a means of enhancing their status and providing a channel for development funds. Another Indian project was one carried out in the early 1980s to organize the lace makers of Narsapur as a method of supplementing their income. The program was designed to prove that housewives could produce for the world market. The stimulus given by publication of the project study by Rounag Jahan, the ILO staff member responsible for it, in *Working Women's Forum,* led to effective local action. The women in the community began to get themselves organized and find direct access to raw materials through the establishment of a cooperative.

Future efforts are being concentrated on such questions as: access to employment and training, emphasizing the need to diversify women's occupations and to combat occupational segregation; development of low-cost welfare facilities; and strengthening the organization of women workers at the grass roots level and encouraging their participation in trade unions.

The emphasis of ILO activities in Latin America differs somewhat from those in either Asia or Africa. They began much earlier and were more closely related to standard setting than to project development. Technical assistance initially took the form of advice to governments on development of social legislation and the provision of welfare facilities for employed women as well as men. Despite relatively high levels of employment, some two-thirds of the working women are in the service sector, nearly half of whom are in domestic service. Moreover, the wide gap between the employment of women in academic and public occupations has resulted in an even wider gap in income. Therefore, the ILO has laid more stress on the development of appropriate institutions and professional training in such areas as management training and workers' education. In selected Latin American countries, for example, there have been a number of projects dealing with the strengthening of workers' organization.

While many of the above projects have been successful, there are a number that have either failed outright or failed to reach the target group. A project on poultry farming by groups of rural youth failed for several reasons. The direct technical advice and support could not be ensured for small informal groups of rural youth; training and supervision were inadequate; and, moreover, quality poultry stock and feed for small poultry farms were not available locally. Another unsuccessful project was carried out by ILO in the United Arab Emirates and Saudi Arabia. ILO sought to train women in traditional handicrafts and to assist in organizing the production and sale of their work. Women did not earn any significant income and production activities were limited to a few social development centers. The high cost of production and the high cost of living made it improbable that this activity could ever serve as a revenue-producing undertaking without a heavy subsidy.

Failure to reach the target group makes it difficult to obtain a true measure of impact based on the number of women reached. Sometimes the final beneficiaries are not those to whom the project was originally intended but rather those who are relatively better off, able to spare the time and effort. Such a project may, at the local level, actually perpetuate inequality.

ILO's technical assistance programs for women have gone through three distinct phases. Prior to 1975 they were rather modest and limited largely to the field of training. During the next five years attention shifted to a specific focus on the fate of women belonging to the poorest groups, especially rural women. This shift was influenced primarily by the UN Decade for Women, the Declaration and Plan of Action on Equality of Opportunity and Treatment for Women Workers, and the World Employment Program (WEP). This last, launched in 1969 as a contribution to the UN Second Development Decade, was designed to harness development through the alleviation of unemployment and underemployment by promoting the fullest possible employment, especially of those in the poorest areas and lowest paid jobs, with emphasis on rural workers. Beginning in the 1980s the stress was on the promotion of income-earning activities for groups of poor women. Included was not only training but the development of women's own organizations in the rural and urban informal sectors as a defense against greedy intermediaries, agents of subcontracting firms, landowners, and sometimes even local authorities.

The focus on the participation through organization of poor rural women does not mean, according to an ILO publication, "isolating women's interests from those of men. But it is based on a recognition that in addition to shared interests of a class, there are particular interests of women which should not be ignored, yet which are often submerged and even harmed in the name of common cause."[7]

Since women play a key role as producers and deliverers of food and other basic necessities, they, inevitably, should form the core of a rural development strategy. This means not only increasing their income but, more importantly, assuring their control of their own labor. To perform adequately, women need access to resources and participation in decisionmaking. A 1988 meeting on the Contribution of Women to Human Resource Development in Industry emphasized the fact that "women in low income families engaged in home-based activities continue to be disadvantaged as development programs generally fail to provide them with access to capital or credit, vocational training, equipment, market outlets and entrepreneurial skill development."[8] One major problem in integrating rural women into the development process is that the bulk of their labor has fallen outside the scope of economic statistics. They are almost entirely responsible for water collection. In a number of places this may involve a five-kilometer or more trip each way—three hours or more of travel. Women are also the major collectors of fuel, another time-consuming exercise which grows steadily worse with the depletion of the forests. Women do the cooking and look after the children. They also play a major role in weeding and also often in other agricultural tasks. Since these activities are not remunerated and do not bring in a cash income, with minor exceptions, they are excluded from development statistics.[9] ILO has been one of the leaders in seeking to assign a monetary equivalent to these activities. A Demography and Employment Project has been concerned with techniques for measuring the value of women's domestic and related tasks, analyzing the role of women and reviewing ways of measuring women's contribution to agricultural production. ILO has included five components in its definition of labor activities. Two of the categories are traditional—payments for services or sales of goods and services. The third category covers the production of economic goods and services whether or not they are sold, thus including subsistence work. The fourth category includes the gathering and preparation of fuel, fetching water, making clothes, and repairing houses. These are activities which are normally bought in the developed countries. The last category includes household tasks such as cooking, cleaning, child-minding, and care of the sick. Using these as the criteria the ILO determined that in two test countries the "productive work burden" for women was 64 percent as against 36 percent for men (Nepal) and 66 percent as compared to 34 percent (Ivory Coast). In another study the ILO analyzed the trade-off between fuel collection and cooking. In areas where fuel is either bought or largely provided by men's labor, women have the time to provide much greater quantity and variety in cooking preparations, thus leading to better family nutrition.

Grass roots discussion and awareness-raising workshops have been used to persuade women to organize themselves. In a number of Third World countries, women workers' societies, landless women's organizations, and groups of poor women have sprung up to take development into their own hands and improve their lot. Thus, for example, in West Bengal, India, village-level women workers' development associations have been created with the assistance of ILO and a nongovernmental organization. These women have used their collective power to discuss such development issues as employment and income generating opportunities, and access to land and to credit facilities. The success of this approach persuaded the state government to encourage the development of other similar bodies.

A woman's development project focusing on agriculture, organized by UNDP and financed by the World Bank involved both the UN Development Fund for Women (UNIFEM) and the ILO. UNIFEM dealt with the self-employment aspects of the project and ILO organized a workshop in Geneva to formulate an employment creation project. UNIFEM also took part in a two-day workshop organized by ILO in Tanzania. The participants on the ILO team dealing with the project were, initially, all men, but ultimately there were twenty-six women participants and beneficiaries.

Such measures can help women to make a vital contribution to development and to developing societies. However, the road ahead is not an easy one. Obstacles include conditions at home, their male counterparts, limited amounts of available time, illiteracy, shyness, legal constraints, cultural prejudices, and practices restricting their mobility. Reservations about the potential equality of women exist even within the sophisticated and internationally minded Governing Body. During its 1988 session the representative of the Libyan Arab Jamahiriya government stated that while "fully appreciating the strategy for the promotion of the status of working women and for their equality, he felt that their biological make-up required co-operation between the ILO and other international and feminist organizations in order to arrive at legislation which would protect women from unsuitable jobs that were prohibited by religious, cultural and social customs."[10]

One approach by the ILO which has received increasing emphasis is the promotion of women's participation in development through cooperatives. A 1987 ILO report dealing with this question discusses a number of areas which are particularly favorable fields of action for women. "First and foremost" are handicrafts, both traditional and modern, based on the national culture, which can be marketed locally, nationally, or even internationally. These have been carried out in Malaysia, Mauritania, the Sudan, Thailand, Turkey, and also in collaboration with the League of Arab States. Such cooperatives, it is pointed out, have strong support from society because the women remain in the traditional family setting.[11]

The promotion of handicrafts, however, has long been a bone of contention between the feminists and many Third World citizens. The former object just because it keeps women in the traditional family setting instead of liberating them and bringing them into the modern world. The latter resent women from Western capitalist countries who say that "integrating women into a sewing cooperative is not really a movement toward emancipation. They feel that real emancipation is having women as *responsible* in the ministries, factories and mass organizations. We agree, but we must begin by putting a woman into a sewing cooperative and not a leadership position when she does not know how to read and write."[12]

Another field is savings and credit. Again, this is an area consonant with local practice since it is usually the women who manage the housekeeping funds. More than half the members of savings and credit cooperatives are women who also serve on boards of management and various action committees.

Two other areas are the sale of foodstuffs in small local markets and consumer cooperatives. The former is particularly important because it both enables women to contribute to the marketing of agricultural produce and promotes paid employment in the poor districts of urban centers. The role of women in consumer cooperatives is somewhat more restricted since membership is almost entirely in the husband's name. However, as it is the women who do the shopping, they benefit from the cooperative shop.

Finally, where there are cooperatives or organized pre-cooperative family and social welfare activities, women have played key roles with responsibility for participation, administration, and management. The barriers to women's full participation in cooperatives is similar to those in other areas. These include lack of access to socioeconomic facilities and decisionmaking and, even where there is access, inability to profit thereby because of lack of information, education, vocational training, and management skills. Another constraint here, as in other income-producing activities, is lack of time. Studies conducted in Sierra Leone and Kenya revealed the fact that the majority of the women—73 percent in the former and over 50 percent in the latter—considered that the competing demands of food production and domestic chores left little time for nonfarm economic activities. The overcoming of these barriers has become a prime target for ILO action in the field of technical cooperation. To this end the ILO has recently made greater efforts to employ women professionals with experience in the field. One example is Gretchen Goodale, a U.S. national with a Ph.D. from Columbia University in anthropology who has served in the ILO Training Department since 1985. She previously worked for ten years on the African continent, primarily in the Educational Resources Center; she worked with the public school system in Cameroon, and for U.S. AID on marketing problems. She was a project director in Burundi where she heard about a new post at the ILO on income generating activities. She has specialized on women's issues; she noted recently that of all the trainers in the ILO Asian program for training in small enterprises, only two were women.

Many of these themes are being carried forward in the project plans for 1990–1995 but with increased emphasis on the plight of women as amongst the most vulnerable to the effects of the prolonged economic recession and the continuing widespread unemployment and poverty in the developing countries—a group that constitutes a large and growing proportion of the labor force. Studies are to be carried out as to ways in which to put women on an even footing with men in industries not traditionally associated with women, such as mining, plantations, building and construction, and transport. In industries such as food and drinks, textiles, clothing, footwear and leather, which employ a majority of women, efforts will be made to improve their conditions of work. The problems of rural women will continue to be a focus of attention, including the protection of casual workers and home-based workers. Practical measures to meet their problems include material assistance in the form of access to markets, training, credit, water supplies, and raw materials.

Specific targets include: improvement of the work environment, occupational safety and health, working time arrangements, maternity protection, child-care facilities and the harmonization of work and family responsibilities; promotion of productive and remunerative employment; vocational and management training; and the strengthening of workers' and employers' organization. Special attention is to be given to combining technical managerial or vocational skill development, or both, with pre-training counseling, guidance, and motivation programs, and post-training placement and advisory services. In developing countries assistance will be given to women entrepreneurs on how to start and maintain businesses, self-employment and self-development, and the dissemination of improved technologies and information on collective investment, ownership, management, and control of such technologies.

In rural areas attention has been directed to time-saving and effort-saving technologies. These include water supplies, stoves, grinding mills, and transport devices. Most of the emphasis heretofore had concentrated on such things as tractors, new seed varieties, fertilizers, and herbicides which are of profit primarily to men and not to women, sometimes displacing the women altogether.

Current efforts are more woman-centered. One ILO project, for example, involved the introduction of improved ovens for smoking fish in Ghana—an occupation in which a substantial number of women participate. Over half of the women who previously bought cooked food now have time to do their own cooking, additional household chores, and time to engage in social and other economic activities such as visiting and farming. In Guinea-Bissau a group of women bought a rice decorticating machine. So much time has been saved that some women are taking health and nutrition classes, some developing practical skills to increase their income, while others are taking courses in pre- and post-natal care or studying midwifery. In the Cameroon, women own and operate cornmills. With the time they have saved they have built roads for trucks to take out their produce, piped water into storage tanks, and built meetinghouses in central villages for the holding of courses. A fairly recent ILO study asserts that if women's work is less efficient than men's this is often because they do not have equal access to tools and other inputs. Where there is equal access women have actually been found to be more efficient workers and managers of resources than men. This highlights the importance of a joint Mali/ILO project on better use of tools by women. UNDP has organized an interagency workshop in Arusha (Tasmania) to identify both women trainers and beneficiaries on the use of tools. Other ILO technology-oriented projects include an effort to measure the impact of improved energy saving technologies on women; pilot field testing of a variety of improved technologies, including efforts to measure their impact; and a joint project with Intermediate Technology Transport on the introduction of improved technologies to lessen the load movement burden of women.

More far-reaching are current plans to prepare guidelines for "the integration of women, both as active agents and as beneficiaries, in the mainstream of the development process." As a prerequisite and basic first step, training workshops are to be held for the ILO staff concerned to ensure more target-oriented and problem-specific formulations of technical cooperation projects. Emphasis is being laid on more effective consultation with employers' and workers' organizations, including the involvement of women as one of the planning partners. "It is important," the ILO has declared, "to ensure the participation of women in tripartite discussions and in the planning, designing, implementation and evaluation of projects." A UN International Development Organization (UNIDO) meeting report declared that women "tend to be only passive members of trade unions and rarely participate in the collective bargaining processes which seek to improve the status of industrial workers."[13]

ILO Institutes for Training

One ongoing ILO institution, designed to improve the technical capacity for both men and women, is the International Center for Advanced Technical and Vocational Training, which was opened in 1965 in Turin with the cooperation of the Italian government. It provides training in engineering and in management, including management of cooperatives and small industries, with emphasis on participants from developing countries. The rising proportion of women attending its worker education courses indicates the growing recognition of women's responsibilities in trade unions. However, the underrepresentation of women in government agencies is still reflected in the overall percentages. In 1984, 15.1 percent of the participants in the regular courses were women, and almost 25 percent of these came from Europe. Of the individual fellowship program participants, 11.9 percent were women and almost 25 percent of these came from the Americas. Subsequently, an American Center for Research and Documentation on Vocational Training (CINTERFOR) was established in Costa Rica, an Asian and Pacific Skill Development Program (APSDEP) in Islamabad, and an Inter-African Center for Vocational Training (CIADFOR—French acronym) in Abidjan, Ivory Coast.

Evaluation of Technical Cooperation

Two ILO bodies oversee the technical cooperation program. It is reviewed annually by the Governing Body's Committee on Operational Programs and about every ten years by the Annual Conference's Committee on

Technical Cooperation which was initially set up in 1967 and meets when a technical cooperation item is on the agenda. The 1987 Conference committee included fifteen women employer participants. Among these were such familiar figures as Anne Mackie from the United Kingdom, Lucia Sasso-Mazzufferi of Italy, and Angela Smith of Grenada. There were also women from Belgium, Canada, Denmark, France, Norway, Spain, Thailand, Trinidad and Tobago, and Turkey. The women workers were less well represented with a total of only seven. In addition to European women from Bulgaria, Hungary, Norway, Sweden, Switzerland, and the United Kingdom, there was an Asian woman worker from Bangladesh. (It is impossible to indicate how many women were government representatives, since as noted previously these are not designated by name.) There were twenty-seven nongovernmental organizations who participated in the committee session but only one woman's organization, the International Alliance of Women. In addition, a substantial number of other women's organizations were active participants in other committees of the conference.[14] Women also participated in the delegations of some of the international trade union organizations and in a few of the international employers' organizations.

Evaluation Proceedings

Since 1979 the Governing Body has called upon the International Labor Office to prepare material as a basis for an evaluation of the impact of projects and the reasons for success or failure.[15] This inevitably is more of an art than science. As the Director-General pointed out in 1988: "It will always be difficult to assess accurately the impact of aid programmes, whether on the economy of a country or on a sector or nonsector" partly because any project is only one small segment and also "because development is by nature a complex process encompassing a wide range of variables." In the short term an apparently successful project may peter out for a variety of reasons or a project that appears to be dormant may take on a new life, perhaps because of a change in the responsible governmental officials or because of social developments or the extension of vocational training facilities.[16]

One critical element in the adequate preparation of a project is the expensive and time-consuming nature of the required research. Because of this "many agencies continue to initiate project interventions which are inappropriate to local circumstances. Impact of the project (positive or negative) is rarely documented—in part because of the lack of baseline data collected prior to project implementation."[17] The ILO is one of those trying to find valid shortcuts for the process of evaluation and has conducted a few experiments.

Many of the problems encountered, be they related to men or women or both, are of long standing. There has rarely been a realistic timetable, for projects frequently need far longer than anticipated. All too often, adequate market surveys have not been made prior to the establishment of a handicraft project, with the result that women were not able to sell their products. Emphasis on income-generating projects has frequently led to activities which are not economically viable, too short-term or small-scale, and lacking in the improvement of skills or technology or irrelevant to the needs of rural women. The World Employment Conference in 1976 emphasized "the participation of the people in making the decisions which affect them through organizations of their own choice."[18] In some cases cultural norms and customs have not been taken sufficiently into account. In one instance, a pedal-type grinding machine was rejected because women had to stand astride, which was considered indecent. Sometimes the educational level of the women had not been realized and in one project it was only after it had been initiated that it became apparent that staff skilled in the communication of expertise to illiterate women would have to be hired. Again, foreign experts may not have assessed the needs of a particular group of women. One pottery project had to be abandoned because the techniques were too sophisticated. Some projects, dependent on community organization, have run into problems because the women were too preoccupied with their home, children, and agriculture to devote the necessary time, or because of a reluctance to break with tradition. It has happened, not infrequently, that trainers of trainers end by training beneficiaries, which obviously eliminates the multiplier effect.

One still unsolved problem is the extent to which projects should be women specific. Do they tend "to marginalise women rather than integrate them in the mainstream of development efforts." It was suggested that "most of the skills training and income-generating activities promoted by the projects for women tend to perpetuate the existing division of labour and unequal social and economic structures by confining women to traditional women's tasks and jobs."[19] However, some of the recipients of women-specific projects argue in their favor. For example, a group of women in Nepal argued that "within the household, women cannot speak openly if men are present; the men drink and mishandle women in mixed village gatherings; villagers will gossip and ruin the marriage chances of unmarried women who participate in mixed groups."[20] It has also been claimed that in mixed projects the men quickly take over and either ease the women out or reduce them to silence.

However, the continuous review process and the experience accumulated over the years have resulted in steadily improving performance. Sometimes too much money has been expended on foreign experts who often took a long time to recruit, and receive relatively long-term contracts. The very length of their stay induced a bias toward doing the job rather than training nationals to take over. When the expert left there often was a vacuum. In the 1986 Governing Body's Committee on Operational Programs repeated emphasis was laid by representatives from recipient countries on the need to use more national experts, be they men or women, now outnumbered by the international experts.[21] Experts from developing countries, it was said, were better equipped to deal with the "complex realities of such countries." Some of the international experts "in fact also lacked the necessary skills and were of inadequate quality." Another criticism advanced was that "reliance on non-national experts in activities requiring subsequent maintenance could result in wastage and failure." Many of these criticisms were reiterated in the discussions in the 1987 Annual Conference—better selection of experts, more short-term experts, and better use of national and regional experts.

One major criticism leveled at the technical cooperation program has been the large number of disparate projects that lacked impact because they were not integrated into a larger whole. Even in 1987 governments complained that there were too many inadequately focused projects. The program for 1990–95 indicates a major shift in emphasis to meet this criticism. The various facets of the ILO's own activities are being integrated into a much more coordinated whole. Instead of a dichotomy between standard setting and technical cooperation, the latter is now to be used as a tool to help governments implement the standards.[22] As was pointed out in the report of a meeting in 1988, while labor laws exist in most countries, they "have not been enforced in Export Processing Zones and in small scale industries." Since these are areas where women tend to be concentrated, improvement in the application of labor laws could have a significant impact on their welfare.

ILO is now striving for full integration of women in all facets of development. The Director-General has also stressed the importance of harnessing more effectively the collective efforts of the whole family of organizations. The steadily increasing demands for assistance, coupled with budgetary stringencies, is reinforcing this trend. This has already been manifest in ILO's imaginative cooperation with the World Food Program. Since this addresses the needs of the poorest sectors of the world's population it is of major importance to women who form a large proportion of this population. If all these matters can be effectively carried out they should go a long way to meet such criticisms as those leveled in 1986 by the representative of the government of Norway, Henriette Munkebye, that the program did not "cover the highly important problem of the integration of women in the development process." It "did not show much awareness of the basic importance of women for development efforts. . . . The integration of women in development implied the participation of women in the planning, implementation and evaluation of projects, the coverage by research and action plans of women's interests and prospects, and the representation of women among the project beneficiaries."[23]

In addition to devoting increased attention to the problems of women as beneficiaries of program activities, it was also recognized that, as a corollary, something should be done about the relatively small number of women experts. The Deputy Director-General reported that the 1986 computerized roster of experts included 8,725 men and only 628 women. Hence, he said, there was "a clear need to encourage women experts throughout the world to make their qualifications and availability known to the ILO." He added that, thanks to a grant from the Norwegian government, a full-time woman official was working with the Technical Cooperation Department to advise units at headquarters and in the field to ensure that due consideration was given to the needs of women, including women in the design of projects.[24]

This development may well have been influenced by expressions of concern about the role of women in the Office during both the 1986 and 1987 meetings of the Governing Body. In 1986 the Canadian government representative had complained about the paucity of women in senior posts in the Office and had urged that a special adviser to the Director-General be appointed to coordinate activities relating to women workers and to implement the Plan of Action. Although this proposal was dropped for budgetary reasons, there was no abatement of interest in the situation regarding women in the Office and Torild Skard of Norway took up the cudgels again in 1987. In connection with the Plan of Action she deplored the lack of information regarding the role of women in the Office itself.

The paper, she said, "contained no indication of how the Office intended to implement the Plan or to improve the recruitment of women and its policies in regard to female officials." It was, she continued, "of the utmost importance that the Office should indicate in the Plan how women would be represented at all levels and in all areas of the Organization."[25]

The post of special adviser referred to above was incorporated in the budget for 1990–91, with "specific responsibility for promoting coordinating and monitoring work on the role of women in development in ILO Technical Co-operation activities." In addition, provision has been made for the appointment of full-time regional advisers on women's questions in all the four developing regions, Africa, Americas, Asia and the Pacific, and Arab States. Finally all technical departments are being required to designate officials with special responsibility for issues relating to women workers.[26] The appointment of the first woman Deputy Director-General in late 1989 is too recent to evaluate, but it should be noted that she has been given responsibility for the Technical Assistance Department and the program as a whole.

Research and Studies

There is a constant interplay between technical cooperation and research and studies. Sometimes a study reveals a need which technical assistance can meet or the means by which technical cooperation should meet that need. Conversely, technical cooperation activities may reveal the need for further research.

Initially, research in the ILO focused on such questions as the employment of older women workers, review of social and economic problems affecting teachers, and opportunities for women in handicrafts and cottage industries. In the 1960s attention was broadened to include the problems of women in the developing countries, in order "to ensure that women in these countries are not left behind in the modernization of their societies, but are enabled to contribute as fully as possible to the nation building process" and "to promote changes conducive to the advancement of women in all walks of life."[27] Many of these studies have dealt with vocational training, with particular emphasis on increasing opportunities for self-employment for women and for improving their wage earning capacity. Others have analyzed problems of discrimination, including equal pay for equal work, and legislation and other national standards regarding equality in respect of employment. Still others have dealt with female-headed households, women workers on plantations, women in the energy sector, migrants, and the participation of women in economic activities, both in general and in particular geographic areas, especially in rural areas. Recently, attention has been directed to women and apartheid, and to the implications for women of technological change.

Automation in factories and offices requires drastic changes in skills and working practices. Women's jobs, it has been pointed out, will be particularly at risk in manufacturing, retail, financial, and clerical sectors. Machines will take over many of the lower-paid jobs traditionally carried out by women and, without special training, the women will be in no position to compete in the area of new technology. One example of this type of training problem is illustrated by the experience of a group in Nigeria who bought a mechanical maize sheller. The women had to be taught not only how to manage the sheller but also how to train their muscles to new patterns and rhythm of movement.

Studies carried out by the ILO in Africa indicate that "with technological change, there is a tendency for the work load for women to increase; rural women tend to work in sectors of production with particularly low levels of productivity; the socio-economic category to which women belong may affect the impact of technological change." Another study concludes that "a technology which is looked upon as a labour-saving device may well put some women out of work altogether, when as improved technology is introduced, men usually take control of it and often do work which used to be performed by women when only traditional tools were available."[28] Some technological change has the effect of reinforcing the patriarchal or entrepreneurial role of the men in the household to the detriment of the women. "Technological advances can mean a setback if, for example, tractors shorten the working hours of men who do the plowing but lengthen the working hours of women who do the winding. 'Modernization' can mean merely more advanced feudalism for women if it disenfranchises matrilineal or matrifocal peoples, or introduces agrobusiness (and training for only men in new farming techniques) in a country where women traditionally have been the landowners, farmers and marketers."[29]

The importance of these studies is reflected in the type of problems that arise on the national level in adapting women to technological change. The problems that can be posed, under certain circumstances, by even the most basic mechanism were vividly described by Joyce Mujuri, who was suddenly appointed minister of sports, youth, and recreation and subsequently women's affairs of Zimbabwe. "I was," she said, "twenty-five years old, just out of the jungle [she was a guerrilla fighter], with only a ninth grade education. I didn't know how to use a telephone or even a desk diary. I could barely speak English and here I was expected to speak political jargon with mature, seasoned politicians." She made it by dint of hard work, night school, and help from colleagues.[30] Mary Tedese, the chief of women's training and research of the UN Economic Commission for Africa deplored the "alarming trend" toward the appointment of young, inexperienced women as women's affairs officers as prejudicial, not only to the individuals concerned and to their jobs, but to the reputation of women generally.[31]

Even in a country like Sweden the problems arising from technological change may adversely affect the situation of women. Accordingly Sweden has set up a program through an agency of the Ministry of Labor. It operates through a network of regional branches and local centers to train men and women to satisfy the specific needs of local employers. Because of their greater need, special one-to-five months' courses have been created to initiate women into nontraditional areas in industry. They are designed to equip women with skills in basic economics, technical knowledge, marketing, and entrepreneurship.

In addition to research on technological change, several women on the ILO staff have made major contributions to the ILO research in the field of rural development and its effect upon women. Zubeida M. Ahmad, a Pakistani who retired in 1985 after thirty years in the ILO, but who has continued to carry out technical assistance missions, and Martha Loutfi are two examples. Much of the information concerning women in rural areas that is analyzed earlier is drawn from studies they have made in the field. Ahmad began her work in the ILO's cooperative section and later went to Africa and Asia as an ILO technical expert. Martha Loutfi, who is now senior economist in the international policies unit of the Employment and Development Department, came to the Office in 1979. She has a Ph.D. from the University of California (Berkeley). Prior to joining the ILO she had worked for the Brandt Commission (Independent Commission on International Development Issues) and before that had been a consultant to the Center for Arab Unity Studies in Beirut. She was also an assistant professor at the American University in Beirut, and earlier (1968–69 and 1973–74) had worked at McGill University in Montreal. Thus, although a U.S. citizen, she has a widely varied background. Both

Ahmad and Loutfi, in addition to their research activities, were successful negotiators, obtaining multi- and bilateral support and funding for a number of regional and interregional programs such as those dealing with rural women.

Another impressive young woman, working in the Rural Employment Policies Branch, is Rounag Jahan from Bangladesh. Prior to joining the ILO staff she spent some time in Bangladesh teaching politics and advocating women's interests. Then she was for two years in the UN Center for Development in Asia and the Pacific, in Kuala Lumpur, with full responsibility for women's issues. She attended both the Mexico City and Nairobi UN women's conferences and chaired panels at each. One of her most interesting projects after joining the ILO was the previously mentioned lace makers of Marsapur.

The World Employment Program

The World Employment Program (WEP) has generated a substantial number of studies, as well as the 1976 Declaration and Program of Action adopted by the Tripartite World Employment Conference.[31] The declaration states as its aim the achievement of full employment and the satisfaction of the basic needs of all people, particularly of the lowest income group by the year 2000. Women are singled out as a vulnerable group, their role in economic development stressed and their needs emphasized. A report issued in 1979 points out that recovery from depression, with structural changes and slow growth, will have different effects on different groups in the labor market, noting their effect on women: "if as expected, those parts of the tertiary sector that were major sources of female employment contract as a result of technological change, while others (clothing and textiles) are increasingly affected by import competition."[32]

Another area of research by the WEP has addressed such questions as: What policies should be adopted toward labor supply, and in particular, female labor supply? How can the different aspects of economic and noneconomic activities and their welfare implications be taken into account in labor market policy design, and more generally in the design of policies to influence the role and status of women? In seeking to answer these questions a large-scale project was developed in 1978 as part of the WEP, whose objectives are:

– To measure and demonstrate to policymakers the important economic contribution made by women.

142

– To establish the effect on women's productive activities of important developmental changes.

– To investigate the effect on women's positions of measures aimed at improving women's status, such as educational programs, cooperatives, income generating schemes and improved job opportunities for women.

– To study the effect on women's productive activities of changes in marriage, fertility, mortality, and family structure, and vice versa.

Institute for Labor Studies

An International Institute for Labor Studies was established by the ILO in 1960. In addition to its own research studies and publications it has provided a link with the academic world, especially in developing countries, and has been responsive to their suggestions. In 1975 it began a new program on women, work, and society with the aim of exploring the question of women and their participation "in a broad sense as referring to the social relationships which govern the actions of both men and women." The program was launched in a symposium on "Women and Decision-making: A Social Policy Priority" which concluded that "the part played by women in decision-making has up to now been insignificant." A second symposium was held in cooperation with the Austrian federal government in 1978 on "Women and Industrial Relations" designed to lead to further research activities aimed at improving the working and living conditions of both sexes. The symposium concluded that, despite the growing awareness of the problems faced by women workers and the emphasis placed on the promotion of equality, "a very real gap exists between the normative intent" of the regulatory processes "and the situation in which women find themselves." A third major step taken by the institute has been the inclusion in its research program of a study of women and industrial relations in the Asian region. The institute's publications now reflect the continuing concern with women workers' questions and include monographs in its research series, bibliographies, and articles in its journal *Labour and Society*.

There are only a few women professionals on the staff of the institute. The most senior is Rose Marie Greve, a Sri Lankan whose father was a former employer member of the Governing Body. A capable, friendly woman, she is critical of many of the articles published by the institute— and because of some frustration with respect to her work, has directed much of her energy to organizing women on the staff to take a more dynamic role both in the staff union and in an independent group, the aim of which is to eliminate—or at least lessen—discrimination against women on the staff. Another woman who heads the institute's research and documentation branch, Christine Smith of Great Britain has, like Rose Marie Greve, joined the special group seeking to improve the situation of women within the Office.

Periodic Publications

A number of ILO serial publications have always carried articles and texts dealing with women's issues. Thus the *Legislative Series,* which dates back to the earliest days of the ILO, has always published national and international laws and regulations concerning women. Moreover, its first editor, Sophy Sanger, was the women who had been responsible for the editing of its predecessor series, published by the International Association for Labor Legislation. Many articles concerning women have appeared, ever since the ILO was established, in the *International Labour Review.* The *Social and Labour Bulletin,* which appeared four times a year, regularly carried articles on "equality of opportunity and treatment," including many items dealing with facets of women's work. Unfortunately, as a result of budget cuts, its publication was suspended at the beginning of 1989. *Women, Work, and Development* is another publication which includes many technical articles on women, especially in the developing countries.[33]

In recent years two women have carried major responsibility for both of these publications. Hedva Sarfati is an Israeli who joined the staff in 1966 to do research in the labor administration branch of the Industrial Relations and Labor Administration Department. When, in the 1970s the publications program was reorganized, and the *Social and Labour Bulletin* begun, Sarfati moved over to become both editor and contributor to the bulletin and to the *Women, Work, and Development* series. Her professional background in industrial relations and research enabled her to publish, and write, controversial articles on women in many fields, especially in developing countries. An example is her article entitled, "Job Equality for Women: Progress, Problems, and Perspectives," which appeared in *Labour and Society,* a publication of the International Institute for Labor Studies in 1985. In 1987 she was promoted to become the chief of the Salaried Employees and Professional Workers Branch—thus joining the limited number of D1 (one of two top posts below the Directorate) women on the staff. (Her predecessor Rolande Cuvillier had been one of the first women to attain the rank.)

Sarfati's successor as chief of the *Social and Labour Bulletin* section was Margaret Cove-Christiansen, a British national who has had an unusual career. Her father from his childhood was a miner; her mother was a teacher with a strong belief in the value of education. Margaret grew up in Wales, where she remembers deliberately failing an exam so as to be able to stay in school an extra year. She obtained a B.A. from Trinity College, Dublin, in English and French. Her first real job was with ICI (International Chemical Company) and then Monsanto. While working, she took a diploma in public administration. She later went to the International Red Cross in Geneva and then transferred to the ILO where she first worked in a clerical category. She entered a competition for the professional category for work in the training section, and in 1979 moved to the *Social and Labour Bulletin* section. In addition to her research and editorial work there, she was a very active member of the staff union and coeditor of their publication, *Union*. In consequence of the suspension of the *Social and Labour Bulletin,* she is taking early retirement.

The first ILO publication dedicated entirely to women's issues, *Women at Work,* was initiated in 1977 by the Office for Women Workers' Questions. However, as noted elsewhere, the unit was abolished under the 1989 reorganization. Its publication, *Women at Work,* which originally appeared three times a year, and then twice, provided invaluable information on women workers throughout the world, including the activities affecting women of the ILO and other international organizations, trade union bodies, employers' organizations, and other nongovernmental bodies. Its final issue was published by a consultant firm in the summer of 1989.

Medium-Term Plans and Program Budgets

A major planning tool of the ILO, similar to that of other UN agencies, is a six-year, medium-term plan, which becomes the principle policy directive for the Organization and a pragmatic basis for budgets. Developing this plan, as well as the program budgets, is the responsibility of the Governing Body. The ILO's plan is formulated by the International Labor Office in consultation with the United Nations and other specialized agencies to ensure a coordinated approach. A special interagency meeting was convened in 1987 to plan a system-wide, medium-term plan for women designed as a follow-up to the Nairobi Forward-Looking Strategies. The ILO was represented by the then director of the Office for Women Workers' Questions, Raissa Smirnova. The Governing Body and the Conference then adopted the program budget which specified how the medium-term plan would be implemented over each two years of the plan. In the period 1982–87 the ILO placed major emphasis on the problems of working women, proposing four main lines for action similar to those adopted in the medium-term plan for 1976–81.[34] These include the following efforts: to improve understanding of "the nature and degree of discrimination against women in employment"; to achieve the greatest possible "equality of opportunity and treatment between the sexes in the field of employment and occupation"; to facilitate the entry of women into working life and to widen their employment opportunities by giving special attention to those sectors where there are large concentrations of women "mainly at low levels of skill, income and employment security." To this end there should be appropriate training arrangements in both developing and industrialized countries; and, finally, the development and improvement of methods to measure and collect statistics concerning the contribution and participation of women in the economy and labor force, particularly in developing countries.

The next step of the ILO in dealing with women's questions is the implementation of its medium-term plan for 1990–95. This plan identifies women workers as one of the main groups likely to be exposed "to the negative effects of restructuring and technological change." They run the risk of drifting "between unemployment and low-paid, insecure jobs with poor career prospects." To mitigate this trend ILO will inter alia promote employment opportunities in both the formal and informal sectors of the economy, seek to improve working conditions especially in agriculture and the services sector, and to strengthen social security.[35]

The next move in implementing the medium-term plan has been the incorporation of new arrangements in the Director-General's Program and Budget Proposals for 1990–91 "to ensure more rapid progress towards the integration of women's concerns into all ILO activities both under the regular program and under technical co-operation programs."[36]

6. The Regional Approach: Women's Role

As membership in the ILO grew in the postwar years, the demands of technical assistance, coupled with the changing nature of ILO membership, led to basic alterations in structure. More and more newly independent countries from Africa, Asia, and the Caribbean joined the ILO, bringing its membership from 55 in 1948 to 150 in 1989. To service these ever-wider geographic areas, a new, decentralized regional structure was set up. In the first phase of decentralization field offices were established in developing or newly industrialized countries. They served primarily as liaison offices for technical assistance. In the second stage they were superseded by area and regional offices which were gradually given wider responsibilities and their scope broadened to cover a larger span of ILO activities in the regions.

Regional Structure

Regional offices have been established in Addis Ababa for Africa, Lima for Latin America and the Caribbean, Bangkok for Asia and the Pacific, and a Beirut office for the Middle East—at the time of writing operating from Geneva. These regional offices are responsible for all ILO programs and projects within the region. There is a director with the rank of Assistant Director-General in each regional office who provides liaison with headquarters and reports to the Director-General in Geneva. In addition to the regional offices there are ten area African offices, eight Latin American and Caribbean offices, and four Asian offices.

Since 1936 formal regional tripartite conferences have been held regularly in different parts of the world. The resolutions adopted by these conferences set the tone for activities in the respective regions, frequently call for actions by the Governing Body and the annual conferences, and reflect the increasing role of the developing countries in the ILO's programs. In addition to the regional conferences and the regional and area offices, there are regional advisory committees whose major task is to voice the views of the regions in the determination of program priorities.

In the late 1960s the regional structure was strengthened by a series of regional teams. These included some dealing particularly with training problems, others with labor administration, and others with employment. The three employment teams undertake some of the research and support needed for many of the employment projects being carried out in the regions. There are also numerous workshops, seminars, and symposia which inter alia implement many of the regional conference resolutions.

While from the outset there has been some limited concern in the regions for women's issues, by the late 1960s programs involving women began to receive much greater emphasis. The most recent change was the appointment of full-time regional advisers on women's questions in all the four developing regions. Along with the increased focus on women's issues, an increased number of women now take part in the regional structure—serving in some instances as directors and frequently as experts and support staff. In addition, the participation of women in the regional conferences has increased geometrically as has the number of women beneficiaries of technical assistance projects. Here too there seems to be a direct relationship between the women's issues dealt with by the ILO, including the role of women in dealing with these issues, and the concerns of the national and regional women's movements. Thus as women's organizations, such as the International Alliance for Women, the Soroptomists, the International Council of Women—and their various national affiliates—began to identify the problems faced by women in developing countries, primarily in the 1960s and 1970s, the ILO and other international organizations gave them increasing attention. But it was not until the mid-1980s that the trade union (and even later the employers') organizations recognized that women trade unionists could be effective in developing countries, and consequently included women labor and employer representatives in regional meetings and gave priority to technical assistance projects encouraging women to join trade unions.

Regional Conferences

As indicated above, the regional structure of the ILO is built upon its earlier experience with regional conferences. The earliest formal regional conferences were those on the American continent, but in 1947 the ILO initiated regional conferences in Asia and the Pacific, while in 1955 it held its first regional conference in Europe. The last series to be initiated was in 1960 when the first African regional conference took place. While the objectives of the various regional conferences were similar, the agenda items differed in accord with the varying concerns of the different regions. With the exception of the European region, where women were accustomed to attending conferences, there were, in most instances, very few women participants until the 1980s. In some cases there were no women from developing countries in the region. This would appear to be a sad commentary on the significance of the conferences to women. However, this is belied by the results. Men from the region did participate and did adopt resolutions directly affecting women, and in many cases national implementation of these resolutions followed. The tripartite structure of the ILO was maintained in the regional conferences, but there were few women labor representatives, reflecting the limited participation of women in trade unions in most of the developing countries. Recognizing this situation, much of the current emphasis of the ILO in these areas is directed toward bringing women into the trade union movement.

Regional Conferences of the American States

The first Regional Conference, held in Santiago, Chile, in 1936, was intended to deal inter alia with conditions of employment of women on that continent. However, very few women participated, as was ruefully pointed out by Frieda Miller, the U.S. delegate, in her report on the conference (included among her papers at the Schlesinger Library). She was elected chairman of the Committee on Women and Children. The only other women members of the delegations were Allamita Diniz-Gonzales, technical adviser to the Brazilian Department of Labor and Maria Ramirez Gomez, a workers' adviser from Chile. Interest focused almost entirely on such traditional concerns as maternity protection, while hours and conditions of work and wages received scant attention, and the concept of equality was not on the agenda.

In all, twelve American regional conferences were held between 1936 and 1986. While most of them dealt with issues affecting women, only a limited number directly addressed women's problems. These latter issues included maternity protection, vocational training, equal pay, welfare facilities in individual enterprises, protection of women in agriculture, and at the 1979 Conference on employment, training, and conditions of work of women.

The second regional conference, held in Havana, in November 1939, served a purpose essentially different both from its Santiago predecessor and all later regional meetings, since it met shortly after the outbreak of the Second World War, at a moment when the wartime role of the ILO was under close consideration. Its chief significance was its reaffirmation of support for the ILO's activities by noncombatant nations during the period of the "phony war"—an affirmation that took the form of the Declaration of Havana. (This was the first time that an ILO meeting had adopted a declaration to express its conclusions.) Its concern with women's issues was indicated in a series of resolutions, which included a statement, to be known as the maternity code of Havana, "to recognize child bearing as having a social value of such a lofty nature that it entitles it to particular care on the part of the public authorities"; a statement of principles concerning the protection of women's wages, including practical rules to achieve better application of "equal pay for equal work"; proposals for legislative measures dealing with industrial homework; and legislation prohibiting dismissal of working women on the ground of marriage. One immediate outcome of the conference was a series of technical missions to assist in establishing and improving Latin American social security regimes.

The participation by women, although larger than that in Santiago, was still small. However, those at the conference played a significant role. Of the nine women coming from three countries, Cuba, Mexico, and the United States, five served as officers of committees.[1]

No other regional meetings were held until after the end of the war. At the third meeting, held in Mexico City in 1946, although representatives of thirteen countries attended only two women—both from the United States—were members of delegations. However, women's issues were high on the agenda. One of the resolutions adopted was entitled "Women" and stated: "(1) Measures including the orientation of general education towards vocational aims and vocational guidance, should be adopted to assure women complete access to all forms of training. (2) It is desirable to investigate women's training requirements for the purpose of determining adequate methods of improving existing training facilities.

Other resolutions dealing with freedom of association, and equal pay for equal work included a provision that prohibited any distinction on the grounds of sex, race, color, and creed. One general resolution dealing with the elimination of discrimination by reason of sex, race, color, and creed urged that all practicable measures be taken to lessen existing wage discrimination.

At the following session in 1949, held in Montevideo, Uruguay, resolutions were adopted concerning the protection of women in agriculture and the need to prevent exploitation of women. The initiative for these resolutions came from the United States. Aryness Joy Wickens, assistant commissioner of the Bureau of Labor Statistics, who had also participated in the 1947 and 1948 annual conferences as assistant to David Morse, then acting U.S. secretary of labor, took the lead in much of the conference actions. She was strongly supported by Beatrice McConnell, chief of the legislative standards and state services of the Bureau of Labor Standards, another old-timer at ILO meetings and the only other woman attending the meeting.

In 1956, again in Havana, and in 1961 in Buenos Aires, only three women attended each conference. The Havana conference had no item on its agenda of special concern to women. The Buenos Aires conference dealt with social security of migrant workers, conditions of life and work in agriculture, and vocational training. Mrs. Oller de Sarasgueta of Panama, director of labor inspection, was chairman of the Committee on Vocational Training—the first women to chair a committee at a postwar regional conference. All three women at the conference took an active role, especially in the committees dealing with social security and with cooperatives.

In 1966, at the Ottawa regional conference, the representation of women had deteriorated further with the only woman present an observer from the Canadian Province of Ontario, the host country. By 1970, at the regional conference held in Caracas, Venezuela, there was some improvement with respect to woman, with one government delegation (Honduras) being led by a woman, two countries (Venezuela and Uruguay) including women in their delegations, and the employers electing a woman vice chairman to a committee. Diana Mahabir, of Trinidad and Tobago, the employer delegate in question, recalls that her election was the source of some embarrassment to many of the Latin American committee members. The conference adopted a resolution urging countries to ratify the equal pay convention, and paid a warm tribute to Ana Figueroa, Chilean diplomat, member of the UN Commission on the Status of Women, and later Assistant Director-General of the ILO.

In 1974, at another Mexico City session, the number of women had gone up to eleven, with Argentina, Brazil, Cuba, Jamaica, Mexico, Peru, and Uruguay sending government representatives—all women who attended a regional conference for the first time. In addition, Colombia sent Maria Elena de Crovo, minister of labor and social security, as "Minister Attending"—a position she had already held at the ILO Annual Conference. Shirley Carr, then newly elected executive vice president of the Canadian Labor Congress, appeared for the first time as Canadian worker delegate, while Mahabir came not as the Trinidad and Tobago employer delegate but, in her role as chief of the Caribbean Employers Confederation, a nongovernmental organization. The three substantive items on the agenda were integrated economic development, the general situation regarding ratification of conventions, and tripartite cooperation.

Five years later, at Medellín, Colombia, the number of women participants shot up to a startling high—from eleven to forty. This was due in part to the impact of the Decade for Women, but also to the conference agenda which included a topic specifically concerning employment, training, and conditions of work of women. The conference had the benefit of a previous meeting of an Inter-American Advisory Committee in Quito, Ecuador, which had dealt with policies and practices regarding working conditions, the environment, and new approaches to training for promotion. The women attending the session comprised ten government delegates and thirteen government advisers; one employer delegate and one employer adviser; and two worker delegates and thirteen worker advisers. Women came from Argentina, Brazil, Canada, Chile, Colombia, Costa Rica, Cuba, Grenada, Haiti, Jamaica, Mexico, Panama, Paraguay, Suriname, Uruguay, and Venezuela, in addition to an observer from Great Britain.

The next conference in 1986, held in Montreal and attended by five hundred persons, including tripartite delegations from nineteen nations, had fewer women participants than at the previous session, partly because there were no women's items on the agenda (by contrast with the previous conference) and presumably because it was more difficult or more expensive for Latin Americans to go to Canada instead of Colombia. However, the Canadian delegation was headed by a woman, Jennifer R. McQueen, deputy minister of labor, the only speaker at the conference to draw attention to the role of women. Thirteen of the countries attending included women in their delegations, sending seven government delegates, two substitute delegates, and eight advisers; and two employer delegates but no women worker representatives—an indication that the trade union movement in the Americas still had few effective women members.

Regional Conferences in Asia and the Pacific

After launching its programs in Latin America, ILO had turned its attention to Asia. In 1947 a preparatory Asian regional conference was held in New Delhi, designed to survey the issues of particular concern to the Asian countries and lay the groundwork for the first formal Asian regional conference, scheduled to be held in China the following year. As a basis for the preparatory discussion the International Labor Office prepared a substantial report, entitled "Labour Policy in General including the Enforcement of Labour Measures." The employment of women was the subject of a major chapter and provided an analysis of the nature of women's employment in almost all the Asian countries, the overwhelming need for greater maternity protection (noting the "alarmingly high level of maternal and infantile mortality and morbidity in Asiatic countries," the absence of an "adequate general system of public health services," and the economic situation of women in general). On a country by country basis the report reviewed the major problems faced by women, including illiteracy and low wages. It concluded, "The position of women workers in Asiatic countries has certainly improved considerably in recent years," adding, "Many of the difficulties encountered by the women workers in these countries in securing employment, in extending the sphere of their economic activity and in obtaining equitable rates of wages are due largely to obstacles raised by tradition and convention, whose effects persist notwithstanding declarations to the contrary in political Constitutions." The report suggested that the China regional conference might deal with: methods of maternity protection; measures to promote the general education and vocational training of women; measures necessary for the "protection of the health of women workers who are still employed on heavy work; and adequate administrative arrangements for giving effect to a policy designed to promote the employment of women under improved welfare and working conditions."[2] The preparatory conference

---

153

adopted resolutions along these lines, emphasizing protection of women in employment and maternity benefits.

As was the case in the initial meetings in Latin America, few women took a direct role in the early Asian meetings. The only woman present in New Delhi was Wen-harem Chen, an employer adviser from the Federation of China Industries.

The second Asian regional conference, held in Ceylon in 1950, and attended by only two women, both from Europe, dealt with labor inspection; facilities for the promotion of workers' welfare; wage regulation; and organization of manpower with special reference to the development of employment services and training. A resolution adopted by the conference called for a detailed study by the Office of how the problem is solved in industrially advanced countries, so as to aid the developing countries in establishing protective labor inspection for women and young persons. Another resolution noted that "benefits of the employment service should be made available on the basis of absolute equality to all workers residing in a country without regard to nationality, sex, caste or creed." This resolution was primarily the work of Mlle Guelfi of France who was labor inspector of overseas territories of France, and a frequent participant in the annual conferences of the ILO.

At the 1953 Tokyo conference the situation of women was only fractionally better, with four women participating: one each from Hong Kong, Japan, and the United Kingdom, in addition to Gertrude Stemberg of the Netherlands, the perennial woman member of the Governing Body who represented the government group of the Governing Body at the regional meeting. The agenda items were of concern to women throughout Asia. In addition to protection of young workers, they included problems of wage policy and workers' housing. The director of the Women's and Minor's Bureau of the Japanese ministry of labor was the reporter of the Committee on Protection of Young Workers and presented its report to the conference.

At the next conference, again held in New Delhi in 1957, Connie Soo Mok Sau-Ha, assistant commissioner of labor of Hong Kong was the government delegate, but no other women were present. The agenda included: labor and social problems of small-scale and handicraft industries in Asian countries; conditions of life and work of sharecroppers, tenant farmers, and similar categories of semi-independent and independent workers in agriculture; and labor-management relations.

In 1962, at the Melbourne session Miss A. M. Stephen, executive officer of the Department of Labor and National Service, was a government adviser, but again, no other woman attended. Here the items on the agenda were: employment promotion with special reference to rural areas; vocational training and management development; and labor management relations and settlement of disputes. Although each of these items was of direct interest to women, neither the special problems of women nor their role were ever mentioned in the debates nor in the resolutions adopted.

At the sixth conference, held in Tokyo in 1968, the agenda included social security—trends and problems; management development with special reference to personnel policies and practices; and a review of the Asian Manpower Plan (which had been outlined at the previous conference). There were seven women participants from Hong Kong, Japan, Mongolia, the Philippines, and the USSR.

Despite the fact that the agenda items, and the resolutions adopted, dealt with subjects directly affecting women, there was no reference to women in any of the speeches, reports, or resolutions.

By 1971, at the Teheran conference, the situation had begun to improve. For the first time some leadership was assumed by the four participating women, Connie Soo Mok Sau-Ha, Felina T. Reyes, who was reporter for the Committee on Worker and Employer Organization, Myatavyn Lhamsuren, from Mongolia, chairman of the government group, and, also from Mongolia, Bavudorjiin Odguerel. However, the only woman related issue was the need for family planning programs in Asian countries.

In 1975, at the Colombo conference, two more women attended, Mrs. G. Braybrook, government delegate from Australia, ministry of labor and immigration (who also began to play a leadership role in the Annual Conference), and Khajorn Sobhon, government adviser from Thailand.

As indicated earlier, the first real recognition of the role of women in Asian regional meetings came only in 1980. At the ninth Asian conference, held in Manila in December 1980, there were more women—thirteen—many of them newcomers. Myatavyn Lhamasuren was again government delegate from Mongolia; and Alison Mary Stephen was the government delegate from Australia. Other countries represented by women were Iran, France (with an employer delegate), Singapore (with a worker representative), Japan, Fiji, Indonesia, and, of course, the Philippines as host country.

The issues discussed by the conference were problems of rural workers in Asia and the Pacific, with special attention to women's work. The conference adopted resolutions recommending a wide variety of measures, including a shift of resources to rural areas, and education about population problems and family health programs, combined with social security and the creation of employment and income-earning opportunities. On the specific problems of women workers in rural areas, it recommended the collection of information, research, and technical and financial assistance to strengthen rural women's organizations, with special emphasis on the need to assist the integration of women in development programs.

The most recent Asian conference (its tenth), held in Jakarta, Indonesia, in December 1985, stressed vocational training and the need for vocational rehabilitation of the disabled as significant factors in the growth and adjustment in Asia. The discussion was based on a comprehensive report prepared by the International Labor Office which stressed the need for retraining and skill upgrading throughout life. Other issues before the conference were employment, productivity, migration, and the problems of women workers. Resolutions were adopted which dealt with the need for equal opportunity for women workers. Some three hundred participants from thirty countries attended. Among these there were eighteen women from nine countries—again an increase. Three were government delegates, and one was a workers' delegate; while there was no employer delegate, there was one employer adviser.

Both the number of women participants and the variety of their nationalities and skills marked the growth of the concern with the role of women in Asia. The ways in which the concerns expressed in the regional conferences have been implemented is discussed below in the section dealing with workshops and seminars.

European Regional Conferences

Although somewhat different in emphasis and approach, the activities of the European regional structure constitute a facet of the decentralization of ILO activities. The first European regional conference was held in Geneva in 1955 with an attendance that included women from five countries—Austria, Czechoslovakia, France, Norway, and Poland. (The French delegation encompassed an employer and a worker adviser; the Norwegian included a worker adviser, as did the Czechoslovak and Polish delegations.)

The second European Regional Conference was held in Geneva in January 1974. Twelve countries—Belgium, Bulgaria, Denmark, France, the Federal Government of Germany, Italy, the Netherlands, Norway, Romania, Switzerland, the United Kingdom, and the Soviet Union—were represented by delegations which included twenty-one women, some from the government sector and some from the employer and worker sectors. In many cases, such as Mrs. Sasso Mazzerufferi and Mrs. Glorioso of Italy they were frequent participants in the Annual Conferences or the Governing Body of the ILO.

At the third European regional conference, which also met in Geneva in October 1979, seventeen countries included a total of thirty-nine women on their delegations. Two countries, Finland and Poland, sent their appropriate ministers to attend the conference—Sinikka Luja-Pentilla, Finnish minister of social affairs and health, and Maria Milczarek, Polish minister of labor, wages, and social affairs. (There were no women in the British delegation, and the European Community with an observer delegation of twenty-one included only three women, Mrs. Barendregt, principal assistant to the vice president for employment, F. Devonić, administrator for employment and social affairs, and Miss K. Imhoff, an assistant in the department.) As at the previous session, a number of the women, like Ursula Engelen-Kefer, were old-timers for whom the sessions were primarily a continuation of the Annual Conference or of the Governing Body, but a number of others came for the first time and found the sessions to be a learning process, especially with respect to women's issues.

While the European regional conferences have met less frequently than those in the other regions, their meetings were of unusual significance because they served as a forum for intra-European discussion, providing an opportunity for the representatives from Eastern and Western Europe to discuss their problems within a continental framework. This has proved useful, especially with respect to such issues as equality for women. While the East European countries have a longer tradition and wider application of legislation dealing with the rights of women, in Western Europe women have been more vocal and articulate in making their demands known.

African Regional Conferences

Machinery to assist African development was the last to be established, the first regional conference having been held in Lagos (Nigeria) in 1960. A resolution adopted by this session called attention to the special problems facing women and young workers in dealing with their living and working conditions. At this session Nigeria was represented by a woman, Malla Ahmed Coomase, O.B.E., while its employer delegate was Jaujeola Aduke Moore, director of the Consultative Association of Employers, who was elected chairman of the employers group; she was also an active participant in ILO Annual Conferences. From the United Kingdom came Anne Godwin, long an ILO stalwart, as a worker adviser.

At the second conference, which met in Addis Ababa, Ethiopia, (now Burkina Faso), in 1964—the same year that the Annual Conference was considering an ILO report on the Status of Women in a Changing World—three significant resolutions were adopted dealing with various aspects of conditions of employment and conditions of work of African women. They noted that women should be "entitled to join trade unions of their choice freely and have the possibility of occupying responsible posts in the unions and of obtaining adequate training for this purpose." The conference also urged that women representatives take part in consultations between public authorities and employers' and workers' organizations formulating employment policies for women to "the maximum extent possible." These resolutions grew out of the Committee on Women's Work, which was chaired by Mrs. Combrary, government delegate of Upper Volta (now Burkina Faso), and had as its vice chairman Dorothee Raharison, workers' delegate from the Malagasy Republic (Madagascar), and as reporter Souad Jedidi, government delegate from Tunisia. The only other item on the agenda was wage-fixing machinery.

Twelve countries—the Central African Republic, France, Upper Volta, Liberia, Gabon, Nigeria, Malagasy, Tanganyika, Tunisia, Ethiopia, Israel, and the USSR (Israel and the USSR were observers), included women in their delegations. All of the women participated in the Committee on Women's Work. (Incidentally, the conference was opened by the emperor of Ethiopia, Haile Selassie.)

At the next conference, held in Accra, Ghana, in 1969 the situation had again changed and only one woman participated—C. Leone Chesson, legal counsel and chairman of the National Labor Office of Liberia, as a government delegate. This may have been due to the fact that there was little on the agenda of particular concern to African women, since the emphasis was on the development of industrial skills and labor administration. Nevertheless, the conference adopted a resolution on employment policy which referred to the need "to reappraise and modify . . . the employment of women."

In 1973 the African regional conference was held in Nairobi, Kenya, where Ethiopia sent two outstanding women as its government delegates, while Egypt and Senegal also included well-known women on their delegations. There were no specifically women's items on the agenda of the session.

At the fifth regional conference, held in Abidjan, Ivory Coast, in September 1977, in spite of the fact that the basic report submitted by the Office called special attention to the importance of meeting women's needs, only five women were present, Maria de Lourdes, government adviser from Angola; Moulikatou Cabirou, director of planning of Benin, who was the government delegate; Brigitte Dable, of the status of women ministry, government adviser, and Mrs. Achio, chief of service in the ministry of technical and vocational education, both of the Ivory Coast; and Tamara Toure Diallo, government adviser of Senegal. The Office report proposed various reforms and strategies for women, which might include "designs of new rural institutions, dissemination of knowledge of improved methods of food farming, market evaluation studies, providing relevant training, introducing groups of women to bankers or other holders of capital, encouraging the basis of women's unionization and advising on further enabling or protective legislation."

The increased ILO programs in Africa were hardly reflected in the level of participation of women in the sixth conference, which met in Tunis in 1983. Aida Gonzales Martinez, Mexican government member of the Governing Body (and former chairman) represented its government group. Cameroon had a woman government delegate as did Djibouti, Mozambique, and Tanzania; in contrast, the Congo and Tunisia sent government advisers. There were no women representatives of either employers or workers.

Although there was no agenda item on women workers, at the request of the African Advisory Committee (which preceded the conference) the Office had included a chapter on women workers' problems in a report prepared for the discussion of working conditions and the environment. However, the chapter dealt primarily with urban women.

The next African regional conference was held in 1987. In preparation for the session the African advisory committee met in February 1987 in Cameroon and recommended that the agenda items should be (1) women's work in Africa; (2) rural and urban training; (3) cooperatives; (4) promotion of small-scale enterprises; and (5) workers' education and assistance to employers' organizations. When the Governing Body determined the final agenda it accepted only two of these items, rural and

Aida Gonzales Martinez of Mexico, chairman of
ILO Governing Body, 1982 *(courtesy of ILO,
Geneva)*.

urban training, and cooperatives. However, it agreed that the Director-
General's report to the conference (item 3 of the agenda) should "inform
it of action taken by the ILO with a view to actively participating in efforts
to resolve" the problems of apartheid, as well as "the situation of women
in Africa." The ground was thus set for greater concern with women's
needs.

In comparing the role of women in the regional conferences, there is
one common denominator. Relatively few women attended any conferences until the 1970s. However, the increased numbers of delegates in the
seventies varied sharply among the regions. Most came from the American
hemisphere. This was a direct reflection of their cultural and educational
status at home, where they won leadership roles in government and in
recognition of their civil and political rights at a relatively early period.

The larger and constant participation of women in the European conferences reflected their economic and political development, as well as their role in the various Geneva national missions and in the many international meetings in Geneva. The more limited participation of Asian and African women stems from the social inhibitions which have limited their activities at home. However, the growth in their attendance at conferences marks progress in their economic and social development.

While the decisions regarding the holding of regional conferences and their location and agenda are made by the Governing Body on the invitation of the government concerned, the initiative with regard to the subjects to be covered comes from the regional advisory committees as well as from the regional departments of the International Labor Office.

Regional Seminars and Workshops

The discussions in the regional conferences reflected a growing concern that more technical aid should be directed to the needs of women in the developing countries. Regional seminars, usually tripartite, and workshops provide a more informal opportunity for a give-and-take between the governmental officials, ILO staff, intergovernmental and nongovernmental agencies, and the local participants. They also provide an opportunity for an exchange of experiences and views among the participants. For each of these meetings the Office prepares comprehensive analyses of the problems to be faced and proposals for national or regional activities to promote the livelihood of the women concerned. Technical missions—some exploratory and some to provide advice on specific problems—are carried out, frequently in cooperation with the UNDP or with multi- and bilateral programs.

Latin America and the Caribbean

With the increasing emphasis on Africa and Asia there have been fewer technical meetings devoted to Latin America. A regional seminar on vocational training for working women in Central America and the Caribbean was jointly organized by the ILO and the Inter-American Center for Research and Documentation on Vocational Training (CINTERFOR) in Costa Rica, April 1978. Under the main theme of equality of opportunity between men and women, the seminar discussed labor and social repercussions of vocational training and its planning, organization, and evaluation in Costa Rica, El Salvador, Guatemala, Honduras, Nicaragua, Panama, and the Dominican Republic. It made concrete suggestions to the ministries of labor and education, official vocational training organizations, and trade union confederations. This was part of a series of meetings held between 1975–79, which approved a project to establish pilot units for coordinating vocational training of women. A follow-up seminar, held in Quito in 1981, reviewed the progress achieved and made recommendations regarding the future of the units. A similar exercise was undertaken for ten Caribbean countries, at a meeting held in Antigua in 1981.

In 1979 two seminars were organized by the ILO/DANIDA (Danish International Development Agency) Workers Education Project under the joint sponsorship of the Caribbean Congress of Labor and the Barbados Workers Union Labor College. The objective was to try to ascertain why women trade unionists did not play a more active role in collective bargaining. This was attributed in part to the attitude of women themselves, lack of education and skills, and lack of day-care centers, and also to legal barriers and the attitude of male trade unionists. Among the proposals for corrective action made at the end of the second seminar was the creation of national and regional women's trade union movements.

An additional seminar, jointly organized by ILO and DANIDA in 1983 in Costa Rica, again dealt with the obstacles women confronted in joining and participating in trade unions.

In 1982 the Trade Union Education Institute (Jamaica), in consultation with the ILO Caribbean Office, conducted two regional seminars. Discussions ranged from women's needs at the workplace to the possibilities for training women for trade union leadership.

A seminar on nondiscriminatory employment practices held in Lima, Peru, in 1983 was notable for the fact that out of twenty participants there was only one woman. Despite the membership, the seminar stressed the bias against women holding managerial or senior positions and declared that trade union policies did not seem to take full account of the need to promote women's involvement in trade union activities.

The impact of new information technologies on women's employment and training in Latin America was discussed at a seminar held in the Turin Training Center in 1985. The seminar reiterated the findings of other groups that women were likely to be the victims rather than the beneficiaries of new technology.

In early 1987 a Latin American regional tripartite roundtable, convened in Lima, Peru, dealt with international migration. Its focus was on the employment of non-nationals in the countries concerned and the employment of their nationals abroad, including the effect of such employment on families. The attendance included one senior government official responsible for migration from each of ten Latin American countries, and five employers and five workers responsible within their organizations for emigration or immigration matters. The roundtable was designed to provide an opportunity for an informal exchange of views on current problems affecting migrant workers, in order to achieve better understanding and closer cooperation among these countries on matters of mutual concern.

Asia and the Pacific

Partly in consequence of the resolutions adopted at the 1964 Asian regional conference, an expanded program was developed in the region to focus attention on the need to integrate women in the overall effort to assist economic and social development in developing countries. This effort led to a series of seminars, workshops, and projects in a number of Asian countries.

In 1972 an Asian regional seminar on labor inspection relating to employment of women and protection of children was held in Singapore. It stressed the need for ministries/departments of labor to establish a focal point for dealing with problems of women workers. As a follow-up, a Japan/ILO Asian regional program for women workers was formulated. It was composed of three parts: preparatory studies in selected countries; organization of a regional workshop; and initiation of advisory services.

In consequence of this program, a Japan/ILO Asian regional workshop on administrative arrangements for the exercise of responsibilities of labor departments with regard to women workers was held in Tokyo, November 18–29, 1974. This was one of the first workshops funded under multi- and bilateral arrangements, and was timed to coincide with International Women's Year, which had been proclaimed by the General Assembly. It was participated in by senior officials from sixteen Asian countries, as well as observers from other UN and aid-giving countries. The participants included ten women (two from Japan) and seven men.

The consultants and lecturers included eleven women from Japan (plus one man), in addition to two women and two men from the ILO. (Among the lecturers was Nobuko Takahashi, former Director-General of the

Women's and Minors' Bureau of the Japanese ministry of labor, and later Assistant Director-General of the ILO.) The organization of the workshop took the form of lectures and discussion, country presentations, discussions with employers, trade union organizations, and nongovernmental organizations, field visits, and the drafting of conclusions. They included the desirability of establishing a separate unit in a government ministry or department to deal with women workers' questions. In defining the unit's functions, the workshop suggested that the actual enforcement of labor standards should be the responsibility of the labor inspectorates, though they should be carried out in coordination with the women's units. One of the major functions of the units should be the promotion and strengthening of equality of women in all spheres of life and the improvement of their status and working conditions. It was also felt that national tripartite advisory bodies to consider questions relating to women workers would be useful. The workshop further recommended that there should be an ILO regional adviser on training and employment opportunities for women.

A somewhat different example was a seminar sponsored jointly by the ILO and the UNDP in 1977 which dealt with employment, under-employment, and unemployment, with an emphasis on women. It was attended by women from Indonesia, Malaysia, the Philippines, Singapore, and Thailand.

Another demonstration of the value of the regional approach was a seminar organized by the ILO and the Malaysian Trade Union Congress in Kuala Lumpur in 1979. Nineteen women trade unionists from nine Asian countries discussed the difficulties involved in women's membership of trade unions. The seminar agreed that women were subjected to various types of discrimination—a reflection of the hierarchical classification of jobs on the basis of sex, stressing the fact that the double standard applied not only in the labor market but with regard to social security and other benefits. The seminar emphasized the need for active participation by women in trade unions, particularly at the executive level.

A somewhat different regional workshop was held in late 1979 by the ILO's Asian and Pacific Skill Development Programme (APSDEP—established in cooperation with UNDP) with twenty-seven participating countries to organize training seminars and workshops on income generating skills for women. The workshop examined studies on women in Bangladesh, Japan, Malaysia, the Philippines, Sri Lanka, and Thailand. The recommendations presented by the workshop included strengthening national training programs, finding ways and means of removing administrative and financial constraints, and establishing training criteria for use at the local level.

Partly as a result of the conclusions of the 1976 World Employment Conference and the proposals of the 1979 meeting of the ILO's Advisory Committee on Rural Development, the ILO initiated an expanded program on rural women in the development of rural employment policies. While this program was worldwide in scope, it was initiated in Asia, and has now been carried out in other areas as well. Although the main focus of the program was on studies and field research, it moved gradually from framing a conceptual approach to information to the dissemination and exchange of information through seminars and workshops, followed up by direct technical cooperation projects. As an integral part of the ILO project "Action to Assist Rural Women in Asia" (financed by the government of Norway), a tripartite Asian regional seminar on rural development and women was held in April 1981 in Mahabaleshwar, Maharashtra, India, financed by the Federal Republic of Germany.[3] The participants came from eleven countries (Bangladesh, India, Indonesia, Malaysia, Pakistan, the Philippines, Sri Lanka, and Thailand, as well as Denmark, the Netherlands, and Sweden). With the exception of the deputy secretary, ministry of local government, rural development and cooperatives of Bangladesh and the program officer for rural development of UNICEF, all those at the seminar were women—and most of the background documents had been written by women.

Each item under discussion was introduced by a woman expert (usually the individual who had prepared the basic document); discussants then identified the major issues, and by the time the seminar ended, it was possible to adopt both general and specific conclusions—more significant in the fact that they emanated from the Asian participants than in the novelty of the ideas expressed. These included the concept "that prevailing models of development tend to work to the detriment of poor rural women, denying them due recognition as producers, and contributing to a growing polarisation and alienation." The seminar also concluded that insufficient or improper investment in the interests of the poor in rural areas causes impoverishment and results in migrations and strains that hurt the children as well as the migrants themselves; and encouragement of work for women in their homes through a putting-out system may help to support families, but may also mean evasion of labor, welfare, and tax laws, along with extremely low wages. There was full agreement on the importance of grass roots, participatory self-reliant organizations to support the interests of rural workers, so that policies which "affect them will be based on their own perceptions and what they express to be their needs and priorities."[4]

Several workshops were held during 1982 as a follow-up of the seminar. These workshops involved the active participation of working women in India, Sri Lanka, and the Philippines. The Sri Lankan workshop dealt with working and living conditions of women in the plantation sector, including assignment of hazardous tasks, low wages, and inadequate social services. Its participants were nominated by the trade unions, while those in the Philippines comprised rural women, representatives from selected governments, and moderators or motivators.

A regional workshop on participation of women in training programs in Asia and the Pacific was held in Islamabad in 1982. It suggested a wide range of action regarding national policy formulation, training systems, and the development of pilot projects for training women in nontraditional occupations.

A regional high-level consultation on women workers was held in Bangkok, January 26–29, 1983. The meeting was a follow-up of the 1974 Tokyo workshop.[5] Its main goals were to enable senior officials from women's units in the ministries of labor or women's bureaus to exchange experiences, ideas, and proposals for strengthening the units and developing or initiating programs for women workers. A second objective was to provide a forum for an exchange of views between the ILO Regional Office for Asia and the Pacific, its regional advisers and regional teams, and the invited participants (almost all of whom were high-level government officers, many of them ministers of labor) in regard to the immediate and long-term problems of women workers in the Asian region. Their aim was to plan a systematic approach to alleviating discriminatory practices and providing better opportunities for the training and employment of women, the improvement of their quality of life, in both rural and urban areas, and to identify new project proposals and ideas for possible ILO aid to the countries concerned.

Seventeen government representatives from Australia, Bangladesh, India, Indonesia, Korea, Malaysia, Nepal, New Zealand, Pakistan, Sri Lanka, and Thailand, and one representative each from workers' and employers' organizations, nominated by the respective groups in the Governing Body, took part in the consultation. Of the total participants, all but three were women. The director, lecturers, and resource persons, as well as the secretariat, were primarily women, with the exception of four lecturers from the regional teams, all the regional advisers/experts and the ILO Assistant Director-General responsible for ILO activities in Asia and the Pacific.

The organization of the agenda permitted the meeting to review and make recommendations both to governments and the ILO, as well as to the employers' and workers' groups on a number of defined issues. The first, concerning the role of women's bureaus, stressed the importance of the coordinating and catalytic role of such units, rather than their direct operations. Consideration of labor standards and labor legislation affecting women workers called for a clearer distinction between measures to promote women's equality within the work force and protective measures which had, in the region, at times been used to prevent women's employment. The differences between the problems of rural and urban women were emphasized and different approaches suggested. The need for a greater role for women in trade unions was also reemphasized, and suggestions were made as to how this could be done more effectively in the Asian region. Finally, a whole series of precise proposals were endorsed for action by governments and for investigation by the ILO.

Another seminar in Bangkok, also in 1983 (April) initiated a series of regional tripartite seminars, to identify practices designed to eliminate direct or indirect sources of discrimination and to promote equality of opportunity and treatment for all categories of workers. (An earlier seminar, as noted, had been held in Lima, Peru.) These seminars constituted a form of implementation of the 1958 ILO Convention and Recommendation on Discrimination in Employment and Occupation. It was recommended that employment services should ensure that discriminatory instructions from employers be disregarded, and procedures be established regarding dismissals and grievances. The Bangkok seminar was followed up by a one-week seminar, held in early 1987, in Jakarta, and attended by government participants from Australia, China, Fiji, Indonesia, Japan, Malaysia, New Zealand, the Philippines, and Thailand.

Another follow-up was a subregional tripartite seminar in Indonesia in 1987 on nondiscriminatory employment practices, which drew representatives from Australia, China, Fiji, Indonesia, Japan, Malaysia, New Zealand, the Philippines, and Thailand. Its focus was also on implementation of the 1958 ILO Convention on Discrimination in Employment and Occupation.

One workshop, held in Madurai, India, in 1985, under the auspices of the Asian Regional Team for Employment (ARTEP), brought together activists, both men and women, who had been involved in organizing poor rural women and provided a new forum for the exchange of experiences.

Africa

A symposium on equality of treatment was held in Dakar in 1977. It dealt with the issue of discrimination against migrant and women workers, examined problems arising from discrimination in both law and practice, and suggested measures to overcome these problems.

A seminar for Southern African liberation movements was held in Lusaka in 1978. In the course of discussion the seminar noted that women in Southern Africa suffered a double discrimination on the grounds of sex as well as of race. This included women workers in rural areas and in the nursing profession, and the discrimination practiced in respect of inability of African women to contract for employment themselves in their own right.

Under the auspices of the Inter-African Center for Vocational Training, CIADFOR (French acronym), established by the ILO, a workshop was held in Benin in 1979 to examine the question of vocational training of women, in order to increase their involvement in economic life. Participants came from Benin, Ivory Coast, Senegal, and Togo. The workshop concluded that much remained to be done to reorient training systems and to change attitudes toward training for women. A follow-up seminar was held in Abidjan in 1981 under the auspices of CIADFOR, the Economic Commission for Africa, SIDA (Swedish International Development Aid), and the ILO. It examined needs in women's training for sub-Sahelian francophone countries.

A tripartite regional seminar on rural development, held in Dakar, Senegal, in 1981, examined various aspects of women's work. These included food production and processing, commercialization and modernization of agriculture, and migration.

In 1985 another Southern African subregional tripartite seminar, in Zambia, dealt with nondiscriminatory employment practices. The meeting was attended by representatives from Botswana, Lesotho, Malawi, Mozambique, Swaziland, Zambia, and Zimbabwe. A representative of the South African Congress of Trade Unions attended as an observer. The seminar recommended inter alia that all countries in the region should incorporate in their national legislation provisions prohibiting discrimination in employment and should establish tripartite monitoring machinery for their enforcement. It also embraced the principle of equal pay for equal work and called for the abolition of taxation systems which discriminate against working married women. In regard to maternity leave, it was urged that the wide variation in the region in benefits and conditions be eliminated.

Middle East

A workshop for selected Arab countries on the vocational rehabilitation of disabled women, funded by the Arab Gulf program for UN development organizations and the ILO regular budget, was held in 1987. Participants included Bahrain, People's Democratic Republic of Yemen, Iraq, Jordan, Kuwait, Lebanon, Oman, Qatar, Saudi Arabia, Syrian Arab Republic, United Arab Emirates, and Yemen Arab Republic. The objective was to determine the basic needs of disabled women and suggest long-term goals for the development of national training and rehabilitation programs and to propose measures to integrate disabled women into productive life.

Another regional workshop dealt with the development of policies and programs for the social and vocational rehabilitation of such women. Also in preparation is a regional training and employment program for Arab women to encourage their greater participation in training programs and income generating activities.

Europe

Aside from the conferences and an occasional symposium such as that held in Brussels in 1977 to exchange national experience of directors of women's bureaus, the European region has served as the locus for a number of global and interregional meetings. In 1984 an ILO panel on people's participation met in Geneva and discussed guidelines and checklists for women in rural development. Since then a number of meetings have been held in Europe dealing with women in rural areas. One of the most important was an international workshop held in The Hague in April 1986 dealing with the rural energy crisis, women's work, and basic needs. One of the findings of the workshop indicated that while many of the women's energy problems could be solved by increasing their access to cash, improved energy supplies are needed to enable women to undertake income-generating activities.

169

The role of the European regional meetings has somewhat declined in relation to the states' members of the European Community (EC). Moreover, the EC, which has power to act by decree, has shown concern for women's issues and has brought some able women onto its staff. The result has been preference for its jurisdiction by many of the women's organizations in Europe. However, the ILO has worked with the EC in developing its programs that affect women in Europe, and the EC participates in ILO meetings held in Europe.

Interregional Meetings

In addition to its regional meetings, ILO frequently organizes interregional workshops and seminars, one example of which is a workshop held in Arusha, Tanzania, in August 1984 entitled, "Resources, Power and Women." It was designed to stimulate debate on alternative strategies to improve rural women's employment conditions in Africa and Asia. The workshop was hosted by Tanzania and funded by DANIDA. Its major objective was to contribute to a dialogue among policymakers, grass-roots activists and representatives of nongovernmental organizations. A number of concrete issues were presented, based on some fifty projects in Africa and Asia, in order to formulate future strategies. Although the project approach was criticized as tending to marginalize women's concerns instead of integrating them in mainstream development, there was consensus on continuing a strategy of special projects for women because most national development plans are broken down into projects. However, it was agreed that women's projects should be changed from "welfare" to "development" and should be based on activities which are economically profitable and viable.

A number of special technical assistance projects are carried out on an interregional basis, some of these over a two- or three-year period, and some in cooperation with other agencies. An example is a special project dealing with the Third World which is concerned with energy and rural women's work. An Africa/Asia interregional project has sought to identify successful methods for improving the employment conditions of rural women, while employment opportunities for rural women through organization have been studied in India, Mexico, Nepal, Pakistan, and Senegal. (Some examples of such projects have been given in chapter 5 dealing with technical cooperation.)

Summing up the effect of decentralization and of regional activities as a whole, it is apparent that their development gradually brought a new group of women into ILO operations and has begun to bring women in developing countries, including some from rural areas, into more significant positions in their own countries. This has included recognition of their potential role in trade unions and of the value to many of social and protective labor legislation. It has called for new measures to implement legislation, and for specific machinery to achieve women's equality with men in the world of work.

Staff in the Regions

Backstopping, and often initiative, for regional activities are carried out by the regional and area offices. Senior staff and experts assigned to these offices are usually not nationals of the country in which they serve but must be acceptable to the host country. Thus the question of nationality (and in some instances culture) must be taken into consideration as well as gender—on a nondiscriminatory basis! There are today a few outstanding women serving in top posts in the regional and area offices. It may be hoped that their number will increase. The director of the ILO Office in Algiers for several years has been a German woman, Karin Schramm. When her appointment was first proposed there was considerable local resistance—and hesitation by the Geneva Office—on the grounds that a woman could not handle the situation in a North African country. In the event, although she has been a great success, it has not been easy and she has refused a renewal of her appointment to this post and has returned to Geneva. A 1988 appointment is that of Cecilia Lopez Montano, from Colombia, who has been made the head of the regional employment program for Latin America and the Caribbean—with the rank of D1. This program is located in Santiago, Chile. As a principal technical adviser, she is responsible for the technical cooperation program throughout the region. Another women, Eugenia Date-Bah, from Ghana, who formerly worked in the African Regional Department (with responsibility in the programming of regional technical cooperation) was transferred in 1988 to the equality of rights branch. Ayse Mitchell, from Turkey, has been both a regional adviser for Asia and an expert on a special post under a multi- and bilateral program in Bangkok. However, she too has now returned to headquarters staff. Sally Christine Cornwell, a young U.S. national, who was the first woman director of the Suva, Fiji, Office has, as discussed later, returned to Geneva as the new special adviser on women's questions, although she had found the Suva assignment very rewarding professionally and a positive experience. The deputy director of the Suva Office is also a woman, Mary Catherine Johnson of Australia, as are many of the local support staff. At the time of Johnson's appointment there was considerable hesitation within the Office about having two senior women in a field office, but this was overcome when the argument was put forward that two senior men served together in most other offices!

Another woman who has made a substantial contribution to the ILO field structure is Maria de Lopez Collado of Colombia who was for some time director of the Costa Rican Office. She had initially been in the personnel office at headquarters, and then for a time in the New York liaison office with the United Nations in New York. Her appointment was supported by the Latin American leadership in the ILO.

Several other women have served not only in the field but also in the liaison office to the United Nations as well as at headquarters. An outstanding example is Marianne Nussbaumer, a Swiss national, who joined the staff in the early 1950s in the clerical category in the Finance Department. In 1954 she went to Istanbul as an administrative officer; following a period in Ceylon as a fellowship program officer (upgraded to the professional category) she returned to Geneva, where she was promoted after winning a competition. She was again placed in the Finance Department, from which she was transferred to the Latin American desk of the Field Department. She later went to Costa Rica as deputy director of the area office and then to Chile as acting director. She returned from the field, to Geneva, as coordinator in the Technical Assistance Department, until she was moved to the UN liaison office in New York, where she was an effective deputy director for several years. Following her return to Geneva in 1982 she was made coordinator of the office for children and young persons (a position left over after women's issues were moved to the Office of Women Workers' Questions) where she found that she had no clear responsibilities, program, or staff. She retired in 1984.

A somewhat different example of the interplay of employment at headquarters and in the regional structure is that of Emma Broisman, a U.S. national who was originally appointed to the liaison office in New York (very shortly after it was established) and whose major career took place not at Geneva headquarters but in the field in the Asian region. She became a member of the staff in 1947, initially as a junior professional but graded in the general services category (although she held a graduate degree from Columbia University and had written a study on the ILO). Her first post was in the New York liaison office with the United Nations. She remained there until 1957, when she took advantage of an opening in the growing field staff and transferred, with a promotion, first to Bangalore and then to Ceylon, as a fellowship and country program officer. In 1963 she went to Geneva, where she initially occupied the Asian desk of the Technical Assistance Department and then worked in the Field Department. In 1968 she returned to the field, serving first as program officer in Bangkok and then as senior personnel, finance, and administrative officer, the first such post in the fully decentralized structure. From 1972–74 she was head of regional programming and relations in Bangkok. In 1975 she was made deputy director of the area office, located in New Delhi, where she stayed until September 1978. During her assignment to New Delhi, she was responsible for country programs in Nepal, Sri Lanka, the Maldives, and Bhutan. From 1978–82 she was back in Bangkok as head of the section of program, relations, and information, and in addition served as coordinator of women and youth programs for Asia and the Pacific. Her final period of service, just after her retirement, was in Bangkok, as a consultant. During her periods in Geneva she was active on the staff union (and served on the Administrative Committee) where she sought to make headquarters aware of the problems of the field staff. Throughout her regional employment she worked with the technical assistance program, not only of the ILO but also of the United Nations, developing close relationships both with the other governmental and intergovernmental organizations as well as with the various nongovernmental organizations concerned with development and with women. After retiring from the ILO she continued these relationships, becoming a representative of the International Council of Women at the United Nations.

Another appointment, made during the same period as Emma Broisman, while the ILO working center was still in Montreal, was that of Angela Butler. A Canadian citizen (though British by birth) she joined the Office in Montreal in 1943 as a typist, then was made a secretary in the editorial section, working under Elna Dutt, described in chapter 2, who taught her basic editorial practices, and in 1946 becoming a secretary, serving in the director's office. Like Emma Broisman and others she could have qualified for a professional post, but none was available, at least for a woman or for a Canadian, then an overrepresented nationality. After most of the Office was transferred to Geneva, she continued in the Montreal Office as secretary of the economic division until its final closing down in 1949. After a brief period in Geneva, she was sent to New Delhi, as the only Geneva staff member of a three-man team designed to set up the first Asian field office on technical training (later expanded to become the ILO's regional office for Asia and the Far East). In October 1950, while still in India, she successfully took an office-wide examination to establish a list of members of the GS (clerical) category capable of being moved into the P (professional) category. Shortly after, she was transferred back to Geneva to a research post in the training section of the manpower division. The following year she was sent as administrative officer of the Asian cooperative field mission in Lahore, Pakistan. She was there only briefly when she returned to the Training Department in Geneva, doing research and documentation. In the 1960s she was promoted and placed in the International Vocational Training, Information, and Research Center. When this was disbanded as an economy measure, she was transferred to the Department of Official Relations. She retired in 1981. She was long an active member of the staff union, serving as a staff representative on a number of the joint committees with the administration. She was particularly concerned with the role of the union in defending the clerical staff and with the efforts of the women staff to deal with discrimination. Since retirement she has been an officer of the Federation of Associations of Former International Civil Servants which represents the staff and pensioners of the ILO as well as other UN organizations in dealing with the administrative organs of the various agencies. She represents the International Federation of Business and Professional Women at meetings of the ILO and maintains close relations with former and present staff.

The decentralization of ILO activities into the regions has enabled many clerical staff members to take on greater responsibilities and to obtain professional reclassification. A few examples illustrate this trend. Eileen Hull began her ILO career in the 1950s in the Personnel Department, working with Anny Lansdorp (see below in chapter 7) on recruiting experts for the field. She then went into the field herself, working first in Bangalore in 1962, and later in Colombo and in Bangkok where she assisted in the establishment of the Office and in the operation of several programs. Winning a competition she returned to Geneva, to handle the Asian desk of the Field Department. She later worked in the Human Resources Department. Subsequently she returned to the field and, during the 1970s, was first deputy director and then director of the Bangladesh Office, where she remained until her retirement in 1980.

Another woman, Eileen Pocock, from Ireland, who began her career in the clerical category at headquarters, went out into the field where she succeeded in obtaining professional classification. Ultimately she went to the Addis Ababa Office, and later became deputy director of the Caribbean Office. More recently she returned to Geneva where, until retirement, she served as one of the senior officers of the marketing and licensing section of the editorial and documentation services.

Several of the young women recently recruited for their technical research and writing skills began their careers in the field. A number are currently employed at headquarters in the employment and the training divisions of the employment branch, but have had wide field experience. One example, discussed in chapter 5, is Gretchen Goodale, a U.S. national, who worked for over ten years on the African continent before joining the ILO staff, where she has specialized in training.

A number of women have been particularly concerned with rural women's employment problems. One of the most impressive, also described in chapter 5, is Rounag Jahan, from Bangladesh, who works in the rural employment policies branch.

A somewhat different example of the role of women who have both worked in the field and at headquarters is that of Hélène Pour, French, now in the employment planning and population branch, who has been part of field missions for many years, and whose work preferences are in the area of public relations. She initially came to Geneva as part of the staff working on the centenary of the Red Cross. Following the meetings she obtained ILO employment in the press section, doing interviews and reports on experts returning from the field. She began at the lowest professional category and remained in that category for almost ten years, during which period she carried out a number of rough assignments on technical cooperation projects in Africa. On her return she was promoted to a higher status. Recently she has been devoting a part of her time to the staff union as a public relations expert.

Women Experts in the Field

In addition to its own regular staff, the ILO, like many other international organizations, recruits special, short-term technical staff to carry out projects in the field. Most of this staff is paid out of special project budgets and they leave after a project is terminated, but some have then joined the regular ILO staff, either at headquarters or in the regional structure. This is an area where one might have expected to find a large number of women, since many specific projects are concerned with women and most of the beneficiaries are women. As of May 1986, the staff roster indicates that most of the women experts and associate experts came from the Netherlands, Finland, Norway, and Sweden, with a few from Belgium, the Federal Republic of Germany, France, Argentina, Chile, India, the United Kingdom, and the United States. The substantial number from the Nordic countries may be partially explained by the fact that these countries are generous in providing associate experts to the ILO technical cooperation projects.

In addition to experts recruited for the duration of a project—usually one to two years—there are a substantial number recruited on a very short-term basis, usually to formulate a project or to get it under way. There are more women in this category—presumably because short-term service may be less disruptive of family life. The percentage of the women experts in 1985 was 5.1; in 1986, 5.7; in 1987, 5.6; and in 1988, 6.4. The percentages for women associate experts is substantially higher for each of the respective years: 36.9 in 1985; 38.4 in 1986; 38 in 1987; and 37.9 in 1988.

Another category of field staff is the UN Volunteers Program which recruits staff to serve on projects concerned with employment, development, and training. A portion of the volunteers are recruited from developed countries and others from the developing countries. In 1986 there were 124 volunteers (149 the previous year) serving in ILO-executed projects in the various regions, mostly in Africa. Only 11 percent of these were women.

The projects to which the women experts are assigned are quite varied in type. Thus one expert is working as a professional rehabilitation expert at the CINTERFOR training center in Uruguay; one is in charge of the self-employment scheme for female headed households in India; another is working on a refugee project in Costa Rica. Other projects to which women are currently assigned are: an adult education project in Fiji; an interregional project for rural women in Gambia; and a woman's program in the Agricultural Machine Training Center in the Sudan. Other areas where women experts are working include a hotel training program in Costa Rica and another in Cameroon; and cooperative programs in Equatorial Guinea and in Gambia.

In addition to the "expert" classification, there are nine women classified as junior professional officers who are working on various technical cooperation projects in the Geneva headquarters, financed from special multi- and bilateral funds given by their countries, while several more are part of the regional teams or working on special regional projects. Two of these, one from Belgium and one from the Federal Republic of Germany, are assigned to the ILO Office in Mexico City, while one from the Netherlands works in the ILO Office in Islamabad, and another from Belgium is stationed in Cameroon at the Yaoundé Office.

While women, even in the lower categories, are a small minority in each location, the fact that there are as many as there are today indicates the extent to which women have progressed in being able to work in so many of the most difficult areas.

As noted in chapter 5, there have been frequent criticisms by members of the Governing Body of the small proportion of women experts—criticisms, it may be added, which are directed not only at ILO recruitment policies but also at national governments who do not make women experts available. However, the substantial increase in their number in recent years indicates some progress. Primarily in response to these criticisms, the International Labor Office is setting up a network of officials to monitor integration of women in technical projects in each region under the direction of a woman named by the technical cooperation department at headquarters.

7. Women Policymakers in the ILO

In chapter 4 we described the ways in which women participated in the discussions of the Conference that culminated in the adoption of resolutions, recommendations, or conventions dealing with technical issues affecting women. These activities represent only a part of the conference program. Approximately half the time of every conference session is devoted to discussion of the annual reports of the Director-General and of the Governing Body. This permits delegates to put forth new program ideas, to criticize the ongoing activities of the ILO, to evaluate the effect of ILO standards on their own countries, and also to provide a forum for worldwide assessment of social and economic, and—in some instances—political issues. At the conclusion of the debate the Director-General indicates what steps he will take to put proposals into practice. This is also the occasion when visiting ministers and other dignitaries address the conference. Increasingly, women from all three groups have spoken, with various voices, and often played an influential role in determining ILO programs.

A number of women who participated in ILO Conferences made their major contribution in fields other than the rights of women. Some were policymakers, often behind the scenes. Some played their role on the committees which guide and delimit Conference activities, and on those such as finance and resolutions which frequently determine future programs, as well as the committee on application of conventions and recommendations which appraises governmental adherence to ILO standards. Others have served on the bureaus of government, employer, or worker groups, which frequently formulate their respective policies in the Conference. Women have also participated in committees which, without regard to gender, deal with issues such as trade union rights, the role of the ILO in attacking apartheid, and, since the 1970s, on the restructuring of the ILO itself. While the proportion of women participants in conferences has gradually increased, the proportion of women delegates to women advisers has hardly varied. Moreover, only in rare instances have women held the top jobs, namely two Conference presidents and one chairman of the Governing Body.

In addition to their conference role, an increasing number of women have been members and officers of the Governing Body which oversees the administration of the Office, including such matters as personnel policy. Women members of the staff also service all aspects of the work and some carry top-level responsibilities.

The participation of women in the conference and their influence behind the scenes since the Second World War reflects the growing role of women on the national scene in developed and developing countries. A number of women now serve as the permanent representatives of their countries in their Geneva missions in Switzerland and participate as delegates in conferences as well as behind the scenes. Two examples of such women were Mrs. A. F. W. Lunsingh-Meijer of the Netherlands and Dame Anne Marion Warburton of the United Kingdom. The former received copies of all correspondence of her government to ILO and maintained regular contacts with the European delegations in Geneva and with the ILO staff. Warburton closely monitored ILO activities and kept in constant touch with the Director-General. She was fully informed by her government of all its communications to the Organization, and was thus in a position to provide delegations to ILO meetings with both information and advice.[1]

Although fewer women rose to prominence in either employer or labor circles, there were exceptions in each. Two French women obtained substantial influence through their close association with the French employer representative on the ILO Governing Body and ILO conferences over many years. One of the women, Marie Françoise Roche, came to Geneva from the National Confederation of French Employers (NCPF) and the other, Paule Roiland from the International Union of Mines and Metals (UINM). They prepared the French employers' positions and assisted the employer representative at ILO meetings. One of the influential worker representatives was Ethel Chipchase, secretary of the Women's Advisory Committee of the British TUC (see chapter 4). Her influence was pervasive over a number of years both in national and international trade union movements, and she played a major role in determining British labor policy in the ILO in the 1960s and 1970s.

The positions adopted by women in the Conference were determined more by the constituents they represented than by their views as women. Women representing employer groups tended to vote and speak one way, those representing the workers tended to vote and speak another, while those representing governments frequently took the middle course. While many women were, or had been, members of nongovernmental organizations, their views did not necessarily reflect those of the organizations. Although all the representatives to ILO meetings are presumed to have knowledge of the technical material under consideration, there is a distinction between those who are more involved in the problems of government because of the role they play at home and those who are essentially experts in a particular subject. The latter help to shape the form, and often the content, of individual instruments but are not concerned with questions of gender as such. They think of themselves as specialists rather than protagonists for the rights of women. This group also includes those who are more concerned with the way the ILO operates than with the substance of the issues.

Conference Officers

Not unexpectedly, the women who served as officers of ILO conferences were among the most politically oriented and were frequently concerned with the rights of women. The first woman president in 1941, Frances Perkins, as we have seen, recognized the potential of women in government and in employment and was concerned with the need to protect workers from exploitation. The second woman president, in 1984, Anna-Grete Leijon of Sweden, had previously been chairman of the Council to Advise the Prime Minister on the issue of equality between men and women. Trained in political science, sociology, and economics, she had carried out research for the Labor Marketing Board, been a Social Democratic member of the Riksdag, and served for several years as minister of labor. When she came as visiting minister in 1975, she called attention to the parlous condition of women who, she said, "according to the ILO, account for two-thirds of all the work—in hours of work—performed in the world. Yet they receive no more than one-tenth of all the incomes in the world, and they own less than one percent of the world's riches."

There were also only two woman Conference vice presidents in the last seventy years—Shirley Carr of Canada, workers' vice president, who

Anna-Grete Leijon of Sweden, president of ILO Annual Conference, 1984 *(courtesy of ILO, Geneva)*.

served in 1985, and Dagmar Molkova of Czechoslovakia, government vice president in 1986 and again in 1989. Both women were concerned with broad issues of human rights. Although Carr was one of the leaders who tried to improve the conditions of women on the staff, her major preoccupation was with workers as a group, irrespective of gender. For fourteen years she was the executive of the Canadian Union of Public Employees. From 1984–86 she was vice president of the Canadian Labor Congress, and in 1986 became its first woman president. She also was vice president of the International Confederation of Free Trade Unions. Even when she cannot attend ILO meetings, she controls the Canadian labor position in the Organization. She is warm in her endorsement of it, especially the fact that it brings trade union movements together—"sometimes as the forum of last resort." In recent years Carr has concentrated on the Committee on Apartheid, serving as its vice chairman from 1981–85. In 1964 the Conference had adopted a declaration concerning the policies of apartheid in South Africa. In late 1979 the Governing Body decided that apartheid should be included on the agenda of the 1980 session of the Conference and that a committee on apartheid should be set up.[2]

The mandate of the Conference committee includes: developments in the field of labor relations; admission to employment and access to training; and the problem of influx control (prevention of black immigrants obtaining housing or land in white areas) and labor matters. One of the specific items for monitoring is "equality of treatment for women workers and advice on elimination of discriminatory labor legislation."

In her first year as vice chairman Carr called on the Conference to make the committee a permanent body and this was done. Two years later she declared that the workers "cannot interpret the employers' silence on this matter as anything but flagrant collusion with the apartheid authorities." The following year, speaking for the workers group, she attacked the attitude toward the committee of some governments and some employers. Their reservations "seem to result from either ignorance of what apartheid actually is or a policy of playing ostrich in order to safeguard heavy financial interests."

The second woman to serve as vice president of the Conference was Dagmar Molkova, deputy minister of labor and social affairs of Czechoslovakia. She participated actively in UN meetings concerned with women. She has been a regular attendant at the Third Committee of the General Assembly and UN Commission on the Status of Women. She participated in the Nairobi women's conference. She has also been concerned with the role of women in the International Labor Office and, like other East Europeans, has urged greater use of the available trained women from that area as technical assistance experts.

Officers of the Groups' and Bureaus' Members

Only a few women have served on the bureaus of the government, employer, or worker groups. Three have been officers of the Government Bureau, Frances Perkins as chairman in 1945, two vice chairmen, Ram Dulari Sinha, minister of labor from Bihar, India, in 1973, and Maria Cristina Salmoran de Tamayo of Mexico in 1960.

For the most part, women officers and members of the bureaus were not primarily concerned with women's rights. Labor representatives sought to strengthen the role of unions both within and outside the ILO. East Europeans of all three groups, in addition to their concern with specific substance issues, fought the efforts of employer and labor organizations to bar the seating of representatives from the socialist countries. One example of this attitude was frequently expressed by Sandra Gereb of Hungary, head of section, International Department of Central Council of Trade Unions. She vigorously attacked allegations that socialist trade unions were mere governmental appendages, and thus not eligible to sit on committees as workers. Pointedly, she urged the "solidarity of all workers" to overcome the problems facing women on the long road to equality.

Another worker representative, Susan A. Berry, president of the Liberian Congress of Industrial Organizations, emphasized the role of trade unions generally rather than the specific issue of women. In discussing problems in Liberia, she pointed to the difficulty of organizing nonmanual workers who were themselves hesitant about joining a union and who faced the determined opposition of employers. A particular problem related to agricultural workers, many of whom worked for the Firestone Rubber Company, the dominant economic force in the country. Firestone had fought a long-standing battle against unionization and had finally achieved legislation debarring industrial unions from organizing agricultural workers.

Larissa Munteanu, secretary, General Council of Romanian Association of Trade Unions, congratulated ILO in her first intervention in Plenary on safeguarding and consolidating the trade union rights of women. She emphasized manpower utilization and the raising of the living standards of workers. To ensure trade union rights and freedom, she called for the adoption of appropriate instruments for the protection of workers' representatives in the undertaking.

There were, however, examples of women on the bureaus who were directly concerned with women's issues. One of the rare African women employers was elected vice chairman of the employers group in 1961. Janjeola Aduke Moore of Mobil Oil of Nigeria was the first woman employer delegate to the Conference. In her maiden speech to the Conference she said she might as well "take this opportunity of championing the long-suffering women." She urged the necessity of approaching "human problems with sympathy and understanding, conscious that we are fashioning not only a new nation but an entirely new environment for the worker." A somewhat unusual speech for an employer.

Committee Officers and Participants

An increasing number of women have served as officers or participants of the various standing committees.

Committee on Application of Standards

The committee in which the largest number of women have participated—some 200—is the Committee on the Application of Conventions and Recommendations (now known as the Application of Standards). This is probably because the committee dealt with the implementation of labor legislation, a field in which a large number of the women sent to the conference were involved in their own countries. Thus, for example, Lucretia Guelfi, inspector general, ministry of overseas development of France, prepared labor codes for French overseas territories and organized labor inspection procedures. She also established a number of social institutions, including professional training centers for Africa, family allowances, medical services for workers, and labor tribunals. She served as reporter of the Standards Committee.

Over the years four other women have served as officers—Diana Mahabir of Trinidad and Tobago; Lucille Caron of Canada, employer and government vice chairman, respectively; Henriette Munkebye of Norway, deputy director, Norwegian ministry of local government and labor, reporter in 1984 and in 1986; and Nieves Confesor, chief of the international labor affairs service of the Philippines who served both as chairman and reporter.

Diana Mahabir, director of the Employers' Consultative Association and, simultaneously, chief executive of the Caribbean Employers' Confederation, served for three years as vice chairman of the committee. She grew up "back of the beyond" in Northwest Quebec, with native Indians, French Canadians, and an assortment of refugees from war-torn Europe. At age nineteen, while studying at McGill University of Montreal, she married a Trinidadian fellow student of East Indian descent. She went to Trinidad with her husband, had four children, worked with retarded children, helped her husband set up and run a taxi business, completed her B.A. at McGill, started to work for a master's degree at the University of the West Indies, and also lectured there in a survey course on the "use of English." She was "still fairly young, foreign born and white in a black newly independent country where 'foreign' was not entirely a concept to be clasped to the national bosom." In addition, she became divorced and was left to cope on her own with four children and shortly thereafter with two foster children.

In her first intervention in the Plenary in 1971 she raised one of the most intractable problems with which governments are faced, a problem that affects women as well as men. This, she said, is that "the ones who need help most are the growing Third World army of the young, the dispossessed, the angry, the militant, the underprivileged, the anti-estab-lishment . . . the hard ones to feed. We must," she concluded, "all learn new values, new ways of seeing, thinking and reacting and new techniques of communication." In a subsequent intervention, in 1978, she pleaded, like many spokesmen for developing countries, for less detailed conven-tions. "As conditions change, the detail of these instruments makes it difficult for many of the developing countries to adapt quickly enough to changes around them to ensure that implementation is kept up, as devel-oping countries are not as flexible in this regard and as responsive to change as the industrial countries."

Lucille Caron of Canada, executive director of the International Affairs Department of the Labor Department, chaired the committee in 1983. Her great-grandfather emigrated from Ireland during the potato famine, and her mother's family were among the first French settlers in the Mag-dalen Islands in the Gulf of St. Lawrence where Caron grew up. After graduating from Carlton College she got a job as an air stewardess, then as a translator in the Labor Department, and later as coordinator in the branch dealing with the ILO. In 1980 she had been chairman of the work-ing party to review the methods of operations of the conference committee on that subject. She felt that the examination by the committee of the reports from developing countries, and the list of procedures by which a country was put on a special list, were too rigid and automatic.

Another woman who served on the committee because of her expertise as an attorney in the solicitor's office of the U.S. Department of Labor was Margaret Pallansch. Her activities were without regard to sex. She was an ardent defender of the Committee of Experts which provided reports for the conference Committee on Standards. The Committee of Experts, as noted in the introduction, is an independent committee ap-pointed by the Governing Body to monitor the steps taken by governments to implement conventions. The experts' findings had been attacked by some governments as being prejudiced and arbitrary, and they sought to subject the findings to a code of procedure. Pallansch, speaking for the

United States, declared that the "great value of the Expert's work lay in its independence and competence." There was "no call for hampering its freedom to adjust its methods of operation to rapidly evolving situations." She stressed the distinction between procedural criteria which could be applied automatically, such as failure to submit to competent authorities or to provide required reports and "the evaluation of factual situations" with regard to the degree of application of a given convention in a particular country. She welcomed the proposal of the Committee of Experts that there be a "system of direct contacts with governments, with the prior agreement of the Government concerned, in cases which have not led to satisfactory results and where prolonged discussion might simply lead to deadlock."

The Committee on Application of Standards and the department of the International Labor Office which services the committee have been a training ground for young staff members, including several women, because the qualifications for employment included a legal background, so the experience enabled the staff to become familiar with the legislative practices both of the ILO and its member governments. An example of the skills required was that of Hilary Kellerson, a British lawyer who went from the Division of Standards to the Office of the Legal Adviser. She drafts well and is liked by the delegations with which she is in contact; although she has frequently served on the drafting committees of technical committees dealing with women's issues, she is not active in the various women's groups nor specially concerned with women's problems.

Resolutions Committee

Another committee on which a substantial number of women participated was the Resolutions Committee. Here there was a much larger percentage of women concerned specifically with the rights of women.

One of the most important actions of the committee in recent years was its recommendation to the 1988 Conference that it adopt the conclusions concerning rural employment promotion which had been prepared by the technical committee dealing with this subject. (Item 7 on the conference agenda.) These conclusions, which call upon national governments in general and the ILO in particular to give a high priority to the problems of rural employment, contain several provisions directly related to women. Talking to national governments, they state that "countries should ensure that: . . . women's central role in rural development is fully recognized and women are given equal access to basic resources, productive assets and property rights. In recognition of women's double work burden related to employment and family responsibilities, measures to provide them with adequate social services and appropriate technologies should be given priority. In parallel, nontraditional productive activities for women [they] should be supported and women's access to decision-making institutions should be facilitated. . . . In designing and implementing rural employment policies, special attention should be paid to enabling women's full participation in the development process." In detailing how this should be done, the resolution calls attention to the need for nations to encourage "women's full integration into rural workers' organization" and to ensure "their full participation and influence in rural development processes, including through women's organisations in the service of the community." With respect to the ILO's own program, the Resolution directs it to give "priority to activities in support of women" and goes on to outline the emphasis that should be given to research on constraints in employment, conditions of work, and differential impact of policies on rural women; to the development of social amenities such as safe water, easy access to fuel, and child care facilities; "to women's access to decision-making bodies; . . . and developing productive non-traditional activities for women."

While some women members of the committee put major emphasis on resolutions of this type, others placed their emphasis on other issues. An example in this category was an employer who played a leadership role in influencing the positions of the employer group. She was Lucia Sasso-Mazzufferi, chief of the Bureau of International Relations of the General Confederation of Industry (CONFINDUSTRIA). In the Conference Plenary, as a spokesman for the employers, she urged the need to strengthen employer associations particularly in Third World countries. She stressed the importance of "dialogues on the mutual rights and duties of social partners." She said, "we are going through a profound crisis which should induce the social partners to reach agreement among themselves on the growth and creation of wealth before thinking of its distribution."

A very different emphasis was given by a worker representative from the United States, Eugenia Kemble, special assistant to the president, American Federation of Teachers, who was deeply concerned with resolutions dealing with freedom of association and trade union rights.

Committee on Structure

Another committee in which women participated actively, not on the basis of gender but because of their deep concern with the way the ILO operates, was the Committee on Structure set up in 1969 to review proposals both to change the tripartite composition (including the number of votes of each group in the conference) and to adapt existing procedures governing the role of the Resolutions Committee. It also was to modify the composition of the Governing Body. While the numbers of members of the Governing Body were increased on several occasions to reflect the changing size of ILO membership, the concept of permanent seats for states "of chief industrial importance" had remained and had long been a bone of contention with the developing states. This committee and the various working parties which preceded it became a critical instrument of self-analysis and evaluation of the operation of the ILO. In 1986 the report of the committee basically altered both the composition and size of the Governing Body and provided for the election of its members on a regional basis.

The adoption of the committee's conclusions by the Conference was considered one of the greatest achievements of the Director-General. He attributed much of the success to three women—Aida Gonzales Martinez (see below under Governing Body), Lucille Caron, and Cornelie Hak. One of the most vigorous and determined women to leave her mark on ILO conferences and on the Governing Body is Cornelie Hak. After graduating from the University of Amsterdam, she started her career in an architect's office, moved to the Metal Industry's Employers Organization, then to a metal industry company, and eventually to the Federation of Netherlands Industries. In her years at ILO conferences, from 1973 on, Hak was the leader of the Netherlands employers' delegation and was always conscious of the need to look after her delegation, socially as well as professionally. She was an excellent negotiator, as the Director-General's comment indicated. She rarely spoke in Plenary because, she said, she talked only "when the basic principles of ILO" were under discussion. She stressed the need for universal standards and hence for greater flexibility "so that the different levels of economic and social development in the member States" could be taken into account. "That so many Conventions remain so far unratified," she said, "gives considerable reason for worry." She complained that instruments tended to be "too sophisticated" instead of "clear, comma, short and flexible." Although often in opposition to feminist movements and against provisions in the ILO Convention on Family Responsibilities, nevertheless she has participated actively in the small group of ILO representatives concerned with problems facing women on the ILO staff.

Other Standing Committees

One woman who played an active role in a number of conference committees and addressed herself specifically to women's problems was Alison Stephen of Australia, assistant secretary, manpower development operations, number 1 division, Department of Labor and Immigration. Speaking in Plenary, she took the occasion to state that "in recent years statistics on women's participation on national delegations show a disheartening regularity from year to year. On the other hand, the absence of significant variation in the number of women delegates between years when there is a so-called women's item and other years may be interpreted as signifying a recognition of the fact that in a modern context, it is no longer possible to identify questions specifically affecting women. Female workers are as much workers as male workers and all the questions on the Conference agenda affect women." Her concern with women led her to bring young women into her department and to foster their careers, including service on the ILO staff. Two examples of the latter are young women, both lawyers by training, who have been playing interesting roles in legally oriented ILO departments, such as those dealing with the Application of Standards and Freedom of Association, as well as in a new group dealing with women's issues within the staff. Christine Elstob is in her early thirties. She was originally placed in the Application of Standards branch, and then, when the Office for Women Workers' Questions was being pressed to come up with proposals for implementation of the Nairobi Plan of Action, she volunteered to work for them to prepare the documentation called for by the Governing Body. She also was coordinator of the women's group, AGE, pressing for better status for women within the Office.

The second example of a woman on the ILO staff who had served under Alison Stephen was Jane Hodges-Aeberhard. She joined the ILO staff in 1978 and one of her major efforts within the staff has been to obtain training for women without fees and on paid time. Meantime, she has been on a number of freedom of association missions—in answer to complaints.

189

Very different concerns were expressed by Zdravka Peeva, an engineer by profession and director of the Amalgamated Industrial Enterprise, "Pirene," of Bulgaria. She intervened frequently in Plenary. Two of her main preoccupations were technical progress and the attitude of the employers' group toward socialist employers. "Technical progress," she said, "has become a matter of concern for every single undertaking" and she urged the importance of further training, deploring the fate of the unskilled worker. Despite her criticism of the discrimination manifest in the employers group, she appreciated what the ILO had to offer as "an accumulation of world experience in the field of labor and social policy."

Drafting Committee

The conference has a small Drafting Committee which is responsible for all legal texts. When it is considering a convention or recommendation, it includes—in addition to the president of the Conference—the Secretary-General and the legal adviser, as well as the members of the Drafting Committee of the committee that adopted the given instrument. One member of the legal department who served for many years on the Drafting Committee was Felice Morgenstern. A young British lawyer, she joined the staff in January 1952 as the result of winning an international civil service competition. She began as the junior member of the small legal staff of the Office, working directly under C. Wilfred Jenks, then the legal adviser. She had been a student of Sir Hersch Lauterpact at Cambridge and was greatly influenced by his concepts of international law. She soon demonstrated her capacity as draftsman, researcher, and negotiator when needed. In addition to the Drafting Committee she staffed many of the other committees of the conference. By the time she took early retirement in 1982 she was respected by all, and might well have become the first woman legal adviser of the ILO (or of any UN agency) had she remained on the staff. She was never concerned with being a senior woman or with the advocacy of women's issues in the staff. She was a substantial writer of legal articles, including one on "Women and the Courts." Since retirement she has continued lecturing and writing both books and articles, and is frequently called upon to advise on legal issues, not only for the ILO but also for many other international organizations.

Visiting Ministers

The tenor of the plenary debates in the Conference is set by the report of the Director-General and that of the Governing Body. The debate on these reports provides a platform for visiting ministers to address the Conference. During the period from 1954, when it became customary for women visiting ministers to address the Conference, until 1989, there were twenty-seven different women who participated in that capacity. Since a number of these women came more than once, the actual number of women visiting ministers at the Conference was seventy-nine.[3]

The country which sent the largest number of women visiting ministers, Finland, was also one of those most concerned with the rights of women. In 1984 Finland had more women in Parliament than any other country (31 percent) although somewhat fewer in government. Since it ratified the ILO Equal Pay Convention in 1962 it has had an equal pay policy which includes the right of women to reenter the labor market after periods of child care. The success of women in Finnish political life has been attributed to the fact that they came on the scene at the same time as most men, before the latter had time to establish a tradition of control.[4]

The first of the Finnish women was Tyne Leivo-Larsson, who came in 1955 as minister of social affairs and health. She was succeeded, over the years, by nine other women Finnish ministers. Many of these placed major emphasis on the importance of improving the lot of women. Thus, for example, in 1970 Alli Lahtinen declared that the ILO should "constantly and effectively work against discrimination against women in the labour market" and she urged the provision of day-care centers and adequate household facilities. A few years later Seija Karkinen talked about equality between men and women which, she said, affected men quite as well as women "like all political issues in society."

Three other Nordic countries—Norway, Sweden, and Denmark—repeatedly sent women visiting ministers. Norway took the lead among this group with women ministers participating in the ILO over a period of eight years. One of the most distinguished of these was Harriet Andreassen, minister of local government and labor. In addition to attending as visiting minister, she frequently attended as a workers' delegate in her capacity as secretary of the Confederation of Norwegian Trade Unions. She has participated on such committees as those dealing with workers with family responsibilities and the social aspects of industrialization. In

1985 she was elected vice chairman of the Committee on Equality of Employment.

Other Norwegian visiting ministers expressed a variety of concerns. Ruth Ryste, minister of social affairs, stressed the growing interdependence of the countries of the world and warned that the Program of Action adopted by the ILO's World Employment Conference could not "be regarded as a substitute for a New International Economic Order, but as one of its elements." Inge Louise Valle, minister of local government and labor, emphasized the need for training. "With high unemployment in most countries," she said, "young people without the necessary skills seem to be the most vulnerable group and this clearly demonstrates the necessity of giving the young generation adequate training." She added that training and retraining was likely to become a lifelong process. Astrid Nokelbye Heiberg, under secretary of state, Ministry of Health and Social Affairs, declared that "we should aim at eliminating child work which leads to injuries to body and mind or spoils the educational opportunities of youth." She supported the Director-General's approach to the question and urged the study of the economic and social background of child labor in order to frame appropriate policies.

Visiting ministers from Sweden spoke from a different background than those from the other Nordic countries. Sweden is in the forefront of policies on women's rights although, according to several sources, its feminist movement is weak because of its collective culture. In any case it is deemed to have the most comprehensive and reasoned policy on women of all the liberal democracies of Western Europe, as well as one of the highest rates of women's participation in the labor force. In addition to an Equal Opportunities Commission and an "equality minister," there is also a special advisory council to the minister consisting of representatives from the largest women's organizations. The national role of Swedish women has for many years been reflected both in the ILO and in the United Nations.

Grethe Fenger Moller, minister of labor of Denmark, exemplified the combination of concern with general issues and the situation regarding women. She focused her attention on occupational health services. International instruments in this area, she said, could have a big impact on large parts of the world where such institutions are as yet only at the preparatory stage. Services in this field might be set up on a medico-technical basis for the purpose of preventing occupational injuries, and increasing the safety and health of the workers. In addition, addressing the significance of the Decade for Women, she declared that its end "must not lead to the misapprehension that work to improve the situation of women in the world has come to an end." She said it was of paramount importance that all the specialized agencies of the United Nations family always keep the conditions of women on the agenda and that they are included in all plans of action.

An active involvement with women's issues was evident in a number of the speeches of other women visiting ministers. One example was provided by Miss Agatha Barbara, Minister of Labor, Welfare, and Culture of Malta. As one of those who objected to the protective segregation of women, she noted with "a good deal of satisfaction, the current expert view that women are not particularly vulnerable to health hazards and do not need any special protection," except where pregnant women were concerned who might be exposed to toxic substances or heavy physical labor. Barbara entered politics as a young woman candidate of the Malta Labour Party in the general elections. She won her seat to be a Member of Parliament, the first woman MP and the only woman to be reelected at every subsequent election. In 1955 she became Minister of Education, again the first and only woman to hold cabinet rank. Coming from a country with a high degree of unemployment she stressed "government's primary responsibility . . . towards the unemployed."

Grete Rehor, Federal Minister of Social Affairs of Austria, stressed the importance of vocational training and declared that only the social adjustment of men and women to industrial society could ensure permanent economic success. She also called for more intensive consideration of the problems of female workers in view of their increasing importance in the economic life of countries and asked that a special women's department be set up as part of the International Labor Office.

Maria Helena de Crovo, Colombia's Minister of Labour and Social Security, discussed the reasons for the discrimination against women. She said that "the main problem in discrimination against women is not only their own self discrimination but also the intellectual ostracism to which they have traditionally been subjected: the lack of confidence in their ability and creative capacity." She also voiced the resentment felt by many developing countries over the imbalance between these countries as "mere suppliers of raw materials and the processors of those materials." She said it would be "necessary to change the outlook of the powerful members of the international community, finding a way of persuading the developed countries immediately that the social development programmes of the countries of the Third World represent an investment and not an expense."

A very different note was struck by Myatavyn Lhamsuren, chairman of the State Committee on Labor and Wages, Council of Ministers, who addressed herself not to problems concerning women's issues but to more general economic issues and to the administration of the ILO. She attended conferences over a number of years, sometimes as visiting minister and sometimes as her country's government delegate. She was an inveterate speaker in Plenary. In one session she declared that "the root of all social evils lies in the unjust acquisition of wealth by a minority of members of society and the unjust distribution of the products of society." Although she appreciated the ILO's standard-setting function, she believed that many of the conventions, such as those dealing with employment, recruitment services, and freedom of association, needed to be updated. As far as the ILO itself was concerned, she insisted that it needed to be made more democratic and less costly. She suggested shortening the length of conference sessions and of documents, and reducing administrative expenses and activities that did not have priority.

The geographic spread among the women visiting ministers in recent years is evidence of the changes in the political landscape. Most of the women ministers over the past fifty years came out of ministries of labor, employment, social security, or social welfare. A number of them also served at one time or another as government or labor delegates. The steady increase in their numbers reflected the growing role of at least some women in a large number of countries. Thus in 1988 for the first time there was a total of five women visiting ministers and the number rose to nine in 1989. These included, in the latter year, four from Africa, two from Latin America, three from Europe, and two from the United States. As influential and articulate members of their own governments, they were leaders in forging links between national and international interests both in the ILO and throughout the UN system.

Women on the Governing Body

As indicated earlier, the Governing Body has major responsibility for administration and program determination, and it has from the beginning been primarily male. This was particularly evident in the prewar years, when only four women played any substantial role. (Violet Carrothers of Canada, Margaret Bondfield of Great Britain, Frieda Miller of the United States, and Gertrude Stemberg of the Netherlands.) In the immediate postwar years Stemberg continued to take an active part. With a few exceptions, the women who participated in the Governing Body were also delegates at the Conference.

Between 1954 and 1967 the role of women increased substantially. Government, employer, and worker members came from both developed and developing countries.[5] An example of the women who came to the Governing Body in these years is Bedia Afnan of the Iraqi mission in Geneva. She served as a substitute and—occasionally full—member of the Governing Body from 1959 to 1965. She became one of the spokesmen for the Middle East nations.

By 1967 the list of women participating in the Governing Body was somewhat longer. One of the women who from that time on has played an influential role is Zagorka Ilić of Yugoslavia. One of the most dynamic women in the last two decades, she participated not only in the ILO but also in all three UN conferences on the Decade for Women and in the Third Committee of the UN General Assembly. She spent a number of years at the Yugoslav mission in Geneva, starting as second secretary and rising to counselor. In the mid-1980s she was transferred to Belgrade. She came from a family with large agricultural holdings, and as a law student developed an abiding concern with the need for women to obtain better employment opportunities and adequate legal rights, both locally and internationally.

Although an increasing number of women participated from time to time during the 1970s, the real change in influence came in 1979 when Aida Gonzales Martinez of Mexico was elected chairman of the government group, and then in 1982 chairman of the Governing Body, while in 1986 Dagmar Molkova of Czechoslovakia became vice chairman. Gonzales Martinez came from a large family living outside of Mexico City. Her father was a rancher and business man, but died at an early age. Her mother was interested in social and economic affairs. Since money was short, Aida Gonzales Martinez went straight from high school to work as a secretary in the Ministry of Foreign Affairs. While working she managed to sandwich in a college degree, joined the foreign service, and by 1965 she became an officer in the ministry. In 1970 she entered law school while continuing to work in the ministry. From then on she worked at different periods for the Ministry of Foreign Affairs and the Ministry of Labor, where she served as coordinator for international labor affairs and representative for women's affairs. In 1982 she was proposed for the chairmanship of the Governing Body by the Tunisian minister of labor, with the support of the whole African group (a rather rare occurrence for a Latin American, and especially for a woman). The workers said she was the only candidate they would accept and the employers welcomed her. She served as chairman in both 1982 and 1983. This was really precedent-setting; a woman in the most influential position (aside from that of Director-General) in the whole ILO hierarchy.

Mrs. Gonzales Martinez deplored the fact that there were few women in the world dealing with labor policy and maintained that this was one of the reasons they did not make a better showing in the ILO. She also felt that many ILO conventions, whatever their original purpose, tended to restrict women rather than helping them. She cited as an example the Charter provision calling for a woman adviser when an item of concern to women was on the agenda. "Why only then?" she queried. (This was the provision that Margaret Bondfield had been so proud of almost seventy years ago.) Despite these strictures she felt that the ILO had made a real contribution to women.

During the 1980s women have come much farther in influencing ILO policy through participation in the Governing Body. Many women who have obtained ministerial or other senior posts in their own countries now use their positions both in the Governing Body and in the other ILO fora discussed earlier. These women come from many continents and from all three groups—although it must be stated that there are currently more employers than workers, a distinct reversal of the earlier period. The number that were reelected or elected for the first time in the 1987 elections indicate the solidity of the change from the earlier periods.[6] Another example of this change was the representation at the Governing Body of intergovernmental agencies. The World Health Organization, the Commission of the European Communities, and the International Atomic Energy Agency were all represented by women. A few examples are given here of the interplay of the role of women nationally and the positions taken by women in the Governing Body.

Among the outstanding women government representatives in the 1980s were Lucille Caron of Canada, Dagmar Molkova of Czechoslovakia, Marie Holmboe Ruge of Norway, adviser for ILO affairs, ministry of local government and labor, Torild Skard of Norway, director-general, ministry of development, Jennifer Dimond of the United Kingdom, and

Marion F. Houstoun of the United States. In 1986 Molkova was vice chairman of the Governing Body. Marion Houstoun, director, Office of International Organizations, Bureau of International Labor Affairs, Department of Labor, has been serving as substitute government representative in the Governing Body. She is one of the few U.S. women in recent years who has come up through the ranks in her department and now has policymaking responsibility in regard to the U.S. positions in the ILO. Significant employer representatives were Lucia Sasso-Mazzufferi of Italy, Cornelie Hak of the Netherlands, Diana Mahabir of Trinidad and Tobago, and Anne Mackie of the United Kingdom. The women workers included Shirley Carr of Canada and Ursula Engelen-Kefer of the Federal Republic of Germany.

Jennifer Dimond of the United Kingdom served as a substitute—and frequently acting—member of the Governing Body between 1981 and 1988. She was principal, Department of Employment, working directly with the under secretary of employment. She was the leader of a group of women who attempted to give the ILO women's bureau a more effective role and to see that women were given a greater role in formulating and designing projects affecting women in developing countries. She worked closely with other women members of the Governing Body in keeping women's issues to the fore in determining ILO's policies and programs. However, her interests were by no means limited to women. Her education and employment background gave her wide-ranging experience in a number of fields. She studied at the University of Sussex and at the London School of Slavonic and East European Studies, where she wrote a thesis on Russian history and received a Master of Philosophy degree. This was followed by a year in Moscow as an exchange student. Having passed the examinations for the foreign service, she came to New York with the British mission to the United Nations and was then sent to Korea as second secretary for three years—the first British woman to be posted to that country. Her next job was as first secretary in Moscow where she had an opportunity to interpret for Gromyko. After a short posting to NATO in Brussels, she went for three years to the overseas development administration and then to the Department of Employment, with responsibility for the international section, including inter alia ILO.

Anne Mackie, O.B.E., is one of the relatively small number of women to be elected as a full employer member of the Governing Body. She is the employee relations adviser of Unilever, consultant on international labor affairs, of the Confederation of British Industries, the chairman of its International Labor Committee, and member of its Multinational Social Affairs Subcommittee. She had worked her way up in what was essentially a male-dominated organization and did not believe that any special concessions should be made to women per se, at least in the industrialized countries. She became a full member of the Governing Body in 1986.

The women who have participated in the Governing Body have come from developing as well as developed countries—from East and West, from North and South. Few of the women have been militant feminists. They have, however, succeeded in keeping women's issues to the fore and have been a real factor in the increasing concern shown by the ILO for dealing with women's problems, emphasizing the women's role in standard setting and in technical assistance. Thus, for example, Lucille Caron was responsible for the introduction of a statement calling for implementation of the 1985 Conference resolution designed to increase the role of women in high-level positions.

Three of the permanent committees of the Governing Body which meet prior to its regular sessions and report to the full sessions have been particularly concerned with women's issues. The Committee on Operational Programs which reviews the ILO's technical cooperation programs devoted a substantial proportion of its time in 1986 to reviewing specifically women's programs, projects, and experts.

Another Governing Body committee whose work bears directly on women's issues is the Committee on Discrimination, which is responsible inter alia for overseeing the problems of apartheid as well as for overseeing the implementation of Conference resolutions dealing with discriminatory employment. For example, the committee in 1986 reviewed the resolution on equal opportunities and equal treatment in employment adopted at the 1985 Annual Conference and discussed at the UN Nairobi conference, concluding the Decade for Women. As a basis for action by the committee the Office prepared the Plan of Action, discussed in chapter 4.

A third committee which has been concerned with the status of women within the Office is the Program, Financial, and Administrative Committee, to which the Office submits a detailed report on the composition and structure of the staff.[7] It is also at this committee, when it is dealing with personnel questions, that the staff representative makes a statement. In her period as president of the staff union, this statement was made by Hong-Trang Perret-Nguyen, of French nationality. She came from a distinguished legal family in Vietnam who moved to France when she was seven years old. She went to school in Cannes and Paris and received a degree from the Ecole des Sciences Politiques. She joined the ILO in 1966, at the age of twenty-one, in the lowest professional grade. She was for several years the head of the staff union, and presented the views of the union before the various ILO joint committees. She is an experienced and effective speaker, expected to take on a greater leadership role. Her professional career includes many years of service in the Application of Standards Branch and in April 1989 she was appointed chief of the Equality of Rights branch, in the D1 category.

The role of women in the administrative functions of the Governing Body is symptomatic of the fact that women are no longer penned within the confines of social issues. However, until the Governing Body achieves much greater equality in its composition, it can only play a limited role with respect to feminist leadership in international organization.

The Staff as Implementers

The role of the Office vis-à-vis the Governing Body and the conference had been established in the interwar years, as had been the position of the staff union in the framework of an international civil service. So, to a large extent, had the status of women staff members become stratified. The return to Geneva from the Montreal wartime headquarters, the development of the UN family of organizations with many joint staff arrangements, and the appointment of a new ILO Director-General, with a background different from his predecessors, brought major changes in the orientation and activities of the ILO. These changes also affected the nature of women's employment within the ILO—and their use, in some instances, in "external relations."

David A. Morse, who was elected Director-General in 1948, was a lawyer who had served with the National Labor Relations Board and with the Allied Military Government for Postwar Labor Policy in Germany, Italy, and Sicily. First as assistant secretary and then under secretary of labor, he had been the U.S. government member of the Governing Body from 1946. He, like Winant some ten years earlier, brought to the directorship more informal staff relationships as well as greater understanding of the varied national groups with which he was dealing than had been the case with his British predecessors.

Morse retired in 1970 and was succeeded by C. Wilfred Jenks, a Britisher, who had been with the ILO since 1931. Formerly legal adviser and, at the time of his election, Deputy Director-General, Jenks had always been deeply involved in standard setting and with the relationship of the ILO with other international organizations. By contrast with Morse's pragmatic approach to technical assistance as a form of direct operations designed to achieve specific objectives in the economic and social fields, Jenks's major concern with research and technical cooperation was their use as a tool to implement and extend standard setting.

Jenks's period of office was dominated by difficulties with the United States. The United States had backed him for the appointment, believing he would take a stronger stand against demands by the Soviet Union than would his opponent, Francis Blanchard. However, interpreting his responsibility as Director-General to mean that he should use his own judgment—subject to later approval by the Governing Body—immediately after his election he appointed a Soviet citizen to the post of Assistant Director-General. The reaction in the United States brought a withholding of U.S. funds to the ILO budget and a series of controversial meetings. Two years after he had assumed office, Jenks died of a heart attack.[8]

Francis Blanchard, of French nationality, who was Deputy Director-General under both Morse and Jenks, was elected to the post of Director-General immediately after Jenks's death. Blanchard served as Director-General well beyond the normal retirement age, until February 1989 when he was succeeded by Michel Hansenne, the Minister for Civil Service (and former minister of labor) of Belgium. Blanchard had joined the staff of the ILO in the late 1940s, coming from the International Refugee Organization. His training as a French civil servant, and then as the director of the ILO's manpower and migration division, brought a more diplomatic and possibly bureaucratic approach to the position of Director-General than that of his predecessors. He seldom challenged the Governing Body of the ILO, or its sister agencies in the UN family, and he increasingly sought ILO leadership in cooperative or joint projects within the UN system. Although he gave extensive public support to women's efforts to obtain equality both within the Office and throughout the Organization there have been relatively few top-level appointments of women in his or his predecessors' regimes.

Assistant Directors-General

In 1960 Morse had appointed Ana Figueroa as the first woman Assistant Director-General, thus acknowledging that it was time to give a woman a clearly policymaking position. As noted earlier, she had previously served on the ILO staff as chief of the women's service and prior to her employment at the ILO she was general supervisor (from 1947–49) for the high school system of Chile, and from 1949–50 she directed the Women's Bureau of the Ministry of Foreign Affairs. In 1951 she became a member of the Chilean delegation to the UN General Assembly and chaired the Third Committee (the Social, Humanitarian, and Cultural Committee). In 1952 she sat on the UN Security Council. Her diplomatic background and rather flamboyant, elegant style and interests enhanced her role as the first ILO woman Assistant Director-General. She carried overall responsibility for women's questions, and served as Assistant Secretary-General of various sessions of the Annual Conference and at several regional conferences. For some years she played an unusual role as the Director-General's adviser on Latin American and other political issues. She had his full confidence and he depended on her judgment in a number of areas. For example, in 1967, when the Director-General convened a meeting of the permanent representatives of Latin American countries in Geneva to consider his decision to be a candidate for another term as Director-General, Figueroa was the only senior staff member present.[9] However, toward the end of 1967 she became ill and retired. She died in 1970. At the Governing Body session immediately following her retirement, an unusual series of tributes were paid to her by members of all three groups. To quote only a few tributes:

> Anita Figueroa knew how to arrange her work. She acted in defense of freedom for more than 25 years. Dedicated also to the creative work of the ILO, she won the affection of all those who encountered her there.
>
> In expressing our condolences on the death of this great lady, it only remains for me, on behalf of the workers of America, to undertake to honour her memory by defending while we live the noble ideals of justice which always inspired her actions and her personality.
>
> Ana Figueroa has a unique place in the hearts of us all. She has the gift of sparkling like Chilean wine. She is for all of us the beloved symbol of the grace and charm, of the warmth and gaiety of Latin America [See Minutes of the Governing Body].

The first woman Assistant Director-General after Ana Figueroa was Nobuko Takahashi. She was named in 1976 by Francis Blanchard for a two-year fixed term and given responsibility for supervising programs for women as well as advising on the ILO activities in Asia. Takahashi, a

Japanese national born in China in 1916, was educated in Tokyo, and became a government civil servant in 1945. After serving for several years in the Women's and Minors' Bureau of the Ministry of Labor, she became its director-general in 1965, and in 1974 a member of the Labor Insurance Appeals Board. During her government service she represented Japan at both ILO Annual Conferences and Asian regional conferences as well as at several meetings of the United Nations. During her term at ILO she served as an Assistant Secretary-General of annual conferences and also as an ILO expert with missions to Bangladesh and Vietnam. After leaving the ILO she became the first female Japanese ambassador to Denmark.

After Takahashi left in 1978, there began another period in which there was no woman Assistant Director-General. This gap was not closed until 1981, when Antoinette Waelbroeck Béguin was named. Her appointment marked the first time that a woman was promoted from the inside to a top-ranking position. As noted in chapter 3, she had joined the staff in the last days of the Montreal Office as a research assistant, immediately after graduating from Wellesley College. The ILO was in her blood; her father had joined the Office in 1919 and at the time of his death in 1944 in a tragic swimming accident in Montreal he was the Assistant Director in charge of all employment programs. Her grandfather (Louis Varlez) had been the chief of the employment and migration section when the Office was first established.

Antoinette Béguin, having grown up in Geneva and Montreal, with Belgian nationality, was bilingual and frequently served as an interpreter. Professionally, she remained in the employment section, and gradually took on increasing responsibilities. From 1976 to 1981 she was chief of the ILO's World Employment Program—the first woman in ILO history to have been a department chief—a position in which she promoted both research and technical cooperation for women in developing countries. This led inter alia to the launching of a new publication series, *Women, Work, and Development,* in which a number of studies and monographs threw new light on the plight of women belonging to the poorest strata in these countries and the factors leading to their exploitation, and, frequently, to the steady deterioration of their position. In 1981 she became Assistant Director-General with responsibility for all ILO activities for the elimination of discrimination and the promotion of equality, including equality between men and women workers.

She was also actively involved in promoting the position of women on the ILO staff. From 1975 to 1977 she chaired a joint working party which investigated the respective positions and opportunities of men and women officials and submitted a comprehensive report with a number of recommendations to the Director-General. This led to a policy statement by the Director-General, followed up in 1980 by an announcement to the Governing Body of a 25 percent target for the share of women in the professional category. Unfortunately this brought little change to the position of women in the ILO. By 1981 a subcommittee of the Administrative Committee (which is a statutory joint body bringing together representatives of the staff union and the administration) was set up to carry out a further study. Antoinette Béguin again chaired the subcommittee which submitted two reports in 1982 and 1983, pointing out the lack of progress and making recommendations that were subsequently approved by the Director-General.[10]

Antoinette Béguin retired, after serving less than two years as Assistant Director-General, when she reached the age of 60—and her post was immediately given to a man. The Belgian government made her a Commandeur de l'Ordre de la Couronne.

Women in Senior Administrative Roles

While there was at the beginning of 1988 only one woman in the top-level administrative or supervisory capacity—category D2—there were a number of women serving in the next category, D1, as chiefs of division or branches. Kate Wild, a Canadian, became director of the Labor Information and Statistics Department as of June 1, 1989. Her job includes responsibility for the expansion of the computerized information facilities, and training, and assistance in library and other information work in the branch and regional Offices. At a meeting in Geneva she was the only woman (in addition to the director of the Paris Office) to play a policy-making role. She participates regularly in most senior staff meetings affecting information questions. Her leadership and potential has from the outset been recognized by the top echelon of the Office, and by many representatives of member states who have drawn upon her services.

Kate Wild was educated at Toronto University, class of 1965, and trained as a librarian in 1977–78. Her ILO history is an example of the advantage of joining the staff as a secure individual who knows she can return to a high career post at any time. She originally came to the ILO on a one-year P4 contract at the suggestion of chief of the Bureau of Information Systems. At the end of the year, when she was acting chief librarian, she refused renewal unless she was given the full title (and responsibilities) and a higher grade than P4, seeking the rank held by past librarians (all men). She won her battle, both with respect to title and grade. Her additional responsibilities included the coordination of the disparate information services which had been carried out by various departments and to assist other intergovernmental agencies to develop similar systems.

She is a good fighter for what she believes in, including staff rights, efficiency (she had no hesitation about getting rid of dead wood), and program planning for better services. The improvement of the whole information service of the ILO is a testimony to her success during the relatively short period (three to four years) since she has been there. Her promotion was a highly deserved recognition of merit.

One area in which only a few women have served in an effective role is that of personnel and administration.[11] Anny Landsdorf, who joined the staff in 1956, is an example of a successful administrator. She is a Dutch citizen who had an unusual career both before joining the ILO as well as in the ILO. On her retirement she was made an *Officier in den Orde van Orangje Nassau* (Officer of the Order of Orange Nassau). She received her education during the war, first at the Higher Commercial School and then at the Higher Textiles School in Brussels. She joined the British Army during the occupation and then was assigned to the Dutch repatriation services as a member of the civilian team.[12]

Throughout her early employment with UN agencies she was in personnel and finance. In 1956 she applied for interagency transfer to the ILO, where she was made chief of the liaison section of the Technical Assistance Department—with the grade of P4. In 1970 she was made chief of the employment branch of the Technical Assistance Department, which became the management branch. She was given both management and personnel functions in the new Technical Cooperation Department, and in 1975 was one of the first women to be promoted to D1. She retired in 1978. Her role in management and administration, where she recruited many of the technical assistance experts and sought to help them work with the Office and the "placement countries," was very much appreciated. Through these years she had maintained close relations with the Dutch government; she was always invited to delegation meetings and functions, and provided useful linkages.

One example of a woman who used considerable ingenuity in circumventing barriers to promotion was Rolande Cuvillier, with dual nationality

(French and British). She joined the UN staff (in New York) in 1953 and transferred to the ILO in 1959 in a medium-level professional category, after winning a competition for the post of translator. After about a year she transferred to the employment branch (she had from the outset sought a technical rather than a language post) and then transferred to the non-manual workers' unit. Finding herself unable to obtain higher status within the direct system of promotion, she took a two and one-half years' leave without pay, in the course of which she worked at the University of Maryland. She also had a degree from the Institut d'Etudes Politiques and was a licenciée of the Sorbonne in Paris. She wrote a series of articles dealing with such subjects as labor problems of professional workers, social security and tax transfers, and copyright and social law. She returned in 1979 to find the scope and staffing of her unit reduced in size but with her position upgraded! She continued to write articles, including one on the economic and social consequences of reduction of working time, which articulated many of the problems being faced by working women. In 1982 she was promoted to branch chief. She also played a leadership role in the staff union, especially with regard to the upgrading of women staff. Her job included responsibility for the work of the Advisory Committee on Salaried Employees and Professional Workers, which is a tripartite committee (analogous to the industrial committees) meeting regularly and giving special attention to the problems of nonmanual women workers.[13] Cuvillier retired in 1987.

Another post of some significance which has in recent years been consistently held by a woman is that of clerk of the Conference—an appointment usually made from the section of the Office responsible for the staffing of meetings, and when possible someone who is expected to work well with the Conference president (who, as we have seen, is usually a man). The present clerk is Nicole Marie de Warlincourt, an attractive and very intelligent French woman who, for several years, staffed the Resolutions Committee.

Branch Offices

A number of women have carried high administrative responsibility in branch offices. These have tended to be in the developed countries and served primarily as information and liaison centers and sales offices for ILO publications, as well as in some instances for the recruitment of technical assistance experts. In small countries where there are no branch offices, the sales function and more limited information functions are carried out by national correspondents. The degree of responsibility carried by branch offices varies from country to country and is determined by the Director-General, in agreement with the host country.

In only two of the branch offices have women played top roles, serving as the director, although in several they have been the deputy or assistant. In many they have been librarians, and in others have carried important administrative duties. In the Paris Office several prominent feminist leaders have served at the top. This, in fact, reflected the role of women in the resistance movement in the Second World War.

The story of the Paris Office is unusual both with respect to the role that women have played and the premises it occupies. A large, high-ceilinged, third-floor apartment in a late nineteenth-century building on the cross-roads of Paris's left bank cultural center, leased by the ILO almost at the moment of its establishment, it seems a fortunate anomaly for an organization such as the ILO. Its wartime history—and that of the Paris staff—is particularly interesting because of the part played by Aimée Morel (formerly Aimée Rommel). During this period she was the acting head of the branch office, although only in the clerical grade. With the occupation of Paris, the ILO staff left with the French government. On July 12, 1940, Morel returned to find that the concierge had managed to prevent the premises from being requisitioned, but by December they were taken over, at the insistence of a former Geneva staff member who had become a German officer, and used as an office for translators by the ministry of foreign affairs. For a few months the ILO was permitted to maintain two rooms, but the staff was deliberately harassed to prevent them from working and then asked to leave, while another German former staff member declared that the ILO was dead. Morel then secretly moved as many files as possible to her own apartment, hid stocks of documents and publications in the cellars of the building, maintained some correspondence, and continued to sell publications clandestinely from her home. As the war progressed many of the publications—coming out in Montreal—were eagerly sought by such leaders of the resistance movement as the secretary of the General Confederation of Labor (CGT), the editor-in-chief of the underground paper, *Liberateur,* and a number of law professors, some of whom were later shot or deported.

Immediately following the liberation of Paris in August 1944 Morel reoccupied the office premises, where she found that many of the publications had been removed but that most of the files remained and all of the hidden material was intact. She immediately obtained authorization to rehire some of the staff—mostly women—and to make available ILO publications which, she reported, were sought by government departments, research bodies, and the trade unions. She complained about the fact that few of the Montreal studies existed in French, and that it was difficult to obtain the Philadelphia Conference publications.[14]

Morel continued as acting head of the Paris Office for several years until, in 1949, she was informed that the widow of Leon Jouhaux, the French labor leader who for many years had dominated the workers' group in the Governing Body and the Conference, had been made director of the Paris Office. (Aimée Morel remained in the office until her retirement in 1963.) Jouhaux's appointment was the first time that a woman was put in full charge of the branch office and carried the title of director. She was particularly important for her ingenious handling of difficult relations which had developed between the ILO and UNESCO, and for working out a compromise that allocated school based vocational education to UNESCO and vocational training to ILO.

Following Mme Jouhaux's retirement in 1971, the Paris Office was directed by a man, Gerald Larrue. Then in late 1979 Micheline Galabert, a political scientist and economist who had occupied many posts in the French civil service, served as counsellor in the French embassy in Morocco, and from 1973–79 as the director of the Center for Employment Studies in France, was named director of the Paris Office. She brought great technical and political skill to the work of the Office which includes representing the Office at meetings in France of UNESCO, OECD and the Council of Europe, as well as being the liaison officer with French authorities, disseminating information in France about ILO activities and in Geneva about French developments within the competence of the ILO. At a recent headquarters' meeting of administrators and directors of branch offices she took a leading role in suggesting changes that would improve the role of the branch offices. A dynamic speaker and advocate, Galabert represented the ILO at numerous meetings of discussion groups held in France, including, for example, the international woman's conference convened by the French government in May 1988 on Equality Between Men and Women: The Role of International Instruments, which was designed to follow up the Forward-Looking Strategies as adopted in Nairobi. Galabert called to the attention of the participants the mandate of the ILO and its contributions to the status of women workers throughout the world.[15] She retired in late 1989 and was replaced by a man.

The only other branch office where women have taken a leading role is that of Washington—and this was only in the prewar and wartime period. All recent directors have been men. Moreover, the Washington women leaders were there primarily because of their usefulness as channels of communication. Ethel M. Johnson had been a former colleague of Winant when he was governor of New Hampshire and an expert on minimum wage legislation in the United States. In 1935 she was appointed, on a temporary basis, to the Geneva staff as a "learning operation" on the understanding that she would then be given a regular post in the Washington Office. She later became its acting director and remained there until 1943, when she was replaced by decision of the directorate, and went to London as special assistant to ambassador Winant. A woman of soft appearance with a will of iron, she was known to many as the Bluebird.

Johnson was followed in the Washington Office by Elizabeth Rowe (wife of James Rowe, Jr.), who was given the title of executive secretary. She played a significant role in the period immediately after Winant's resignation in the somewhat difficult negotiations between the Acting Director, Edward Phelan, and Frances Perkins and Carter Goodrich representing the U.S. government, concerning the role of the Office with respect to wartime activities. One of her problems at this time was dealing with the French staff, including Marguerite Thibert, who were outstationed in the Washington branch Office, because as French citizens they had been forbidden by the Vichy government to go to the Montreal headquarters in a belligerent nation. At the time of the Philadelphia Conference Rowe was "attached" to the Secretary-General, and in 1945 she served as liaison and information officer at the Paris Conference. She resigned shortly thereafter.[16]

Up until 1988 there have been no other senior women staff in ILO branch offices and only two national correspondents, Brighid Stafford, former representative of the Irish government at several ILO conferences, and Katakin Bereczky of Hungary. Most of the librarians and other support staff continue to be women. The role of women in the ILO branch offices clearly reflects their status in the countries concerned and to some extent the attitude of these countries to women's employment.

Senior, Nonprofessional Categories

Another category of "women's employment" which has often been an open path to influence (and even to leadership) in governmental as well as nongovernmental bodies is that of administrative assistant to such senior officials as the director-general, the under directors-general, and the assistant directors-general. In the ILO only a very few women have actually filled this role, primarily because of the attitudes of the senior officials involved. However, there have been a few personal secretaries or assistants who were successful in being upgraded to the professional category and moved to different responsibilities. One in the early years was Miss Duncan, secretary to Harold Butler, both while he was Deputy Director and later Director. A typical British civil servant, she easily adjusted to international service and was also highly respected. Another was Kay Carew, secretary to Butler and later to Phelan. Two others were Morse's secretaries, Edith Boyer and Holly Crosby. The latter carried very substantial responsibilities, and later was transferred from the cabinet to the International Institute of Labor Studies. Mrs. Giddy, Jenks's secretary for many years, was a woman on whom he relied very extensively. Most recently, Blanchard's administrative assistant Yvette Verchere, has, in fact, served at a higher level than that of secretary and played a substantial leadership role. But because of the cabinet system, instituted by Albert Thomas at the beginning of the ILO, the top-level role in this category is carried not by the personal secretary or administrative assistant of the director but by the chef de cabinet (principal private secretary) who, in practice, has always been a man.

Rather similar responsibilities to those of private secretary are carried by the staff assigned to the bureaus for employers' and for workers' activities, respectively. While the professional positions in both of these bureaus have always been occupied by men, a number of women at the top of the nonprofessional category have in practice frequently run the services, and, in fact, earned higher salaries than the men in the lower professional grades. One outstanding example is that of Edith Bode, a German national, who, until her retirement in 1988, was the focal point for all employer activities—as well as problem solver. Another woman, a Dutch national, Miryam Stahl, research and editorial assistant, who joined the staff in Montreal was a second generation staffer, her father having headed the workers' bureau in the early days.

Office for Women Workers' Questions

As indicated earlier, a service for women and children was set up under Marguerite Thibert in 1926, was upgraded to a section under Mildred

Mary Chinery-Hesse of Ghana, Deputy
Director-General, ILO, 1989 *(courtesy of ILO,
Geneva)*.

Fairchild in 1948, and then after her retirement became the initial responsibility of Ana Figueroa. In the late 1950s and early 1960s, with the
changing attitude toward women workers in the ILO as well as the world
at large, Elizabeth Johnstone was made coordinator of women, youth, and
aging questions, and given broad responsibilities for policy determination
with respect to these three groups. During the period when Nobuko Takahashi was Assistant Director-General, a new Office for Women Workers'
Questions was set up with a mandate to disseminate information about
women, to promote employer, worker, and government action, work with
the ILO technical departments, and ensure liaison with the UN family. A
new function of this office was the publication of *Women at Work,* a
bulletin published twice a year to provide information on developments
concerning women workers throughout the world. This publication was
suspended as of 1989 and was not expected to be continued.[17]

The first chief of this unit, named in 1976, was Ekaterina Korchounova, who had been a senior research assistant at the USSR Institute of State and Law. She had served as a government adviser to the 1955 and 1957 sessions of the Conference. She left her post in 1982 and a year later was replaced by Raissa Smirnova who directed the office until her retirement in December 1988. She was one of the few women with a D1 rank.

During its ten years of activity the Office for Women Workers' Questions did not have sufficient staff or influence to fulfill the kind of role as catalyst and monitor that had been envisaged when it was created, and this situation had been of concern to several members of the Governing Body. Nevertheless, various members of its staff have written valuable technical reports and serviced the conference and a number of regional conferences when dealing with women's issues. Some of these women had begun their service either prior to the war or immediately after and reached retirement age in the early 1980s, while others were either transferred or recruited from different areas of the ILO. As of January 1, 1988, the office was abolished as part of efforts to refocus ILO activities for women and to streamline and coordinate activities by various departments. It was replaced by a special adviser on women's questions. The duties of the special adviser, as described in the 1990 budget proposals, seem to be more or less the same as those held several years earlier by Elizabeth Johnstone as coordinator of women and children's questions. Sally Christine Cornwell, director of the ILO Office in Fiji (described in chapter 6), has been appointed to the new post. The overall resources for women workers' questions will increase in the 1990–91 biennium with the appointment of four regional advisers and a staff member in the technical cooperation programs. The special adviser on Women Workers' Questions reports to the Deputy Director-General for technical cooperation and field programs, a post filled in 1989 by the appointment—by the newly elected Director-General, Michel Hansenne of Belgium—of Mary Chinery-Hesse from Ghana, the ILO's first woman Deputy Director-General.

8. Women Organizers Within the Office

Provisions concerning women that the founding fathers put in the ILO Constitution, largely in response to the First World War role of women, and the efforts of Margaret Bondfield at the Paris Peace Conference, as noted in chapter 2, included the explicit statement that there shall be women on the ILO staff without specifying proportion or status. We have noted in earlier chapters the role women in the Office have taken in ILO conferences, in providing technical assistance, and in the regional structure. We have also called attention to their relatively limited leadership positions on the staff. In this chapter we examine the efforts made to upgrade their status within the Office.

How, over the years, and under the leadership of eight different directors, have women prospered as members of the staff? What has been the role of the staff union with respect to women? What role have women played within the staff union? Has any true collective bargaining been possible within the framework of an international civil service? Is the status of women any greater—or less—than in other international organizations? Is there any correlation between the role of women in the Office and prior careers in their own countries? Does the status of women nationally—and in national or regional policymaking bodies—affect their role on the ILO staff? Have women participants in ILO Governing Body and conferences influenced the staff role of women? Have the efforts of other bodies—such as the UN Status of Women Commission—helped women on the ILO staff? Unfortunately, there are too many variables and intangibles for definitive answers to most of these questions, but some general lines for future action may emerge from the exercise.

Although women have, as is generally true in most international organizations, and elsewhere, occupied more than half of the nonprofessional positions, only a few have achieved policymaking status throughout the seventy-plus years of ILO existence. There has been little or no differentiation on the basis of sex with respect to initial salaries for people hired in the same grade but men tend to be hired into higher grades and to be promoted more quickly than women. Many of the problems faced by women center around the relatively rigid division of the staff into clerical and professional categories—with some privileges going only to the senior international professional levels and full diplomatic perks only to the directorial staff. Staff in the lower professional grades, which encompass the major portion of the women professionals, do not have privileges, such as tax-free gas for example, enjoyed by the senior staff (D1 and above). On the clerical level there were initially problems arising from the fact that international staff were paid more than local staff, even when their duties were clerical (rather than "housekeeping") and often required multilingual skills. This problem no longer exists at headquarters since local scales have been eliminated but many continue for staff recruited in the field. In the early days, in contrast to today, a far larger proportion of the clerical and other staff in the general service category was male.

An early problem of discrimination was whether or not wives of ILO staff could be employed and whether a woman would have to resign if she married a member of the staff. Here the decisions were for a long time clearly in favor of men but the situation is now much improved.

The Staff Regulations and the Staff Union

Almost as soon as the Office was organized a staff union was established as an essential element in its administrative structure with a formal statute defining its rights and providing for the election of an expanded staff committee. The statute called for the establishment of a joint committee composed of six delegates, three to be nominated by the Director and three elected by all the staff "with the exception of chiefs of service and chiefs of section." The Deputy Director (Harold Butler) was to serve as chairman without a vote. A short time thereafter the election took place (181 members of the staff of two hundred voted in the election) and nine men and two women were elected—Genevieve Laverriere, who received the second highest vote, and Sophy Sanger, both of whom were discussed in earlier chapters.[1]

Although an initial structure was thus in place, the real role of the staff union had still to be worked out. Implementation of the new provisions did not prove easy. ILO was a public international organization with staff regulations based on the British civil service and concepts emanating from French administrative practice. In an effort to harmonize two, often conflicting, modes of operation, Royal Meeker, a U.S. economist, director of the first ILO research division with long experience as a U.S. government employee, devised an international civil service for the ILO. An immediate question was how a staff union could function within the parameters of an international civil service. The issues involved have been identified in a recent study of international staffs; "the conditions of work are not determined as in the private sector, by a process of negotiation but by a process of consultation; and the dialogue is not with the actual authority (a legislative or executive authority), but with an executive head who is in the position of an intermediary."[2]

While one of the first tasks undertaken by the staff committee and the administration was the determination of specific employment conditions, such as working hours for the staff as a whole, the major early problem was to devise the machinery needed to deal with staff issues as they arose. One precedent-making decision was that union activities be recognized as official duties and a system developed by which departments or sections concerned received some compensation in budget terms for time not worked on professional duties—a concept described as "time off for union activities."[3]

As the Office grew in size and more and more "rights" and "privileges" became part of the staff regulations, the role of the staff union increased. New machinery was devised to meet various contingencies, such as pensions, staff recruitment and promotion, and welfare activities including financial assistance. Thus an Administrative Committee (which replaced the original joint committee) was charged with advising the Director on (1) appointments, transfers, and discharge; (2) the applications of the Staff Regulations; (3) any amendments to the said regulations; and (4) any question which the Director decides to refer to it. Its composition was that of a chairman (the appropriate Assistant Director) with three members and three substitute members appointed by the Director, and three members and three substitute members appointed by the Staff Union Committee. Joint committees could be set up in cases of grievances, with specifications as to hearings. Special joint juries were set up by the Administrative Committee (with equal participation by the staff union and the Administrative Committee) to determine qualifications for candidates for vacancies and organizing examinations. The agreement that recruitment of new staff—other than the top level—should be subject to a jury was introduced in the early days of the ILO, and has been continued up to the present time.[4]

From the time that formal staff regulations were adopted (in 1920), the chapter dealing with appointment and promotion began as follows:

a) The staff of the International Labour Office shall be chosen by the Director, who shall select officials of different nationalities in so far as this is compatible with the maintenance of efficient service.

b) All positions in the Office shall be open equally to men and women as provided in Article 7 of the Covenant of the League of Nations.[5]

In the early days there was no differentiation between the concerns of men and women since the first staff issues affected them equally, and the discrimination regarding salaries and promotions had not yet become apparent. By the end of the first decade discrimination had become clear to many of the women members of the staff. But the staff union expressed little concern about this issue—and few, if any, of the formal grievances with which it dealt particularly affected women. The questions of nationality and the situation of the "stateless" more often formed the basis for discussion. However, one issue that arose almost immediately and has only recently been resolved was the employment of the spouse of a staff member. It is no longer prohibited, although in practice the ILO does not usually allow two members of the family to serve in the same department.

The Postwar Civil Service of the UN Family

With the establishment of the United Nations and the effort to provide for comparable staff regulations and conditions of employment within the whole family of agencies, interagency bodies—such as the Administrative Committee on Coordination (ACC)—were set up to implement provisions outlined in the formal agreement of December 1946 between the United Nations and the ILO. This agreement provided, among other matters, for the development of a single, unified international civil service and for consultation concerning matters of employment to secure "as much uniformity in these matters as shall be found practicable." In 1947 the Governing Body of the ILO established a Staff Questions Committee to consider changes in staff categories, methods of classification, salaries, pensions, and other conditions of employment that would be needed to bring the ILO arrangements into conformity with those being established for the United Nations and for other specialized agencies. Neither the ACC nor the Staff Questions Committee (now the Program, Financial, and Administrative Committee) of the Governing Body were as much concerned with the position of women as they were with respect to nationality distribution. At about the same time, with the beginning of the expanded technical assistance program, further interagency bodies were established. These impinged on staff issues, especially with respect to technical assistance experts and the staff that was either outstationed to field offices or was locally recruited. Gradually their conditions of employment also became a concern of the ILO staff union.

Women did not become a clear issue until the UN Commission on the Status of Women began to look into their role in the United Nations and the specialized agencies, and called upon the Secretary-General and the heads of the specialized agencies to provide information on the numbers of women employed. Only much later was information requested on salaries and job classifications.

As the new "comparable" classification system came into effect, the ILO staff, particularly those in what was formerly the "intermediate" category (a group which comprised many more women than men) felt they had lost considerable status. Some found themselves in the new P1 classification which had been initially designed for new recruitment, and others in the broad "general services" category which had previously been the second division and had comprised both internationally recruited clerical staff and much of the locally recruited staff. For a considerable period the staff committee was preoccupied with these issues, as well as with the general issues of decreased perks, or diplomatic status.

The Drive to Improve the Status of Women

By the early 1970s a new phase began both in the ILO and in the United Nations. In 1971 the Governing Body gave new responsibilities to its Program, Financial, and Administrative Committee. It called upon the Office to submit statistical information concerning the staff, broken down so as to show its distribution by function and grade, place of assignment, category and type of contract, numbers of officials by region (from 1964 on), and current distribution by age, sex, and grade of officials in the professional category (P1–5) and grades D1 and D2, both at headquarters and in external offices. This information, which is published annually, is supplemented by the recommendations for promotion and recruitment made by the Selection Board. (The latter is now a joint body, composed of one member and one substitute appointed by the Director-General from the Personnel Department; one member and one substitute appointed by the Staff Union Committee; two members and two substitutes appointed by the Director-General on the joint recommendation of the Personnel Department and the Staff Union Committee. It is responsible for filling vacancies through external and internal competitions, under the general supervision of the Administrative Committee.) The annual document on the composition and structure of the staff enables both the Governing Body and the staff union to consider staff problems, as well as to deal seriously with discrimination issues and the lack of equality between men and women. Since then there have been frequent references to these issues by the staff representatives, who are enabled to speak both in the Committee on Programme, Financial, and Administrative Questions and in the Governing Body itself.

In April 1975, partly it may be assumed in preparation for the Mexico City Conference opening the UN Decade for Women, the ILO Director-General, Francis Blanchard, appointed a working party on equality of opportunity and treatment for women in the ILO. Its goal was to identify procedures and practices "which may give rise to discriminatory treatment of women especially as regards, but not limited to, appointment, job satisfaction and career advancement." The working party was chaired by Antoinette Béguin (then the director of the Employment and Development Department, but not yet Assistant Director-General) and was composed of six members: three nominated by the Director-General and three by the staff union. In addition, the staff union nominated two substitute members. One of the administration members was a woman, as was the chairman, one of the staff union members, and one of the substitute members.

The working party made a comprehensive review of the situation based on statistical tables recorded by computer as of May 1975 and September 1976 and a survey by the staff union.[6] Unfortunately this survey elicited only a limited response (20 percent of the 1,400 officials who received the questionnaire and 46 percent of the sample survey, or 24 percent if combined).[7] The report of the working party showed the divergencies in employment between men and women: (1) 70.7 percent of the men served in the professional category, while 82.4 percent of the women were in the general services category; (2) both professional and general service women were usually recruited at lower grades than men within the same category, and both, as indicated above, have slower promotional careers and, as a result, rise to less high levels than men, even when starting from the same grade; (3) marital status has an impact on women's employment—married women reach higher grades more slowly than single women; and (4) women appear to have had greater difficulties than men in taking advantage of training opportunities. The report concluded that "the position of women in the ILO reflects, by and large, their position in the world at large." It also pointed to the large proportion of women in linguistic posts and the relatively small number in technical posts. This partly reflects the inadequate training program open to women, both in the ILO and in the world at large from which they are recruited.

The report made a series of specific recommendations as it had been mandated to do:

(a) a statement should be issued by the Director-General "re-affirming" that equality of opportunity for men and women in the ILO "is a guiding principle of personnel policy";

(b) a ten-year "target of 30%" should be set for women in the professional category (such targets to be treated not as quotas but as internal tools of management applying to recruitment, assignment, and promotion);

(c) specific measures should govern recruitment (including clear definitions of qualifications and requirements to be stated in notices of vacancy) to encourage the number of appropriate applications from women;

(d) a system should be devised for "career trainees and special efforts to enable women to participate in career development programs";

(e) every effort "should be made throughout the Office to increase the number of women in high-level decision-making posts";

(f) measures should be taken "to offset . . . any harmful repercussions upon their employment that might derive from their entitlement" to maternity leave and attention to other family matters.

The report of the working party was given due consideration; the Director-General's statement was issued; but the results were not particularly satisfactory from the point of view of women on the ILO staff. Clearly the overriding concern of ILO with the broad issue of the status of women throughout the world, as indicated in the Declaration and Plan of Action adopted by the June 1975 Conference, and its participation in the Mexico City Conference on International Women's Year, did not extend to the staff itself.

Meanwhile, the problem was also being approached on an interagency basis. An ad hoc committee on the status of women in the international civil service was set up by FICSA (the Federation of International Civil Servants Associations), which held two sittings on May 13, 14, 1975, under the chairmanship of Rolande Cuvillier of the ILO, with participation from ECA, FAO, IAEA, ITO, UNESCO, UNIDO, UNDP, and the United Nations. The discussion was based on a number of documents, one of which, "The Status of Women in the United Nations: Problems and Action Programme," was prepared by the special adviser on the status of women in the international civil service, who had been appointed by the staff committee of the ILO. Another of the documents was the preliminary report of the ILO working party. The committee dealt with various forms of discrimination, including the need to protect women's rights, to establish policies in the field of human resources planning, recruitment, training, promotion, and careers that would bring about a better balance between the sexes. The issue of target establishment was the subject of divergent views, some feeling it would be a useful tool and others that it would be contrary to the dignity of women. It was clear in the discussion that there was great variation in emphasis and in the policies carried out by the different members of the UN family of organizations, some of the variation being the result of the location of headquarters in different countries, where national practice influenced the international personnel standards. Similar discussions have been on the agenda of FICSA meetings ever since, but it is difficult to evaluate their effect.[8]

The various initiatives at this time also led to a series of reports by the Joint Inspection Unit (JIU) of the United Nations, the first of which was published in 1977 and submitted initially to the ACC and then to the UN General Assembly, on *Women in the Professional Category and Above in the United Nations System*. The JIU has continued the series, publishing a progress report in 1980, a further full report in 1982, and another in 1985. The reports contain information on developments respecting women's employment and related issues in all the major international organizations, and recommendations by the Secretary-General and the heads of the agencies concerned to improve the situation—taking account of the budgetary situation.[9] These reports present a rather grim picture of the frustrated effort to bring women into leadership roles as the combination of geographic guidelines and budgetary crises ate into the initial progress achieved in the 1970s.

Joint Subcommittee on Equal Opportunity

A new phase began in 1981 and continued through 1983. A joint subcommittee on equal opportunity was established by the Administrative Committee, again under the chairmanship of Antoinette Béguin. The subcommittee was composed of four persons—two appointed by the administration and two by the staff union. In each case they included one man and one woman. The second joint group used the statistics developed by the previous study and compared them with the situation in 1981. These showed that the overall situation of women in the professional category and above had not improved in the previous five years, and in some instances had deteriorated. The subcommittee agreed that a number of measures should be taken to redress the situation, including the implementation of the targets. The subcommittee took the Director-General's target of 25 percent by 1985 and worked out what it would mean (and require) in practice to achieve, using different hypotheses concerning staff growth. The subcommittee concluded on the basis of its study, without an "affirmative action" program aimed at increasing the representation of women in the higher professional category, "the latter would progress only very slowly." This view is reinforced by a comparison of the 1981, 1984, and 1986 figures. In 1981 the proportion of women professionals was 15.4 percent; in 1984 it had dropped to 15 percent and as of November 30, 1985, it had grown to 17.4 percent. In the year ending December 30, 1986, forty-six professionals were recruited, of whom only eight were female (all in grades P2–4), while the thirty-eight males included one Assistant Director-General, one D2, four D1's, seven P5's, and one director of a branch office.

With respect to the general service category, the subcommittee pointed out that there is "relative stability in the structure by grade—contrary to what is happening in the Professional Service and above: one might even wonder whether this contrast is not partly due to the fact that in one case—the Professional Service category—it is chiefly men who are better at improving their position in the hierarchy that are involved, while the other group—the General Service staff—comprises mainly women, whose structure by grade is better controlled."

The subcommittee also dealt with some of the difficulties faced by women staff members in obtaining training as an access to promotion, and deplored the inadequacy of the training budget, and in particular the further reductions foreseen for the 1984–85 budget. The subcommittee concluded its report with a number of recommendations, hoping "that they will meet with a better response than those of this its first report— to which it draws attention once again—up until now." The recommendations again emphasized measures to improve both internal and external competitions for vacancies, noting that preference should be given to women, other things being equal. They urged the Office to take steps to attract young and competent women likely to make a career in the ILO, and added that a larger proportion of senior posts (where appointments are made directly by the Director-General) should be filled by "competent women, either from among qualified serving staff or through external recruitment." The recommendations also dealt with the promotion problems of the general service staff. Among the criticisms leveled at the relative stagnation of women in that category were the lack of adequate career development and training facilities and the fact that women were assigned to routine tasks, providing little opportunity to demonstrate their potential. In addition they called upon the Personnel Department, "in consultation with department chiefs . . . to draw up plans designed to improve the representation of women at all levels over the next three years."[10]

The recommendations of the subcommittee were never fully implemented, although the Director-General approved them in principle.

In 1983, when Béguin was retiring, she was asked by members of the staff union for her assessment of the situation. Despite the hopes aroused by the Director-General's circular, she said, there had been little visible progress. What was lacking was "the will to change things." Some excuses advanced were the difficulty of inducing women to move to Geneva and the lack of qualified women in the developing world. Some department heads demanded that experienced women should be recruited "who were immediately employable." The requirement that women be experienced meant, in practice, that they be at least 30–35 years of age. At that age many women were married, had children and, therefore, their transfer to Geneva posed obstacles.

Béguin went on to say that in fact there were qualified women in the Third World and elsewhere but if "one waits passively until candidates present themselves, there would naturally be very few." In the World Bank there is active recruitment of women. ILO does not do this. When asked why this was the situation, Antoinette Béguin suggested several reasons. Men are more at ease among themselves, on the same wavelength, and spontaneously they assign to their masculine colleagues jobs which would test them and open the door to promotion. One should not forget, she said, that "most of our masculine colleagues have wives that do not work. This model of the woman is carried over into the Office, including the idea that women's work is secondary. Hence it is men for whom career advancement is essential."[11] She also pointed out that the membership of the Selection Board (the body now responsible for assessing candidates and determining recruitment procedures) included few women in the professional category and those only as deputy members. Nor did it appear that a woman of an appropriate grade was automatically included in selection committees which assessed candidates participating in a competition. (This situation has in fact been somewhat improved during the last few years.)

The Action Group for Equality (AGE)

In 1985 women staff members began to take matters into their own hands. Following the retirement of Antoinette Béguin, the three other members of the subcommittee resigned in protest because Béguin was not replaced by a woman and because no action was taken on the subcommittee's recommendations. An ad hoc group for women, chaired by Rose Marie Greve, was established and, backed by the staff union, sent out a questionnaire to female staff. "The old familiar comments came tumbling out"—absence of career prospects, blocking at the top of the general service grades and categories, absence of recognition of qualifications, and discrimination in management courses, training, and promotion. Proposals for action included the creation of a support group amongst women committed to the idea, "regardless of category and grade," which could serve as an "old-girls network" and could show "the ILO administration ways of better utilizing the human potential at its disposal." It was also suggested that the ad hoc group draw up a list of candidates for top appointments on decisionmaking bodies. There was a call "for a suitably senior office within personnel to monitor and actively remedy the situation." As evidence of some progress, reference was made to the Director-General's announcement of his personal commitment to changing the position of women in the Office.[12]

Meantime, the ad hoc committee on women was transformed into the Action Group for Equality (AGE). After well attended general meetings at the end of 1985 and the beginning of 1986, contacts were made with the ILO administration. The group began to organize its activities and to issue informative newsletters. Membership in AGE is open to all officials of the ILO. While it cooperates with the administration and staff union, it is an independent, informal network to encourage contacts among women staff members. It concentrates on "practical, self-help measures." A four-member steering committee was named (at one of the early meetings), comprising a convener of meetings, a coordinator of activities, a treasurer, and a membership secretary. A small annual membership fee was agreed upon.[13]

One of its first specific acts was the preparation of a draft resolution concerning equal opportunity and treatment which was submitted to the Annual General Meeting of the ILO Staff Union (October 1986). The resolution noted the concern of the union that the ILO has made less progress than its sister agencies, both at headquarters and in the field, in meeting the target for representation of women in the professional category, and that any substantial progress in the advancement of women in the general service category is lacking. It asked for: "the establishment of a joint official body to implement necessary measures to ensure equality of opportunity and treatment of all workers in the ILO, including those recommended in both reports of the Equal Opportunity Sub-Committee in 1982 and 1983, and the immediate appointment at the Directorate level of a person responsible for developing, implementing and monitoring a concrete programme of action for equality of opportunity and treatment in the ILO." The resolution, and a statement contained in the body of the Annual Report concerning employment of spouses, which noted the gap between the 25 percent target set by the Director-General in 1981 for the professional category and the 17.3 percent figure which had been obtained by 1985, were duly adopted by the meeting and transmitted to the Director-General.[14] While, as of 1988, it did not seem to have had direct results, the 1989 election of a new (Belgian) Director-General has brought some clear improvements in the situation.

The Road Ahead

During 1986 and 1987, as part of the follow-up of the 1985 and 1986 conference Resolutions, the Nairobi conference ending the Decade for

Women and the work of the recent sessions of the UN Commission on the Status of Women, as well as in consequence of the work of the staff union and the action group on equality, the Governing Body of the ILO has, following innovative Canadian leadership (especially Lucille Caron), taken an active part in seeking to improve the situation of women in the ILO.

The representative of the staff union, addressing the Governing Body in March 1986, pointed out that the Director-General's 25 percent target for women by 1985 had fallen far short. Only 8 percent of officials recruited in that year were women and the total figure now stood at 17.7 percent. One of the reasons, he alleged, for this situation was the limited amount of funds spent for staff training—"an important factor in career development." While the Consultative Committee on Administrative Questions (CCAQ) had set a target of 2 percent of staff costs for training in international agencies, the ILO allocated only 0.2 percent. He went on to say that another problem was the increase in direct selection. Between 1981 and 1985, out of 183 cases of external recruitment in professional and higher categories, only 26 posts had been filled by competition.[15] Direct selection need not necessarily have been a problem with respect to the appointment of women if the directorate had used the power of direct appointment to name a larger proportion of women. Unfortunately this has not been the case.

During the November 1986 and March 1987 sessions of the Governing Body the place of women in the ILO was discussed at length in its Committee on Discrimination. The Canadian government pressed for the appointment of a special adviser to the Director-General whose responsibilities would include the promotion of women within the staff, "monitoring" the ILO's implementation of the Nairobi Forward-Looking Strategies, its implementation of Conference actions relating to equality and other women's issues, and following up on the execution of its Plan of Action. Because of the financial crisis throughout the United Nations and the specialized agencies, no action was taken on these suggestions, on the grounds of their budgetary implications for 1987–88.

One of the key problems affecting women in international bureaucracies, including the ILO, is the emphasis on geographic distribution. As has been pointed out, governments "fear that efforts to recruit women for the professional and higher categories may adversely affect the outcome of steps taken to achieve the overriding objective of a strictly quantified balance of nationalities in the composition of the staff."[16] Indicative of this emphasis and also, perhaps, the growing reluctance to treat women as a separate category is the change of ILO staff regulations. They no longer provide that all positions be open equally to men and women. Instead they provide that, with respect to the filling of vacancies, due regard shall be paid to the importance of maintaining a staff selected on a wide geographic basis. "Officials shall be selected," they provided, "without distinction as to race, creed, or sex" (Article 4.2 (a)).

Another problem facing women is the multinational composition of the staff. To some degree and in some places, cultural and social conditions place barriers on women abroad. Nevertheless, there has been progress, however slow, particularly in the last decade. Despite the target figure of 25 percent, the maximum actual figure reached was 20.15 percent on November 30—excluding the directorate and officials in branch offices or on short-term contracts. Exactly comparable figures are not available for the UN staff or the other agencies in the UN system, but the ILO now appears to have moved up to place above the median. The most recent figures submitted to the February–March 1989 session of the Governing Body show the professional staff distribution as of November 30, 1988:

Grade	Male	Female
D2	24	0
D1	49	6
P5	181	12
P4	179	48
P3	97	55
P2	16	17
P1	1	0
Total	547 (79.85%)	138 (20.15%)

If the directorate is included, the number of males goes up to 557, the percentages change to 80.14 and 19.86, respectively.[17] However, the promotions that took place in the first quarter of 1989 again bring the women's percentage up, since there is now one female D2 (replacing a retiring male D2), and several more D1's, so the total women's percentage falls between 19.86 and 20.15. In November 1989 it had increased to 20.34 percent.

At the time of his retirement, on November 30, 1988, ILO Deputy Director-General Bertil Bolin was interviewed for *Union,* the bulletin of the staff union. In response to questions concerning women and the trade union movement, he noted a growing influence, especially in the service sector, and forecast that within twenty years the AFL-CIO, like the Swedish trade union confederation, might be headed by a woman. He was then asked if he saw any progress being made in the ILO toward "the expressed aim of the UN to have 30 percent of professional posts filled by women." He responded, "It has not been easy to make the plan of action for women workers fully appreciated in this Office, partly because it's male-dominated especially at the management level, where the impulse has to come from. It is hard to find women officials on a high level, which is extremely regrettable." He added that the ILO should have an equal type of recruitment policy and career possibilities and "see sex distribution in the same terms that we see geographical distribution. The ratio could be 60 women to 40 men as well as the other way round." While he did not believe it "will happen during the next ten years," he concluded that "it's a big mistake not to use the enormous resources in terms of intellectual and other capacities we have in possible women officials."[18] The composition of the Office under the new Director-General's leadership will be closely watched with respect to the appointment of women, particularly as several of the male senior staff reached retirement age in the final quarter of 1989. When interviewed in June 1989 Michel Hansenne indicated that he hoped to appoint a woman as Deputy Director-General but added, significantly, that in order to meet the geographic distribution factors, she would have to come from Africa. He fulfilled his wish in appointing Mary Chinery-Hesse from Ghana and putting her in charge of the "$125 million a year technical cooperation program, channeled principally to the developing countries of Africa, Asia, the Americas and the Arab States."[19]

9. The International System and Nongovernmental Organizations

The Forward-Looking Strategies for the Advancement of Women, adopted by the World Conference in Nairobi, to Review and Appraise the Achievements of the United Nations Decade for Women, opened a new chapter in the search for equality of women. The findings asserted that the "need for women's perspective on human development is critical, since it is in the interest of human enrichment and progress to introduce and weave into the social fabric, women's concepts of equality, their choices between alternative development strategies and their approach to peace, in accordance with their aspirations, interests and talents." The 1985 Conference and its two predecessors also brought nongovernmental organizations into prominence and there has been increasing recognition of their role as partners in development.

Long past are the days when the ILO stood virtually alone as a multilateral organization concerned with labor and social issues, including the problems of women workers; when the only voices raised on behalf of women came from a handful of courageous working women, social workers, and suffragettes. Across the whole range of ILO activities in the 1920s and 1930s there were only four intergovernmental organizations that impinged in any real way on the ILO. There was the League of Nations, to which it was attached by the 1919 peace treaties, the Committee on Intellectual Cooperation in Paris, the International Institute of Agriculture in Rome, and the Conference of American States, which subsequently became the Organization of American States. The body most directly concerned with ILO activities was the League of Nations.[1] ILO specialists were invited to submit reports on the social aspects of questions on the agenda of League committees and participated in meetings both of the Mandates Commission and of the Child Welfare Committee. The terms of reference of the Permanent Health Committee included the workplace and accordingly there were joint ILO League appointments such as that of Dr. Alice Hamilton, discussed in chapter 2.

Intergovernmental Agencies in the Postwar Period

The war and its consequences altered the face of the globe both politically and economically. One result of direct concern to the ILO was the proliferation of new intergovernmental bodies. By 1947 the ILO was one among many, although it was the only one to operate on the basis of a tripartite structure where the representatives of employers and workers—nongovernmental organizations—constitute an integral part of the intergovernmental organization. The new intergovernmental bodies included specialized agencies such as the United Nations Educational, Scientific, and Cultural Organization (UNESCO), the World Health Organization (WHO), and the Food and Agriculture Organization (FAO).[2] There was also the UN Commission on the Status of Women. But these represented only the tip of the iceberg. In 1946 the United Nations established a Children's Emergency Fund (UNICEF) to utilize some of the residual funds of the United Nations Relief and Rehabilitation Administration (UNICEF was made a permanent body in 1953); a Population Commission, also in 1946, and later a United Nations Population Fund (UNPF, 1967), and a High Commissioner's Office for Refugees (UNHCR, 1949). Five UN regional economic commissions were set up between 1947 and 1973: ECE, Economic Commission for Europe (1947); ECAFE, Asia and the Pacific (1947, later renamed ESCAP); ECLA, Latin America and the Caribbean (1948); ECA, Africa (1958); and ECWA, Western Asia (1953). In addition to the agencies of the UN family there was also established in 1957 what is now the most powerful independent regional body, the Commission of the European Communities.

An expanded technical assistance program was created in 1949. This program was transformed in 1966 and became the United Nations Development Program. Finally, to mention only two more postwar intergovernmental bodies of particular concern to the ILO, there were established in 1966 a United Nations International Research and Training Institute for the Advancement of Women (INSTRAW) and, in 1977, the United Nations Voluntary Fund for the Decade for Women (renamed in 1985 the UN Development Fund for Women—UNIFEM).

228

A UN Commission on the Status of Women

For ILO the multiplicity of organizations raised questions regarding their respective competence as they affected women. This arose in its sharpest form with respect to the Commission on the Status of Women. The creation of such a body, it will be recalled, was proposed at the San Francisco Conference, where the concept split the ranks of women and continues to do so today. In the case of the ILO the question still arises as to whether women should be treated as a separate category for special attention or should their concerns be merged with those of workers generally—both men and women.

However, the existence of a Commission on the Status of Women is now an established fact. When its proponents won the day, the Commission assumed a sweeping mandate, as detailed in chapter 3. At its first session the Commission asserted that it intended to "raise the status of women, irrespective of nationality, race, language or religion, to equality with men in all fields of human enterprise, and to eliminate all discrimination against women in the provisions of statutory law, in legal maxims or rules or in interpretation of customary law." It added "women should be given equal rights with men with respect to labour, wages, holidays and other economic and social rights."[3]

The Commission tended initially to look at the ILO with a measure of distrust and a determination to maintain its supremacy. The ILO, for its part, had no intention of abdicating the role it had played since 1919 as the only intergovernmental organization with responsibilities for working women. After some initial skirmishes, accommodation was achieved and from that time on the Commission, for the most part, limited itself to urging governments to implement the instruments approved by the ILO and to making an almost unending flow of requests for information and for special studies on a wide variety of subjects.[4] Thus, for example, the ILO was asked to deal with the following points when studying the question of equal pay for equal work: the rate for the job, irrespective of sex; technical training and guidance; access to jobs and promotion on a par with men; and abolition of legal or customary restrictions on the pay of working women. (As noted in chapter 4, a convention and a recommendation on equal remuneration were adopted by the ILO Annual Conference in 1951.) In 1952 the Office was asked to collaborate with the Secretary-General on studies on part-time employment and older women workers. The following year the Commission asked for materials on cottage industries, handicrafts, and seasonal agricultural work. When the ILO report on this subject was received the Commission urged governments to make extensive use of the facilities of ILO and other intergovernmental organizations in developing their own resources.

In the mid-1950s the Commission turned its attention to working women with family responsibilities, and the UN Secretary-General, the ILO, and other specialized agencies were asked to report on activities in various countries for improving the employment situation of such women. In 1961 the Commission asked the ILO to consider the extent to which discrimination in employment in different countries was attributable to the fact that the cost of all or some social benefits, particularly maternity benefits, were defrayed by employers and not by public funds. Subsequently, the ILO was asked to include on the Conference agenda both the question of vocational training and guidance for women, and the effects of scientific and technical progress on employment and working conditions of women in both developed and developing countries.

While the number of such requests put a strain on ILO resources and, in some instances, had little effect on the course of work already in progress, they did serve as a continuing prod to the ILO to strengthen its activities affecting women and a reminder to governments not to ignore the rights of women. This type of relationship continued in the years that followed, and was accentuated during the Decade for Women.

Representatives of the International Labor Office, usually women, regularly attended sessions of the Commission. Moreover, a few members of the Commission were also active in ILO meetings. These included Hanna Bokor of Hungary, who, as previously mentioned in chapter 4, served as vice chairman at several sessions of the Commission and was also a member of the ILO's Committee of Experts on the Implementation of Conventions; and Aida Gonzales Martinez of Mexico, later to become chairman of the ILO Governing Body. On the Commission there were also several other members of the Governing Body from Argentina, Byelorussian Soviet Socialist Republic, Czechoslovakia, and the USSR. Two members of the Commission later joined the ILO staff—Mrs. Ana Figueroa of Chile, who became the first woman Assistant Director-General, and Ekaterina Korchounova of the USSR, who became the chief of the office for Women Workers' Questions.

At its April 1989 session the Commission adopted an unusually large number of resolutions, most of which dealt with the implementation of the actions taken during the Decade for Women and a number urged the various specialized agencies and nongovernmental organizations to take appropriate actions to advance the status of women. Two resolutions were concerned with the ILO; one urged governments to "endeavour to meet the relevant provisions of the ILO Conventions, especially those relating to equal pay and working conditions, ensuring in this way the awareness of their rights by women in all sectors of economy, both formal and informal" and recalling the ILO's "Plan of Action on Equal Opportunities and Equal Treatment for Men and Women in Employment"; and the other calls upon governments "to give high priority to programs that will ensure women's access to the labor market, eliminate sex segregation in the labor market, provide equal pay for equal work, and increase "women's participation in trade unions."

Collaboration and Conflict in the UN Family

The major area of collaboration between the ILO and the United Nations has been the development of standards and treaties affecting human rights. An early example concerned the provisions regarding working women in the Universal Declaration of Human Rights. When the provisions of the Declaration were incorporated into treaty form, the ILO helped to shape the provisions in the Covenant on Economic and Social Rights relating to workers. While the ILO played a role in the drafting of the covenants, its role in their implementation is limited by the fact that it cannot be a signatory. A similar situation obtained in relation to the UN Convention on the Elimination of Discrimination against Women. A somewhat different situation exists with respect to two conventions, one dealing with the rights of the child adopted in 1989 and one still pending, dealing with migrants. With respect to the rights of the child, the ILO made a major effort to prevent provisions concerning age of admission to employment, conditions of child labor, and recruitment to armed services from undercutting existing ILO standards. In the migration field the situation is somewhat ironic because in the 1950s efforts were made by a number of governments to transfer responsibility for conditions of migration from the ILO to other agencies, including the United Nations. Today, however, some of the same governments have sought to exclude from the United Nations draft convention provisions protecting the rights of migrants on the ground that this falls within the province of the ILO. The Organization for its part has taken a positive role in assisting in the drafting.

231

There is close cooperation between the ILO and the Social Affairs and Statistical departments of the United Nations which rely on the ILO's classification of occupations and similar statistical tools. In addition the ILO prepares materials for UN reports such as the World Social Situation. The 1989 report includes a chapter on the advancement of women, which concludes that "trade unions and employers determine many job opportunities available for women."

Specialized Agencies

A jurisdictional problem that occurred early in the day concerned the ILO and UNESCO. One of the three facets of the latter's mandate was education, and the ILO was involved in the education of workers, including women. After some rather protracted negotiations, it was agreed that UNESCO would concentrate on academic education, while the ILO concentrated on vocational training. That this distinction had grey areas was clear, both in terms of their respective programs and the frictions that developed over their implementation. A number of recommendations were addressed by the Commission on the Status of Women jointly to ILO and UNESCO. These dealt with the training of girls and women in rural areas and the broader field of technical and vocational education, and training in general. Special attention was called to the need for increased attention to the integration of women in social and economic life within the framework of technical progress.

In some cases ILO and UNESCO carried out joint activities. Examples were an ongoing Committee of Experts on the Status of Teachers and, in 1980, an international congress in Bonn on the situation of women in technical and vocational education. When UNESCO established a number of fundamental education centers, the ILO cooperated by providing training in regard to cooperatives and handicrafts.

Collaboration initiated between the ILO and the health section of the League of Nations has been continued between ILO and the World Health Organization. A joint committee on occupational health meets periodically and a number of joint projects have been carried out in this field. In 1979 a joint seminar with WHO and OCAM (Communal African and Mauritanian Organization—French acronym) on women in rural Africa was held in Benin. The seminar urged that agricultural extension and training programs be open to women as well as to men; that suitable facilities for water and fuel supplies, and improved tools to lessen tiring and unproductive work be provided; and that income-earning activities based on a market study of outlets with an organized distribution network be introduced. Stress was also laid on functional literacy and education in health and nutrition, as well as training in the administration, upkeep, and repair of facilities.

Few issues are more critical than that of repair and maintenance. Thus, for example, WHO has estimated that up to 80 percent of all new hand pumps for water break down within three years and the sufferers are mostly women. One problem, stemming perhaps both from ignorance and the fact that repair and maintenance fall outside the scope of traditional activities, is the reluctance of women in developing countries to undertake such tasks. UNICEF reports that in southern Ghana, where women had been helped to buy grinding mills, they "dislike the bother attached to maintenance, getting hold of spare parts and diesel, keeping accounts etc." They prefer a service run for them by a male owner.[5]

Several Yugoslav government departments, ILO, and WHO jointly organized an international symposium on occupational safety and health of migrant workers and their families—a matter obviously of concern to the wives and mothers of migrants as well as to the men. In addition ILO and WHO have collaborated on a number of conventions and codes. At the ILO's request a committee examined the medical provisions for a proposed revision of the maternity convention, and convened a consultant group of medical experts to consider medical care provisions in proposals on minimum and advanced standards of social security. In 1949 WHO also helped ILO on the revision of the Convention on Migration.

The relationship between the ILO and FAO with regard to women's issues has been more limited, but in the area of cooperatives a joint agreement was worked out specifying the respective roles of each organization. There has been consultation on such issues as the importance of crop and cattle insurance to the maintenance of income security, conditions of work of fishermen, conditions of employment of agricultural workers, and the cooperative movement. While these do not as a rule concern women directly, they do affect their well-being. The 1979 FAO Conference on Agrarian Reform and Rural Development adopted a program of action, some of whose provisions concern rural women. In 1981 the World Food Program (WFP), established in 1963 under the joint auspices of the United Nations and FAO, launched a project to develop training and income-generating activities for Indonesia and similar activities in the Syrian Arab Republic. One of the joint ventures of the ILO and WFP has dealt with women dependents in Bangladesh. Since then collaborative programs have increased substantially in both Asia and Africa. Many of these deal with the organization and management of cooperatives.

A rather unusual example of cooperation was a 1977 joint ILO meeting with the Universal Postal Union and the International Telecommunication Union on the effect of technical change on conditions of work and employment in the postal and telecommunications services. It was noted that women workers were more subject to job changes than other workers, primarily because they occupied manual and operator positions. Moreover, because of their family responsibilities, women were not so easily redeployed, particularly to a different geographic area. It was suggested that special programs be provided for women to qualify them for new jobs resulting from technological progress, even if they were considered as "men's work."

United Nations and Its Subsidiary Bodies

While UNICEF has its closest relations with WHO and UNESCO, it cooperates with the ILO on some of its projects regarding children and women's support services such as pre- and postnatal maternity care, teenage pregnancy programs, and child care. The ILO, as mentioned above, participated in the drafting of the UN Convention on the Rights of the Child—an instrument for which UNICEF and the Commission on Human Rights have shared responsibility. ILO was primarily responsible for the provisions relating to age of admission to employment and conditions of work. In 1988 ILO/UNICEF and international nongovernmental organizations sponsored a regional conference on Child Abuse and Neglect, organized by the National Youth Bureau of Thailand.

One of the more interesting pages of ILO's history concerns its involvement in the population question—an issue which had a troubled history both in the ILO and in the United Nations. Although a United Nations Population Commission had been established under ECOSOC in 1946, its role was long restricted to demographic questions—with little practical impact on men or women. It was not until 1966 that the population division of the Secretariat was allowed to expand its functions and to place increasing emphasis on regional activities and technical assistance, directed to both men and women.

Meantime, beginning in 1950, the ILO Director-General's reports had made occasional references to the problems caused by rapid population growth and, in 1964, the Annual Conference adopted the Recommendation on Employment Policy which contained a discreet reference to population growth and the adoption of "economic and social policies that make for a better balance between the growth of employment opportunities and the growth of the labour force." Two years later the Swedish government representative came out openly in favor of ILO involvement in family planning. He introduced a resolution which suggested that family planning education be included as a part of vocational training programs, and that a comprehensive study of the problems of population growth be undertaken. This was vigorously opposed by France and the French speaking African countries which declared that the ILO had no business becoming involved in the provision of family planning services or the promotion of contraceptives among workers. Their views prevailed.

However, at the regional level, the fight had been launched earlier. At the conference of American States' members of the ILO in 1966 the United States argued that "efforts to promote the development of human resources would be wasted if they failed to take into account the forces required to educate and equip the rapidly growing population." This was countered by the Argentine representative on the grounds of "the sacred right to life." To which Wilfred Jenks, the ILO's Deputy Director-General, replied that it "was precisely respect for the sacred character of human life which imposed an obligation to ensure population growth did not outstrip the resources required to provide everyone with a full and useful life."

The same year the ILO's Asian Advisory Committee urged that "countries should consider the adoption of a population policy suited to national considerations." Its report was adopted by the Governing Body over the objections of Mrs. Mironova, the USSR member, on the grounds that this was not an area in which the ILO should be involved. At its June 1967 session the Annual Conference unanimously adopted a resolution stressing the role of governments and organizations of trade unions and employers in creating awareness of the population problem and requesting the Governing Body to arrange for a study in cooperation with other agencies.

While the study was wending its way rather slowly, the Asians again pressed for action. At the Tokyo regional conference a resolution requested the Governing Body inter alia to authorize the provision of technical assistance to deal with population problems as a complement to the Asian Manpower Plan. However, it was not until a UN Fund for Population Activities was established in 1967 and extended, two years later, to include the specialized agencies, that the ILO became actively engaged.[6] Among the joint activities with the ILO was a subregional seminar in Dacca on the interrelationship between the status of women and population questions. The discussion dealt with family planning programs, and suggested methods of involving women in the formulation and implementation of such programs, the creation of institutional structures to facilitate the participation of women, and proposed further research on links between the status of women and their fertility pattern. With UN Fund financing, the ILO has been carrying out a number of projects relating to labor and demographic variables. Most of the ILO projects in this area have focused on Africa—the Cameroons, Ethiopia, Guinea, Kenya, Mali, and Somalia—but there have been a few in Latin America, Asia, and Cyprus. While they have not targeted women specifically, several have been of direct concern to them. These include population planning and human resources and development.

To strengthen its activities for women, UNFPA has set up a special unit for women, population, and development. The unit is responsible for promotional advocacy, the development of policies and procedures, technical support, and coordination of the activities of the fund to ensure that due attention is given to women.

The United Nations High Commissioner for Refugees (UNHCR) is active on a number of fronts that involve women refugees. These include health care centers, water supply, programs for women in agriculture and livestock rearing, assistance in seeking employment in existing labor markets, vocational training, and formal education. UNHCR has funded several ILO projects. These have included the economic integration of urban and semiurban refugees in Costa Rica, vocational training for Afghan refugees, and provision of an expert on income generating activities for refugees.

The International Research and Training Institute for the Advancement of Women (INSTRAW) has given priority to improving statistics and other data relating to women. In cooperation with the UN Statistical Office it has prepared two manuals on compiling statistics and indicators on women. Like the ILO and others it has been concerned with methods of evaluating women's work in the informal sector and several expert group meetings have been held to examine this issue. In 1985 an important joint statistical survey was made on women in economic activity, attempting for the first time to quantify activity in the informal sector. It has also been involved in encouraging women's participation in cooperatives, and in promoting, in Africa, new and renewable sources of energy. At a 1986 meeting in Geneva on water resources there was an INSTRAW/ILO sound-slide presentation on minimum evaluation procedures, and a representative from the ILO Turin Training Center explained how women could be acquainted with the maintenance of water resources such as irrigation canals and traditional wells. In November 1986 the chief of ILO's Rural Employment Policies branch, Employment and Development Department, visited INSTRAW for consultations on employment policies for women.

UNIFEM, as noted earlier, is the only UN mechanism for development cooperation set up specifically to channel financial and technical resources to women. Its mandate is to ensure the appropriate involvement of women in mainstream development activities and to support innovative and experimental activities benefiting women. Its current emphasis is on strengthening national institutional capacities to address women and development, with particular reference to planning ministries and nongovernmental organizations. As of 1987 it became engaged in joint programming with the International Development Association (the soft-loan partner of the World Bank), the Inter-American Development Bank and the International Fund for Agricultural Development. UNIFEM has cooperated closely with the ILO on a large number of projects, especially in Africa. In April 1987 it participated, along with DANIDA (the Danish International Development Agency), at a meeting at ILO headquarters on "the integration of women in technical cooperation projects." Guidelines were developed for incorporating experience with women in development projects with mainstream development programming. An example of the results of this consultation is the participation of UNIFEM in an ILO self-employment and employment creation mission to Nigeria to ensure that women are taken into account in the work of the mission. UNIFEM funded a joint Mali/ILO training project on the better use of tools by women and participated with the UNDP in the self-employment aspects of a broadbased interagency program which included a Geneva round table and a two-day workshop (organized by the ILO in Arusha, Tanzania). Approximately one-third of all UNIFEM projects are carried out by nongovernmental organizations. Participating organizations include local and national women's organizations and grass roots groups.

In a recent UNIFEM paper on the impact of time- and energy-saving technologies on women, it reported that ILO seemed to have the greatest involvement and interest of all the agencies it had contacted. Five examples cited deal with efforts to measure the impact of such technologies on rural women; field testing a variety of such techniques; rural transport prob-

lems; and ways to measure women's contribution to agricultural production and management training based on upgrading women's skills. Each
of these projects were carried out by members of the ILO staff, most of
them young women.

The UNDP's contribution to projects for women was slow in coming.
Not until 1977 did it give women any priority. That year its administrator,
Bradford Morse, declared that one of the subjects to which he attached
the highest importance was the role of women in development and added
that liaison officers in each of the regional bureaus would insist that proper
attention be paid to the needs and potential of women. Ten years later
UNDP set up a new division for women in development to ensure and
monitor throughout UNDP's programs the role for women both as active
participants and as beneficiaries of its projects. (The director of the new
division is a Norwegian woman with long experience in the Norwegian
technical assistance program for women.)

Examples of ILO projects funded by UNDP are the promotion of women
in management in Equatorial Guinea; the development of textile workshops in Kampuchea; development of rural cooperatives for women in
Senegal; and technical and technological support for handicrafts, also in
Senegal. Other projects, not exclusively women centered, are of direct
concern to them. These include vocational training; small-scale industry
development cooperatives in Burma; hotel school training and management in Angola, Antigua, Cameroon, Tanzania, and Thailand.

Despite such examples of cooperation between the ILO and other agencies—such as those mentioned above—there are a number of areas of
concern to the ILO which are dealt with by agencies other than the ILO.
From the point of view of ILO this obviously complicates programming.
Geographic areas overlap and frequently the prospective participants are
the same. Thus, for example, WHO has held a number of meetings dealing
with the health care of working women, FAO the same on the integration
of women in agriculture and rural development, UNESCO and the regional
economic commissions the same on handicrafts and allied subjects, as
well as on the participation of women in political, economic, and social
development, women as producers, managers, educators, health agents,
income earners—some in cooperation with UNICEF—and UNIDO the same
on the development of branches traditionally employing women and on
their environmental protection. ILO does not always participate in such
meetings.

The ILO and the Decade for Women

One effect of the UN Decade for Women was to weave these multifarious strands into a more coherent whole. The focus of this effort was the UN Commission on the Status of Women which became the preparatory body for the various conferences held during the Decade. In 1975 the Decade opened with the Mexico City conference, and throughout the Decade the ILO played a positive role, working with the Commission and providing reports and recommendations. Just prior to Mexico City, the ILO's Annual Conference adopted, as was seen in chapter 4, a declaration and a program of action dealing with measures to promote equality between men and women. This was the ILO's contribution to the Mexico Conference, opening the Decade for Women.

At the midpoint of the Decade, during the 1980 UN Conference in Copenhagen, the ILO representative warned that it would be difficult to "shape the basic principles and values unless fundamental policies of our society towards women, such as not ignoring their work, rewarding adequately their labor and integrating them equally in such areas as social security schemes and taxation" were altered and modified.

In the aftermath of the conference the ILO declared that the conference had provided a basis for strengthening and reorienting some of its ongoing and future activities and the Governing Body discussed the implementation of the Plan of Action at meetings in both 1980 and 1981.

Before the Decade for Women ended in 1985 the omnibus resolution adopted by the Annual Conference summarized the successes and failures and included a ten-point action program. (See chapter 4 for discussion of the resolution.)

The year following Nairobi, partly in consequence of the report and resolutions adopted by the conference, the UN General Assembly substantially expanded the functions of the UN Commission on the Status of Women. Its tasks now include: monitoring the implementation of the Forward-Looking Strategies to the year 2000, and the implementation of the world Plan of Action. It has been designated as the preparatory body for world conferences to review and appraise the progress achieved and has been urged to review the evolution of the employment of women in the secretariats of the United Nations and the specialized agencies. At the suggestion of the Secretary-General, the Commission decided to base its future agenda on fifteen priority themes, grouped under its three objectives of equality, development, and peace as follows:

A. *Equality* 1. National Machinery for monitoring and improving the status of women; 2. Equality in economic and social participation; 3. Equality in political participation and decision-making; 4. Vulnerable women, including migrant women; 5. Elimination of *de jure* and *de facto* discrimination against women.

B. *Development* 1. Problems of rural women including food, water resources, agricultural technology, rural employment, transportation and environment; 2. Women and education, eradication of illiteracy, employment, health and social services, including population issues and child care; 3. Negative effects of the international economic situation on the improvement of the status of women; 4. National, regional and international machinery for the effective integration of women in the development process, including non-governmental organizations; 5. Integration of women in the process of development.

C. *Peace* 1. Access to information, education for peace, and efforts to eradicate violence against women within the family and society; 2. Full participation of women in the construction of their countries and in the creation of just social and political systems; 3. Women in areas affected by armed conflicts, foreign intervention, alien and colonial domination, foreign occupation and threats to peace; 4. Refugee and displaced women and children; 5. Equal participation in all efforts to promote international cooperation, peace and disarmament.

In its efforts to rationalize the work of the UN system and to make its own activities more effective, the Commission proposed to study the themes with the assistance of the regional commissions and the specialized agencies. Its priority themes for 1987–88 were the first under each of the three objectives—national machinery for monitoring and improving the status of women; problems of rural women; and education for peace, including efforts to eradicate violence against women within the family and society. A proposed system-wide plan on women and development is being formulated as a framework for the preparation of plans and programs of the system as a whole.[7] The Economic and Social Council at its May 1987 session reviewed the proposals of the Commission and transmitted them to the General Assembly which endorsed them in November 1987.

Nongovernmental Organizations as Partners

The impact of the Decade for Women extended far beyond the UN family of organizations. Many women attended the three official conferences and hundreds participated in the nongovernmental parallel meetings. Called the Forum, or alternately the Tribune, these meetings provided women with a platform for the expression of their views, for a critique of conference proceedings, and a chance to exert some influence on the official delegates. Many of these women were organizational representatives, but many came as spokesmen for grass roots groups and still others came as individual protagonists of women's rights. The opportunity to exchange opinions and experiences and to enjoy the mutual support of those with similar goals lighted brush fires that continued to grow long after the conferences had closed their doors. One direct outcome of the Decade was the creation of new nongovernmental organizations—international, national, and local. Another was the establishment of new units for cooperation with nongovernmental organizations by intergovernmental bodies and by national governments. A third was a broad extension of the concept of networking among these organizations at every level, including grass roots groups.

Relations with nongovernmental organizations have been built on a long tradition, first with the League of Nations and later with the San Francisco Conference and the establishment of the United Nations.[8] Subsequently all the intergovernmental bodies formulated rules and regulations for cooperation with approved nongovernmental organizations, determining their rights and privileges with respect to attendance at meetings, and oral and written submissions. While many of the same organizations have continued since the League of Nations days their numbers have swelled substantially in recent years, where they now number in the hundreds. Many of the old established women's nongovernmental organizations continue to make important contributions, as do many of the community based and religious organizations with special programs for women. These organizations are not only faithful attendants at most of the major intergovernmental meetings of the UN family, but also participate in collaborative projects. Thus, for example, the Associated Countrywomen of the World (ACWW) prepared, with FAO funding, a teaching booklet entitled "Food and Health," and a survey on nongovernmental organization community action for rural women through national ma-

241

chinery in Cameroon, Ghana, and Sierra Leone. A seminar on population and the role of the family was jointly organized by ACWW and the World-view International Foundation in Vienna with UNFPA funds. ACWW water projects in Africa, Asia, the South Pacific, and Latin America were funded by UNESCO.

The International Alliance of Women held two regional seminars, one on "Better Family Living," and one on the "Use of Hitherto Unused Foods," in Papua New Guinea and Gambia, with funds from UNFPA and Gambia. A workshop on "Language, Sexism and Education," funded by the EEC, UNESCO and the government of the Federal Republic of Germany was held in Berlin. The Alliance has played a leadership role in organizing cooperation among nongovernmental organizations for work, both at headquarters and in the field.

The International Council of Women has a series of international standing committees covering a wide range of subjects including child and family, the status of women, and women and employment. These deal with such subjects as action to promote literacy, health education, human rights, and participation of women in decisionmaking on both the local and national levels. In carrying out these projects ICW has had the benefit of advice, participation, and sometimes financial support from a number of specialized agencies, including UNESCO, UNIDO, FAO, and WHO, as well as UNICEF, UNDP, and UNFPA. Its Committee on Trades, Professions, and Employment has closely followed the work of the ILO and has regularly made its contributions to the discussions. Among the conventions to which it addressed itself in the interwar years were the Minimum Wage Convention because of its concern with raising the standards of the poorest classes and the Night Work Convention which it felt should be revised to permit the employment of certain categories of women employees during the night. In the 1950s it turned its attention to the problems of job assessment. In fact, its interests have ranged over most of the ILO conventions relating to women—domestic and agricultural workers, older and part-time workers, unpaid workers in the home, and the impact of technology on women.

The International Federation of Business and Professional Women has affiliates in sixty-three countries, comprising more than one-quarter of a million employed and self-employed women. In connection with the United Nations, its special interests center on the Commission on the Status of Women, the Commission on Human Rights, the Commission for Social Development, and the Population Commission. It has taken action to promote implementation of the Convention on the Elimination of All Forms of Discrimination against Women as well as the Forward-Looking Strategies for the Advancement of Women adopted by the Nairobi World Conference, which concluded the Decade for Women. The International Federation has close working relations with the ILO and other specialized agencies. For example, in cooperation with four other international organizations, it is involved in vocational training, as part of the UNESCO Co-Action Program, in Mexico, India, the Philippines, Thailand, and Zimbabwe. At the local level, income generating programs have been carried out by its Ghana affiliate, working with UNIFEM, and by its Australia affiliate in cooperation with UNICEF.

The Pan-Pacific and South-East Asia Women's Association has committed itself to activities and programs under relevant UN resolutions and plans of action. Among the activities of its national affiliates are: a program in Malaysia to mobilize woman power as a pressure group in influencing positive community action on matters affecting the family; in Taiwan a panel discussion on the role of women in the family combined with their role at work; and in Thailand a vocational promotion project for women and children. These are obviously only a few examples of the role of nongovernmental organizations but they provide an indication of the scope and nature of their cooperation with intergovernmental bodies (for their relation with the ILO see below) and their contribution to improving the situation of women on a global basis.

The emphasis of many of the new nongovernmental organizations that emerged from the Decade tends to be on more specific and limited objectives. One example is Women's World Banking (WWB), established in 1979 as an independent, international financial body with a mandate to advance and promote entrepreneurship among women throughout the world. By 1988 it had affiliates in sixty countries. WWB attempts to address the central problems facing women in developing countries—namely the lack of capital. Most women have no collateral to obtain bank loans and, in any case, few banks are interested in small loans. Thus women have difficulty in obtaining money to buy seeds or fertilizers, or start up small businesses. WWB vets applications for small loans and, if approved, recommends the project to a local cooperating bank. Since the international WWB guarantees half the loan and the local WWB one-quarter, the banks have little risk.[9] By 1987 over 4,700 guaranteed loans had been approved, half of them for agriculture. The first loan went to a woman in Colombia to expand her bicycle repair shop. Examples of other loans were: to the Kikapi Weavers, a fruit stall and an eatery, all in Nairobi; and in Thailand funds were allocated to a dairy farming agribusiness.

Another nongovernmental organization created the same year and concerned with a similar type of problem is the United States–based Trickle Up Program (TUP) which has received financial support through UNDP. Its distinctive feature is that it addresses the smallest group and the poorest of the poor. A grant may be made of $100, payable in two instalments, to any group of five or more people who have a project they have planned themselves, that anticipate a profit for the group, and promises to reinvest not less than 20 percent. Furthermore the group guarantees to devote one thousand hours of self-employment within three months, and to send reports on their enterprise to TUP. The program now has functioning businesses throughout the world. A UNDP publication declared that TUP "has developed carefully designed forms and simple procedures and with its creative use of micro-computers, TUP is able to manage a widely spread programme of activities in a large number of countries with a minimal staff resulting in *impeccable financial accountability* and reports on accomplishments."[10] Although this program is not specifically designed for women, they are the major recipients of the grants—67 percent as against 33 percent for men in 1987.

In 1982 an organization called World Wide Working for Women was launched. It is an international membership agency, based in Washington. Its mandate is to strengthen the role of women in environmental policy formulation, to educate policymakers about the effect of the degradation of the environment on women, and to increase the inclusion of women and their environmental perception in development projects. It publishes a monthly *World Wide News* as well as a directory of women environmental experts from around the world. It holds fora, acts as a seeker of funds for specific projects or as a locator for technical assistance, and it disseminates information on demonstration models.

A different type of organization inspired by the Decade is the Association for Women in Development. The United States–based organization was created by a group of scholars, practitioners, and policymakers in 1982, designed to strengthen research and action by increasing interaction among these groups in both the private and public sectors. It seeks to improve the practice of multilateral, bilateral, and private institutions in the integration of women as both agents and beneficiaries of development and to improve communication and education to a widening audience on the problems and solutions relating to development.

To provide for more coordinated and effective presentations by the disparate nongovernmental organizations to intergovernmental bodies, they established a Conference of Non-Governmental Organizations in Consultative Status with the Economic and Social Council of the United Nations. This had a rather slow and stormy start because of nongovernmental organizations' fears of infringement of their sovereignty. Over time the advantages of a forum for the exchange of views was recognized with the proviso that CONGO, as it came to be called, did not take positions on substantive issues. Today CONGO operates through an annual general assembly, an executive board and a series of committees dealing with issues such as the Decade for Women, the aging, youth, family, and more general problems such as human rights, disarmament, and narcotics.

Intergovernmental Structure for Cooperation

The growing prominence of the nongovernmental organizations and especially of women's organizations, much of it stimulated by the women who attended the Decade conferences, led, as mentioned above, to a number of international organizations creating units to collaborate with them.

Noting the fact that "non-governmental organizations are playing a key role in development and their contributions are increasingly recognized by Government," UNDP has established a division for nongovernmental organizations at its headquarters and has appointed "focal points" for organization relations in the regional bureaus and field offices. Grant awards of $25,000 per country are made for innovative projects to support grass roots development, activities to strengthen indigenous nongovernmental organizations, and projects involving cooperation among UNDP, the host government and the nongovernmental organization community.

One indication of the emphasis being placed on the partnerships of these organizations in fostering the integration of women in the whole development process is the establishment within the United Nations Industrial Development Organization (UNIDO) at its Vienna headquarters of a coordinator for the integration of women in industrial development. One of its most recent activities was a meeting held in 1988 in Vienna, Austria. This was the first meeting of UNIDO to focus specifically on women's issues in industrial development. It was attended by fifty-two representatives of international and national nongovernmental organizations. The range of concern with women's problems was evidenced, not only by the participation of almost all the major women's organizations and other organizations dealing with women's issues, but also key international labor unions such as the World Confederation of Labor, the International Confederation of Free Trade Unions, and the World Federation of Trade Unions. The groundswell of national movements was evident from the organizations from which the resource persons came. From Asia came a member of the Policy Research for Development Alternatives of Bangladesh; Action for Asian Cultural Forum on Development, Thailand; Center for Women and Development, Nepal; and Center for Women's Research, Sri Lanka. The Nigerian resource person came from the International Women's Grail Movement, and from Peru, the Flora Tristan Women's Center.[11]

Of all the UN agencies, UNICEF has had the longest and closest relations with nongovernmental organizations and, necessarily, with women at risk. A section of UNICEF not only assists these organizations on an ongoing basis, but provides support staff for meetings, and assists in the publication of an organizational periodic paper. In addition to attending board meetings, a UNICEF nongovernmental organization committee holds parallel fora, dealing with some of the items on the board agenda, in which board members actively participate. With respect to women staff members, as of 1987, the overall proportion of women in international posts was 29.2 percent—an increase from 24.7 percent in 1985. This proportion surpasses the United Nations target of 25 percent. For national professional officers, the proportion increased from 26 to 31 percent. UNICEF was the first agency in the United Nations family to reach the goal set by the UN General Assembly.[12]

In addition to the growing partnerships with nongovernmental organizations in general and with women in particular being developed by the global intergovernmental organizations, there has been a parallel development on the regional level. This applies to the regional economic commissions of the United Nations as well as other organizations such as the European Economic Community (EC). This last is one of the most effective of the promoters of women's welfare. Article 119 of the Treaty of Rome (which established the EC) stipulates the application of the principle that men and women should receive equal pay for equal work.

The Commission of the European Communities Program proposes European legislation and carries out common policies. A Women's Employment and Equality Office is responsible for drawing up and implementing EC policy. A women's information service maintains constant contact with women's groups, associations, and movements and informs them about EC activities of interest to them. In 1982 an Advisory Committee on Equal Opportunities was established to assist the commission in implementing its measures in favor of women. In addition to its general program, it prepares annual reports on the implementation of the positive action program for the commission's female staff. The European Social Fund (ECF) cofinances programs for training, reemployment, and first-time employment for men and women without discrimination. Between 1986 to 1988 it spent close to 1 million ECUs (approximately $1.25 million) to help launch businesses created by women. It also helps to finance specific training programs for women, particularly those in nontraditional occupations. In 1985, of the ECF's beneficiaries, 38 percent were women. Developments such as these have been accompanied by a series of directives binding upon the member states. In 1975 an EC directive imposed upon members the requirement that they revise their laws so as to exclude all discrimination on grounds of sex, particularly in systems of occupational classification. Complainants may bring their grievances to a tribunal. The commission itself has brought member states who were in default before the Court of Justice of the European Communities. While the early directives applied only to salaried workers, a 1986 directive (applicable as of 1989 and in some cases 1991) orders the elimination of direct or indirect discrimination against independent women workers, including agricultural workers. Even with this unique armory of enforcement measures, the commission is keenly aware of the need to enlist the support and partnership of "governmental representatives, women's associations, the social partners and other interested groups."[13] In early 1989 a European Network of Training Schemes for Women (IRIS) was initiated by the commission as a tool for the exchange of training methods among women working in the field. It has held a series of conferences in national centers such as Barcelona, Spain, and its usefulness has been recognized throughout the European scene. In 1990 a women's lobby was created with the help of the European Commission. Its aim is to interest and integrate women in European politics and to advance their interests by means of a steady dialogue with the EC institutions. Another tool of the commission is its research program, which has resulted in a number of outstanding studies including Child Care and Equality of Opportunity, published in 1988 which updates experiences throughout Europe and concludes with a series of recommendations to governments and employers for establishing and financing day care. Much of the commission's program owes its effectiveness to the work of one of its commissioners, Vasso Papandreou, who is the member responsible for employment, social questions, education and training, industrial relations, and human resources.

Because of its tripartite structure, the ILO's relations with nongovernmental organizations and women's groups are inevitably different in many ways from those of other intergovernmental bodies. Since the employers' and workers' groups form an integral part of the Organization, the interaction is closer and more constant. Within the International Labor Office separate units exist to deal respectively with employers, workers, and other nongovernmental organizations. While the international federations of both employers' and workers' groups exert major influence upon the ILO, many national associations participate directly on the delegations of member nations in the Conference and Governing Body. The international federations also enjoy participatory rights in ILO meetings. In addition the ILO has special relations with the international and national associations of employer and worker groups in individual industries, including their participation in the various industry committees.

Employer organizations in developing countries have frequently requested ILO assistance in strengthening their organizations. In an effort to increase understanding of the role of such employer organizations, the ILO has emphasized the services that they can offer to enterprises (especially small- and medium-sized enterprises) in improving industrial relations, "management training in general and staff management in particular and problems arising in connection with the working environment."[14]

All of the major international labor confederations, such as the World Federation of Trade Unions, the World Labor League, and the International Confederation of Free Trade Unions (ICFTU), as well as many of the International Trade Secretariats, have at some point established women's committees, and in most cases special women's bureaus. These have been concerned with the way in which women's issues are handled in all the UN bodies, but have concentrated much of their attention on the ILO. One illustration is the ICFTU, established in 1949. In 1950 women represented 7 percent of the membership, a number which had risen to 33 percent in 1988, out of a total membership of some 87 million.

In 1952 ICFTU set up a women's committee but it was not until 1984 that it was made a statutory committee, with a mandate to examine all plans and policies relating to women's activities and to draft proposals for action by ICFTU affiliates (national and international). The chairman and vice chairman are members of the executive board—on which very few women have served. The only woman officer of the executive board in 1988 was Shirley Carr (one of thirteen vice presidents). The committee is composed of leading trade unionists, representing ICFTU-affiliated organizations, and International Trade Secretariats as associate members. At the time of its establishment its members were not entirely clear as to what activities it could most usefully initiate and in 1956 Esther Peterson was asked to help them develop a program, including a pamphlet stating "the West's program for working women relative to 'equality' of the sexes." Since then the committee has met periodically and determined the stands that ICFTU has taken on women's issues in the United Nations and many specialized agencies—with stress on the activities of the ILO. One of the activities undertaken under the auspices of the women's committee is the convening of a series of world women's congresses. Four were held between the 1960s and early 1980s and the next is scheduled for 1991. These congresses provide a global opportunity for working women to make their views known.[15]

At the 14th World Congress of the ICFTU—the central decisionmaking body of the federation—held in Melbourne, Australia, in 1988, only some 80 of the 430 participants were women. The congress adopted a strong resolution supporting the ILO's tripartite structure, and deploring "the growing tendency among governments and employers to press for a slowdown in the standard-setting activities." The resolution called on all member states to respect fully the obligations deriving from the ILO's Constitution and to fulfill their financial obligations to the ILO. The congress also adopted a resolution calling for a program of action for the integration of women into trade union organizations.[16]

Priority has been given by the ILO to promoting representative and independent workers' organizations through workers' education. A number of steps have been taken to improve the status of women workers within unions. One recent example was a regional seminar on African women for female trade union leaders from anglophone African countries. The participation of women in unions has been particularly weak because so many women work in occupations that have never been unionized.

The influence of the ILO on unions in developed countries has been much more limited. There women have often had to rely on their own initiatives. Thus, for example, in the United States in March 1974 over 3,200 women from 58 national and international unions met to form the Coalition of Labor Union Women (CLUW) in order that they might more effectively organize unorganized women and encourage unions to be more responsive to the needs of women. It has concentrated on getting more leadership positions for women in unions.[17]

Six years after the creation of CLUW, its president, Joyce Miller, became a member of the AFL/CIO Executive Council—the first woman to breach this male stronghold. As vice president of the Amalgamated Clothing Workers, she attended two ILO conferences in 1980 and 1981, sitting on the Committee with Family Responsibilities. However, in the United States as in other countries, the battle for equality in trade unions is far from won. The percentage of working women who have joined unions is about half that of men, and they lag well behind in leadership roles. However, in many countries the fact that the major increase in union membership has occurred in the service sector may well result in that sector playing a key role in giving women a greater influence in the trade union movement and more effective participation in international organizations.[18]

The ILO Looks to the Future

As it surveyed the current scene with respect to women, the Governing Body, on the basis of a paper prepared by the International Labor Office, concluded that the advancement of the equality of women required a restructuring of international economic relations on a just and democratic basis. It was also noted that development policies should integrate women's concerns in all elements of development and not deal with them merely "in small-scale, transitory projects relating to women."

In his report to the 1987 Conference, the Director-General of the ILO has indicated some of the problems which need to be overcome by the UN family of agencies as they look to the future, whether the programs concern women, or men, or both. International cooperation, he said, must "be aimed at achieving a convergence of policies and the programmes of each of the institutions concerned, each contributing to the success of the others." What is still lacking, the Director-General continued, is "the necessary convergence of economic, financial, monetary and social policies."[19]

Conclusion

In the preceding chapters we have looked at the role of women in the ILO and the role of the ILO in regard to women over the span of seventy years. To set this role in perspective we have also looked at the activities of other intergovernmental and nongovernmental organizations and the status of women in various parts of the world. We have sought to identify their major concerns and attitudes. While hard and fast conclusions are elusive, there are trends and manifest influences that emerge as one surveys the record.

With respect to the ILO itself, how have its concepts about women in society changed over the years and how has the participation of women within the Organization evolved? What has been the ILO's response to change? For roughly the first thirty years the major emphases were on protecting women against exploitation—both for their own sake and because their cheap labor posed a threat to male workers—and on women as procreators of the next generation. To protect them against labor injurious to their health and to foster their childbearing under the most favorable conditions were the prime objectives. Such protective measures, initially restricted to industrial workers, were extended to women in agriculture and on plantations, then later to part-time workers, teachers, nurses, and to certain aspects of domestic employment. Gradually the emphasis shifted from protection to such questions as equal remuneration and the abolition of discrimination in the range of jobs open to women. There was also a growing recognition that women, too, had human rights. The next and latest step concerned equality in the broadest sense—the integration of women as equal partners in the whole fabric of society and in economic development. One aspect of this has been the recognition of the mutual responsibility of both parents for child rearing and other family obligations, coupled with provisions such as child-care centers and flexible hours of work, to facilitate this integration.

The impact of the ILO legislative measures is not easy to ascertain. There is the record of ratifications of conventions, very spotty on the whole. However, this does not tell the whole story as it does not take into account the numerous recommendations and resolutions that buttress and amplify the conventions. Moreover, ratification and government compliance is only the first step. While, as we have seen, the Committee of Experts appointed by the Governing Body and the Conference Committee on Standards examine in detail national compliance with the provisions of the conventions, analysis of the changes that have been wrought in the status of women is much more elusive. If one looks only at the record of ratifications, whether they apply to men or women, one is struck first with how slow the process is in most cases. Thus, for example, in the ten-year span between 1976 and 1986, only one convention adopted during that period achieved thirty ratifications and the balance substantially less. Another finding is that only 9 of 168 conventions adopted by 1989 had been ratified by more than 100 countries. Protective legislation for either sex has received short shrift, except with regard to Underground Work for Women (1935) which 88 countries ratified and somewhat smaller numbers for the Night Work for Women and its revisions—59 for the 1919 version and 37 and 62, respectively, for the 1934 and 1938 revisions. The most encouraging aspect of this somewhat bleak picture regarding ratification of conventions is the fact that so many of those that commanded major support dealt with equal rights for women. For example, the Equal Remuneration Convention (100) as of 1989 had been ratified by 109 countries, and the Convention on Discrimination in Employment and Occupation by the same number.

As noted previously, international legislation seldom prescribes new courses of action. It provides standards against which national laws and procedures can be measured. Thus the ratifications of ILO conventions are manifestations of what governments are in a position to live with. Recommendations tend to go one step farther in indicating desirable progress toward implementation, and resolutions look to desirable future action. One hurdle which has not yet been surmounted is the fact that many instruments were drafted primarily with Western concepts and practices in mind. The influx of new states into the ILO with different and, sometimes, skeletal administrative structures, and different mores and customs has made acceptance and implementation of ILO instruments difficult for these countries. There have been repeated calls for greater flexibility but little clear definition of how to make instruments more applicable to what is now the majority of its membership and this has been a matter of continuing concern to the Office.

The legislative facet of ILO's work, however, is by no means the whole story. Between 1919 and 1988 over 4,000 women representatives from governments, employers' and workers' organizations were sent to ILO conferences. Until recently, they seldom averaged more than 4 percent (currently around 10 percent) of the total number of delegates and served predominantly as advisers rather than delegates. However, they were on the whole a distinguished group of women who left their mark on the ILO. Not unexpectedly, despite some brilliant exceptions, the industrialized countries—France, the Netherlands, the Nordic countries, the United Kingdom, and the United States—included the largest number of women in their tripartite delegations. Norway sent the highest number of women delegates, and the only woman to hold that position in 1919 was Betzy Kjelsberg, president of the National Council of Women and an inspector of factories. The predominance of women from the Western nations reflects their longer trade union tradition. But the variations in individual countries have been a direct reflection of the position of women in their own countries. Reference was made earlier to the high level of women in the Nordic countries. France, which rarely sent full women delegates to ILO conferences, had one of the earliest battles for equal rights in 1791 but was one of the latest of the European countries to obtain women's suffrage, and this only by the edict of General de Gaulle in 1944. Another factor which obviously influenced the number of women conference participants was the fact that the ILO was located in Geneva. This latter consideration was particularly evident in the case of France which often rotated its participants during a single session. Of the eleven other countries which have sent substantial numbers of women, five are West European, two East European, two Latin American, one Asian, and one Canadian.

In the last forty years the overall geographic spread of women participants has changed markedly, as did the membership of the ILO. The initial leadership by the Western countries was sharply modified in the late 1950s by the arrival of representatives from other geographic areas. Asian and Latin American women began to appear, not only in increasing numbers but also as conference officers and as members of the Governing Body. Particularly outstanding has been the role of Mexican women, both in terms of women delegates and Governing Body participation.

One indicator of the role of women in the ILO is the part they have played in the Governing Body, the major administrative organ of the ILO. In the early years it was male dominated—both in terms of membership and of policymaking—with outstanding exceptions. From 1919 until the early 1950s four women—from Canada, the Netherlands, the United Kingdom, and the United States—participated significantly in sessions of the Governing Body. During the 1950s and 1960s there were also a few women from other countries, including government representatives from Argentina, Iraq, and the USSR.

In 1979 the situation changed dramatically. A Mexican woman was elected chairman of the government group and then in 1982 became chairman of the Governing Body itself, a position carrying the highest policymaking authority in the ILO. Throughout the 1980s there were some very effective government, employer, and labor women, coming from both developing and developed countries, from Eastern as well as Western Europe. The backgrounds of the women participants have varied from ministries of foreign affairs to academic research. Almost none have been professional "feminists." Almost all are articulate women who have taken leadership roles in their own countries. While the major direction of the Governing Body is still masculine, this is less clearly so than in the past.

In the wake of decolonization in the 1960s, African women began to play significant roles as representatives of government, labor, and employers. In the 1980s, although developing countries provided the majority of women delegates and women visiting ministers (women heading ministries of labor, social affairs, or social policy), Western women again took leading roles in the functioning of the Conference and Governing Body.

During the entire history of the ILO there have been only two women conference presidents (government delegates from the United States and Sweden) and two vice presidents (the Canadian labor delegate and the Czechoslovak vice minister of labor and social affairs). Twenty-one committees have been chaired by women, forty-one had women as vice chairmen and twenty-seven had women as reporters. Within the group structures there have been three officers of the government group, one employer vice chairman, and twelve members of the bureau of the workers' group. One indicator of changing attitudes toward women is the growing number of visiting women ministers and the range of countries from which they have come. The first and only visiting minister in 1954 was the minister of labor and social affairs of Israel. For seven of the next fifteen years there were no visiting women ministers, and only one or two in the other years. From 1969 the situation changed. 1972 was the only year without a woman visiting minister, and in 1989 there were nine. Overall the total number between 1954 and 1989 was seventy-nine coming from twenty-seven countries, including a growing number from the nonindustrialized world.

Another indicator has been the steady increase, despite fluctuations, in the number of women participants during the seventy years of ILO existence. Until 1952 the number of women never totaled thirty, and usually fell substantially below that figure. In the 1950s and most of the 1960s it varied between thirty-one and thirty-five, with the exception of 1964 and 1965 when the number of women more than doubled and, as was pointed out earlier, in one committee, there were about three times as many women as men. This was due, in large part, to two items on the conference agenda of direct concern to women. Discussions of both items resulted in resolutions of broad import. One dealt with women in a changing world; the other with the economic and social advancement of women in developing countries. The following year saw the adoption of a recommendation on the employment of women with family responsibilities.

After this the participation of women in the conferences dropped until 1975 when it reached well over one hundred and there were more worker women representatives than at any time previously or subsequently. At that session a recommendation was adopted on human resources development and a resolution on equal status and opportunity in occupations and employment. This, it should be recalled, was also the year that the United Nations launched the Decade for Women at the Mexico City conference, in which the ILO participated (and whose coordinator was a woman who later became the first woman chairman of the ILO Governing Body).

In 1978 the women took a backseat as there was no conference action of particular concern to them and the total dropped back to 5.4 percent. After this the figures rose steadily. The next peak in women's participation in an ILO conference came in 1980 when the Conference prepared a convention, adopted the following year, on men and women workers with family responsibilities. This was the high point of the effort not to discriminate against women by treating them as a separate entity but instead as equal partners in a common endeavor (except, obviously, for childbearing). At this time women's representation was around 10 percent of the conference attendance. Again the date coincided with a benchmark of the UN Decade for Women—the conference held at midpoint in Copenhagen. Moreover, the previous year the UN General Assembly had adopted a convention on elimination of all forms of discrimination against women and opened it for ratification by states.

By 1985 participation in the ILO Conference increased, sharply rising to 153 government, 23 employer, and 60 worker representatives. The sizable representation of women was a direct consequence of the fact that the conference agenda contained an item on equal opportunities and equal treatment for men and women in employment. Its conclusions took the form of a resolution calling upon both the Organization itself and the governments to implement its provisions. The resolution was also transmitted to the UN conference at Nairobi concluding the Decade for Women.

The increases in the number of women represented in part the growing number of countries who became members of the ILO, but even more the social changes that had been taking place all over the world. Many states, even some European ones, did not send women until long after they joined the ILO. As might be expected since the trade union movement is so new in the developing countries, government representatives outnumbered workers by a substantial margin. There was even a larger discrepancy between women workers' and employers' representatives, the latter amounting to about one-third of the former. This reflects the fact that only recently have women been admitted to the upper ranks of business. In some of the early years there were no women from employer organizations. However, the number of such women has grown steadily, while there has been a relative decrease in the influence of women from trade unions. An increasing number of women have achieved leadership roles in management of industries and in employer organizations. The growing preoccupation of women labor union members, however, with their role in their own national unions, coupled with the continued reluctance of male unionists to share the stage with their female counterparts, has lessened their influence in the ILO. Another reason for the relative decrease in female trade union participation is because so many women workers in developing countries have not yet been unionized. In recognition of this fact ILO has launched a vigorous campaign, including educational seminars in a number of developing countries, to stimulate union membership. This, as noted previously, has become a dominant trend—technical assistance linked to legal instruments.

The conferences have clearly provided women with an exposure to the concerns of other women and men around the globe, affording the solidarity of shared problems and insights into methods for addressing their problems. For some, attendance at these meetings also served as a plat-form for the expression of their own ideas. However, this is a far cry from saying that women have achieved equality. Even in 1985, when there were 236 women participants from governments, employers, and workers, they constituted about 12 percent of the total. Thus the proportion of women to men increased at only a snail's pace. Moreover, there are still a con-siderable number of countries who have never sent a woman during their entire years of membership. True, most of these states—fifteen in num-ber—are small, many of whom sent very few, and sometimes no partici-pants to the conferences. A few, however, were larger states which have successfully resisted the growing demands for women's rights. These in-clude Burma, Morocco, and Saudi Arabia. There are also another twenty-three states which have sent three or less women, a token representation. These include four relatively small Caribbean countries, four Asian states, including not so small Pakistan, two Middle Eastern states, ten African, among which are Mauritania and the Sudan, two Latin American, and one European state.

Given the above statistics, one might be tempted to say that these are all states with small respect for women, but there is a catch which makes obvious conclusions less obvious. Some countries which sent few women in their delegations sent a higher percentage of full delegates than did countries with a large female participation. Thus Benin, for example, sent eight of its nine women government representatives as delegates; Mada-gascar eight out of eight; Kuwait four out of five; and Mozambique and Papua New Guinea four out of four. Almost half of the women represen-tatives from Trinidad and Tobago as well as from Uruguay were govern-ment delegates. Malta, which was represented in conferences by only three women during its entire membership, sent a visiting minister over a period of six years, a record only equaled or surpassed by three Nordic countries.

A few East European countries, such as Bulgaria, Byelorussia, and Czechoslovakia, sent a high proportion of their women as full delegates. In the case of Bulgaria, in addition to three government delegates, all seventeen women employers and seven of their workers were delegates. This contrasts with the overall position of women from Eastern Europe, relatively less in number than their Western counterparts and less influ-ential—mostly advisors.

There were also quite a few employer and worker delegates from Third World countries; the former included Haiti, Liberia, Nigeria, Somalia, and Trinidad and Tobago. Women worker delegates came from all the continents, from Afghanistan and Bangladesh in Asia, to Guatemala and Nicaragua in Latin America, to Liberia and Madagascar in Africa.

The role of women with respect to conferences took many forms. Some were concerned with the substance of issues under consideration, and some were primarily interested in the way in which the ILO functioned. Some were protagonists for the rights of women, while many acted as specialists, irrespective of gender. In addition to participation in annual conferences, a growing number of women from their posts as head of Mission or within their own governments influenced the scope and direction of ILO programs. Some of the women participants in the annual conferences, along with many others, were active in ILO's regional conferences and other meetings. Recently women participants from within their respective regions were afforded an opportunity to shape programs consonant with the local needs of the area. Although only 2 women participated in the first regional conference in Havana in 1936, the number grew to 43 in 1979 (at Medellín, Colombia), with a total participation in all regional conferences of 195 by 1986.

In some instances the position of women in ILO conferences appears to adhere more to her own prominence than to the general situation regarding women in her country. Thus, for example, when the woman minister from Malta (Agatha Barbara) ceased coming, participation of women from her country dwindled. Even in countries with a good overall record there have tended to be one or two dominant women. In the early days there were, for example, Bondfield and Hancock from the United Kingdom, Raffalovich from France, Stemberg from the Netherlands, and Perkins from the United States. Somewhat later there were Afnan of Iraq, Moore of Nigeria, Mahabir of Trinidad and Tobago, Engelen-Kefer of the Federal Republic of Germany, Gonzales Martinez of Mexico, Stephen of Australia, Carr and Caron of Canada, and Leijon of Sweden.

Another comparison which throws some light on the role of women around the world is their participation in ILO conferences and in missions to the United Nations in New York. Thus Barbados, for example, which sent only one woman employer adviser between 1967 (its date of entry) and 1987, had a UN Mission headed by a woman ambassador, and, in 1987, its small staff included two other women, a first secretary and an attaché. Morocco—no women sent to ILO conferences—had a woman as a first secretary in 1987; Guyana, with only three women at ILO conferences, had a woman counsellor in the Mission; while Lesotho, with only four participants in ILO conferences, had a counselor, a third secretary, and two attachés in the Mission—all women. Singapore, which sent ten women observers, had as of 1989 a woman ambassador as head of Mission. How does one explain such discrepancies between the participation of women in ILO conferences and UN missions in New York? Is the explanation perhaps that the diplomatic service has provided more opportunities for women and been more consonant with their education and more socially acceptable than the trade union, social, and economic preoccupations of the ILO?

Another anomaly between the role of women in ILO conferences and in the missions in New York is the relative prominence of West European and North American women in the ILO, and the relative prominence of women from Third World countries in the missions. As we pointed out in the beginning of this book, the seven countries which sent the largest number of women to the conferences—over one hundred each—all came from Western Europe, except for the United States. Finland, although it sent somewhat fewer participants, sent more visiting ministers than any other country—a total of eighteen. By contrast only seven of these countries in 1988 had a woman as counselor or above in their missions. Both Finland and the United States had deputy permanent representatives with the rank of ambassador. Austria and Sweden each had a minister while France, Italy, and Spain listed one counsellor each. With very few exceptions the women under the rank of ambassador were assigned administrative rather than substantive tasks. Of the other countries, there were thirty-four who had counsellors or above in their Missions. These were mostly from the Third World countries. Women from Barbados, Singapore, New Zealand, and Senegal all had the top ambassador post of permanent representative. In the Mexican Mission, although the top post was held by a man, the alternate permanent representative with the rank of ambassador and a minister were both women. Have relatively more women found their way into the diplomatic services in Third World countries than in the West?

Another curious facet of the global scene is, as we have pointed out, the relatively small role played by East European women, despite the full equality claimed by these countries. There have certainly been prominent and distinguished women in ILO conferences but the overall numbers have been substantially less than from the West. With regard to employers and workers, this might be attributed to the reluctance of the West to accept them as entities independent of their governments. However, this does not explain their almost total absence from UN missions, with the exception of Czechoslovakia and Yugoslavia. All of these anomalies point to the need for caution in using participation in intergovernmental organizations as a yardstick of the national role of women.

The second facet of ILO's concern with women, as we have said, is the approach adopted to achieve the objectives. In the early days ILO activities were centered primarily in Geneva and legal instruments provided the basic means of influencing national attitudes and national actions. This began to change in the 1930s when, following the death of the first director, Albert Thomas, Harold Butler took over the ILO. Butler had always sought to widen the scope of ILO membership and activities to encompass active programs in the Americas and to strengthen the ties of Asia to the ILO. His first success was the entry of the United States in 1935, followed by the first Regional Conference of American States in 1936 (in Santiago, Chile). From the mid-1930s the need to adapt European concepts to the cultures and practices of other areas brought a new approach to ILO activities, although international legal instruments and standard setting still dominated much of the ILO program. The change in emphasis necessarily meant that the different cultural concepts with respect to women emerged in the conference debates, but were slow to obtain national and international implementation.

In the years immediately following the war decentralization became the order of the day, to permit adaptation of programs to the diversified needs of the increasingly universal membership. The legislative approach gave way to the more practical concepts of technical assistance and operational activities such as the actual establishment of departments of labor, or of training camps for migrant or indigenous workers.

Regional, area, and country offices were established throughout the world and, although much of the decisionmaking was retained in Geneva, operational responsibility and technical expertise were delegated to the various regions and programs developed to meet their specific needs or objectives. Many of the former colonial areas lacked the infrastructure and traditions which had grown up in the Western countries in response to the nineteenth-century industrial revolution. Although postwar decentralization on a large scale had been initiated by the World Health Organization, major credit for the changes in the ILO structure belongs to David Morse, the first postwar Director-General, who made operational activities the cornerstone of his regime.

How then did decentralization affect women? Slowly, especially with respect to policymaking, but vitally with respect to operations, since women workers were the key to agricultural development and to the economic situation in developing countries. Thus their needs were increasingly emphasized and their economic and societal role changed as they began to see the advantages of organization and to learn the language of equality. Issues such as human rights and freedom of association became a rallying point and a new approach to national and international instruments for standard setting.

If one turns one's attention from the role of ILO in promoting the advancement of women in the world as a whole to the position of women on the staff, the situation remains somewhat unsatisfactory. While many of the women staff members of the ILO, both at headquarters and in the field, have made major contributions to ILO activities in general as well as in so-called "women's programs," they have not obtained many top policymaking positions nor have they surpassed the level of equality garnered by women in some of the other international organizations. Moreover, in spite of strong efforts by the staff leadership, declarations by the Director-General, and resolutions of the Governing Body, there are only a few more women in top-level positions, and only a moderate improvement in the percentage of women professionals as compared to men, as against the situation some years earlier. In all, there have been only three women Assistant Directors-General—one from Chile, one from Japan, and one from Belgium. The last is the only woman to have spent her whole career in the ILO—entering as a research assistant and retiring as Assistant Director-General. Although there were no women serving as Assistant Directors-General in 1989, the first Deputy Director-General was appointed that year. There was only one D2, although there were twenty men in that category; and half a dozen or so women as D1's, compared to close to forty men. The target set in 1975 as a goal to be achieved by professional women in international organizations during the Decade for Women was 25 percent. In November 1989 the proportion of female professionals in the ILO was 20.34 percent (143 female as against 560 male).

The contrast between the ILO's efforts on behalf of women—especially of employed women—throughout the world, and those in relation to the staff is rather striking and in fact somewhat discouraging when consideration is given to the promises or objectives set out in the ILO's Constitution and staff regulations. How can this be assessed or explained? Perhaps because it still seems to be true that relatively few women have entered the fields of international economic and social concern, so that it is difficult to counter the often repeated statement that appropriate women are not available for appointment to the posts under consideration. Another possible answer is that a number of such women have not continued in service for as long periods as have their male colleagues. But in weighing this response one must note that men in the ILO have consistently been promoted more rapidly then women. Moreover, although there are an increasing number of women in the field, it is frequently more difficult, especially for married women and those with family responsibilities to remain away from headquarters for long enough periods to obtain leadership posts. However, there are some signs of a brighter future. There seems to be a marked increase in the number of able highly trained young women who may well move up at a faster rate than in the past. A revitalized women's organization within the ILO and new impetus by some of the women members of the Governing Body may yet provide more opportunity for women to obtain more leadership roles and something closer to equality in the Office. This is certainly warranted in view of the fact that most of the women think of themselves as professionals, doing the same jobs as their male colleagues and assuming that they will be treated as equals.

If one contrasts ILO's contributions with those of other intergovernmental and nongovernmental organizations, what does one find? There is little doubt that the influence of the UN Decade for Women far outstripped any other efforts. Because it was woman-centered and addressed all women—housewives, workers, propagandists, and politicians—in developing as well as developed countries, it stimulated woman and galvanized them into action as nothing else in peacetime had ever done. This was one occasion when talk fests paid handsome dividends. The ILO was, of course, a contributor to this effort but its own activities have never stimulated a similar grass roots reaction. This is not a criticism of its programs but is rather due to their very nature. Standard setting provides the sinews of progress but a relatively small group of women are privy to them. The drive to use technical assistance to achieve and implement standard setting should strengthen both facets of its activities. However, as the ILO itself has pointed out, the diversity of the projects undertaken makes it extremely difficult to assess the average number of intended beneficiaries, still less to appraise the impact on those beneficiaries. In regard to ILO's research there is general praise for its scope, which provides both the basis for new standards and information for their implementation. A number of participants in ILO meetings have stated that they consider its research program its major contribution. Its statistics have won high praise and are used by national and intergovernmental bodies.

The ILO, as well as the other intergovernmental organizations, is placing increasing reliance upon the network of nongovernmental organizations which function in most countries of the world through national affiliates and other local groups. The budgetary stringencies which are affecting all the UN family of organizations makes such cooperation increasingly imperative. This is also bound to have the salutary effect of depending more on indigenous efforts than on the sometimes misdirected cerebrations of distant headquarters. However, the other side of this coin, which creates some concern, is the possible uncoordinated dispersion of such efforts.

Although the ILO retains the leadership in regard to employer and worker groups, the European Community is seen increasingly as the pacesetter for women's rights. Its mandatory powers, the limitations of its geographic scope, and the relative homogeneity of its members obviously provide it with a much easier task. Faced with the approach of 1992, the EC is redoubling its efforts to strengthen the role of women and to equalize their treatment in the different states. It remains for the ILO and other concerned bodies to translate this model into terms valid for the rest of the world. Clearly there is a long road ahead—gender segregation leading to lower pay for similar work and frequently lower skilled jobs, as well as longer hours in rural areas and the fragility of women's positions in periods of economic depression with its effect on employment. This was painfully evident in the 1930s throughout Europe and unemployment is still having its effects. In many regions women are reluctant to join trade unions or to participate in joint activities with men, either because of the uncertainties and contumely if they break with tradition or because of the likelihood of losing jobs in a shrinking labor market. The debate about protective legislation has its repercussions in developing countries, but the issue is over the pragmatic consequences and not the political rights of women. In such areas proponents of protective legislation proclaim it protects them against abuse (especially male) in the workshops while opponents fear being excluded from jobs because of the additional costs to the employer.

It is clear that no effort to improve the status of the masses of the population in most developing countries can have more than a limited effect until the economic base is substantially improved. For this the prospects are still very questionable. In most of the developing countries feminism as it is expounded in Western democracies has few echoes even among the elite.

To isolate the role of the ILO from other forces at work, nationally and internationally, and from the efforts of other international organizations is an almost impossible task. What is clear is that ILO is in step with the approaches being generally adopted by the intergovernmental organizations concerned and the representatives of women's groups. It also seems probable that women involved both in UN and ILO activities have probably benefited from mutual reinforcement. There is certainly a growing awareness among women throughout the world that they are not necessarily condemned to be beasts of burden or procreators. In many, but by no means all, parts of the world the status of women has improved and they are beginning to assert themselves as partners in a common enterprise. The avalanche moves, even though slowly, eroding the habits of centuries, toward the achievement of the "impossible dream."

Appendixes

Appendix 1.

Year	Women's Participation				Conference Action
	Governments	Employers	Workers	Visiting Ministers	
1919	13	1	8	0	Convention 3: Maternity protection
					Convention 4: Night work (women)
					Recommendation 4: Lead poisoning (women and children)
1920	0	0	0	0	Maritime Session
1921	11	0	7		Recommendation 12: Childbirth (agriculture)
					Recommendation 13: Night work (women, agriculture)
					Convention 13: White lead (industry)
					Convention 14: Weekly rest (industry)
					Other Maritime Conventions
1922	3	0	1	0	Recommendation 19: Migration statistics
1923	11	0	1	0	Recommendation 20: Labor inspection

Year	Women's Participation				Conference Action
	Governments	Employers	Workers	Visiting Ministers	
1924	8	0	1	0	Recommendation 21: Spare time use
1925	4	0	1	0	Convention 17: Workmen's compensation
					Convention 19: Equality of treatment (accident compensation)
1926	5	0	1	0	Convention 21: Inspection of emigrants
1926b	0	0	0	0	Recommendation 26: Migration (protection of females at sea)
1927	9	0	3	0	Convention 24: Sickness insurance (industry)
					Convention 25: Sickness insurance (agriculture)
					Recommendation 29: Application (women)
1928	10	0	3	0	Convention 26: Minimum wage-fixing machinery
					Recommendation 30: Minimum wage-fixing machinery
1929	9	0	3	0	Dockers' Recommendation and Convention
1929a	2	0	0	0	
1930	11	0	2	0	Convention 29: Forced labor
					Convention 30: 48-Hour week (commerce)
					Recommendations 37/38: Hotels, hospitals

Year	Women's Participation				Conference Action
				Visiting	
	Governments	Employers	Workers	Ministers	
1931	12	1	14	0	Convention 31: Hours in coal mines
1932	10	1	2	0	Convention 33: Minimum age (nonindustrial employment and dockers)
					Recommendation 41: Conditions of work of dockers
1933	8	0	2	0	Convention 34: Fee-charging employment agencies
					Convention 35: Old age insurance
					Convention 36: Invalidity insurance
					Recommendation 43: Widows' and children's benefits
1934	11	0	4	0	Convention 41: Night work (women) revision
					Convention 42: Occupational diseases
					Convention 43: Sheet glass works, working hours
					Convention 44: Unemployment provisions

Year	Women's Participation				Conference Action
	Governments	Employers	Workers	Visiting Ministers	
1935	13	0	2	0	Convention 45: Underground work (women)
					Convention 46: Work hours (coal mines)
					Convention 47: 40-Hour week (general principle)
					Convention 48: Migrants' pension rights
1936	12	0	4	0	Convention 50: Recruitment of indigenous workers
					Convention 51: Hours of work (public works)
					Convention 52: Holidays with pay
1936a,b	2	0	0	0	Maritime Sessions
1937	13	0	4	0	Resolution re Women Workers
					Convention 60: Minimum age (revision)
					Convention 61: Hours of work (textiles)
					Recommendation 52: Nonindustrial minimum age (revised)
1938	11	0	2	0	Convention 63: Statistics, wages, hours
					Resolution re Women's Employment

Year	Women's Participation				Conference Action
	Governments	Employers	Workers	Visiting Ministers	
1939	10	0	1	0	Recommendation 57: Vocational training
					Convention 64: Indigenous workers
					Convention 66: Migration for employment
1941	4	0	1	0	New York "Informal Session"
1944	12	0	3	0	Philadelphia Session
					Recommendation 67: Income security (includes maternity benefits and age of retirement for women)
					Recommendation 69: medical care
					Recommendation 70: Dependent territories
					Recommendation 71: Employment (transition, war to peace)
					Recommendation 72: employment service
					Recommendation 73: Public works planning
1945	18	0	5	0	Paris First Postwar Session
					Recommendation 74: Dependent territories

Year	Women's Participation				Conference Action
	Governments	Employers	Workers	Visiting Ministers	
1946	19	1	3	0	Montreal First Canada Session
					Convention 77: Medical examination (young persons' industrial employment)
					Convention 78: Medical examination (young persons' nonindustrial employment)
					Recommendation 79: Medical examination (young persons)
					Convention 79: Night work (young persons)
					Convention 80: Revision of constitution
1946a	4	0	0	0	Seattle Maritime Session
1947	14	0	3	0	First Geneva Postwar Session
					Convention 81: Labor inspection
					Recommendations 81 and 82: Labor inspection resolution re women workers
					Conventions 82 and 83: Nonmetropolitan territories
					Convention 86: Indigenous workers

Year	Women's Participation				Conference Action
	Governments	Employers	Workers	Visiting Ministers	
1948	12	1	2	0	San Francisco session
					Convention 87: Freedom of association and right to organize
					Convention 88: Employment service
					Convention 89: Night work (women, revision)
					Resolution re Conditions of Employment of Domestic Workers
1949	17	1	5	0	Geneva Conference Sessions
					Convention 90: Night work (young people, revision)
					Convention 95: Protection of wages
					Convention 96: Fee-charging employment (revision)
					Convention 97: Migration for employment (revision)
					Recommendation 85: Collection of wages
					Recommendation 86: Migration for employment (revision)
					Recommendation 87: Vocational guidance
					Convention 98: Right to organize and collective bargaining

Year	Women's Participation				Conference Action
	Governments	Employers	Workers	Visiting Ministers	
1950	11	1	9	0	Several Seafarers' Conventions
					Recommendation 88: Vocational training
					Resolution to Put Equal Remuneration on 1951 Conference Agenda
1951	17	3	7	0	Resolution on Unemployment
					Recommendation 90: Equal remuneration
					Convention 99: Fixing minimum wage (revision)
					Convention 100: Equal remuneration
					Recommendation 91: Collective agreements
					Recommendation 92: Conciliation and arbitration
1952	20	1	10	0	Convention 101: Holidays with pay
					Convention 102: Social security (minimum standards)
					Convention 103: Maternity protection (revised)
					Recommendation 93: Holidays with pay
					Recommendation 94: Plant-level cooperation
					Recommendation 95: Maternity protection

Year	Women's Participation				Conference Action
	Governments	Employers	Workers	Visiting Ministers	
1953	14	1	3	0	Instruments to Amend Constitution (Governing Body Enlargement)
					Recommendation 96: Age of employees in coal mines
					Recommendation 97: Health protection in plans of employment
					Resolution: Economics of Underdeveloped Countries
1954	14	1	6	1	Recommendation 98: Holidays with pay Resolution on holiday facilities, hours of work, technical assistance for physically handicapped
1955	21	2	7	1	Resolution re Part-Time Employment of Women and Employment of Older Women
					Resolution re Employment of Women with Dependent Children
					Convention 104: Abolition of penal sanctions
					Recommendation 99: Vocational rehabilitation of disabled
					Recommendation 100: Protection of migrants in underdeveloped countries

Year	Women's Participation				Conference Action
	Governments	Employers	Workers	Visiting Ministers	
1956	21	0	8	0	Resolution re Abolition of Sex Discrimination in Field of Remuneration
					Recommendation 101: Vocational training in agriculture
					Recommendation 102: Welfare facilities
1957	19	2	9	0	Convention 105: Abolition of forced labor
					Convention 106: Weekly rest (commerce and offices)
					Convention 107: Indigenous and tribal populations
					Recommendation 103: Weekly rest
					Recommendation 104: Indigenous and tribal populations
1958	16	1	6	0	Convention 110: Plantations (maternity protection)
					Recommendation 110: Plantations (equal remuneration; social security)
					Convention 111: Discrimination (employment and occupation)
					Recommendation 111: Discrimination re employment and occupation
1958a	4	0	0	0	Maritime Session

Year	Women's Participation				Conference Action
	Governments	Employers	Workers	Visiting Ministers	
1959	13	0	4	0	Recommendation 112: Occupational health services in places of employment
1960	16	1	8	1	Recommendation 113: Consultation between public authorities, employers, and workers' organizations at national and industrial levels
					Recommendation 114: Protection against ionizing radiation
					Resolution re Females Protection vs. Iodizing Radiation
1961	25	1	9	1	Convention 116: Revision of final articles in conventions
					Recommendation 115: Workers housing
					Resolution re Freedom of Association, Apartheid (South African Withdrawal), Freedom from Hunger, Holidays with Pay, Older Workers, Employment Policy
1962	24	0	8	0	Convention 118: Equality of treatment (social security; maternity benefits)
					Recommendation 116: Reduction of hours of work
					Recommendation 117: Vocational rehabilitation

Year	Women's Participation				Conference Action
	Governments	Employers	Workers	Visiting Ministers	
1963	22	3	6	1	Recommendation 118: Guarding of machinery
					Recommendation 119: Termination of employment
1964	53	9	26	0	Convention 122: Employment policy
					Resolution re Women in a Changing World
					Resolution re Economic and Social Advancement of Women in Developing Countries
					Resolution re Part-Time Employment
					Resolution re Maternity Protection
					Recommendation 120: Hygiene in workplace
					Recommendation 121: Employment injury benefits
					Recommendation 122: Employment policy

Year	Women's Participation				Conference Action
	Governments	Employers	Workers	Visiting Ministers	
1965	57	5	24	0	Recommendation 123: Employment of women with family responsibilities
					Resolution re Implementation of Recommendation 123
					Resolution re Conditions of Employment of Domestic Workers
					Recommendation 124: Minimum age underground
					Recommendation 125: Conditions of employment of young persons
1966	24	3	6	2	Conventions 125 and 126: Fishermen (crews and competency)
					Recommendation 126: Vocational training of fishermen
					Recommendation 127: Cooperatives (developing countries)

Year	Women's Participation				Conference Action
	Governments	Employers	Workers	Visiting Ministers	
1967	32	2	10	1	Convention 127: Maximum permissible weight
					Recommendation 128: Maximum permissible weight
					Recommendation 130: Grievance procedures
					Recommendation 131: Invalidity, old age, survivors
					Resolution re International Cooperation for Economic and Social Development
1968	32	4	7	2	Resolution re Girls Vocational Preparation
					Recommendation 132: Tenants and sharecroppers
1969	38	6	10	2	Convention 129: Labor inspection (agriculture)
					Recommendation 133: Labor inspection (agriculture)
					Recommendation 134: Medical care sickness benefits

Year	Women's Participation				Conference Action
	Governments	Employers	Workers	Visiting Ministers	
1970	35	4	11	3	Convention 131: Minimum wage fixing machinery
					Convention 132: Holidays with pay (revised)
					Recommendation 135: Minimum wage machinery
					Recommendation 136: Special youth schemes
1970a	7	0	0	0	Maritime Session
1971	37	6	10	1	Convention 135: Workers' Representatives Protection
					Convention 136: Protection against benzene poisoning
					Recommendation 144: Benzene poisoning
					Recommendation 143: Workers representation
1972	31	1	2	1	Resolution re Women Workers
1973	37	6	6	2	Convention 137: Dock workers
					Convention 138: Minimum age
					Recommendations 145 and 146: Dock workers

Year	Women's Participation				Conference Action
	Governments	Employers	Workers	Visiting Ministers	
1974	44	8	8	1	Convention 140: Paid educational leave
					Recommendation 148: Paid educational leave
					Resolution re Paid Educational Leave
					Recommendation 147: Occupational cancer
1975	93	20	66	2	Convention 141: Rural workers' organization
					Convention 142: Human resources development
					Recommendation 150: Re human resources development
					Declaration on Equality of Opportunity and Employment
					Resolution re Plan of Action for Equality of Women Workers
					Resolution re Equal Status and Opportunity in Occupation and Employment
					Convention 143: Migrant workers
					Recommendation 151: Migrant workers, Equality of Opportunity and Treatment
					Recommendation 149: Rural workers' organization
1976	75	16	37	1	Recommendation 152: Tripartite consultation

Year	Women's Participation				Conference Action
	Governments	Employers	Workers	Visiting Ministers	
1976a	18	4	0	0	Maritime Session
					Resolution re Employment of Women on Board Ship
					Three Seafarers' Conventions
1977	91	10	39	4	Convention 149: Nursing personnel
					Recommendation 157: Nursing personnel
					Resolution re Application of Standards to Nursing Personnel
					Convention 148: Working environment
					Recommendation 156: Working environment
1978	69	10	19	2	Convention 150: Labor administration
					Recommendation 158: Labor administration
					Convention 151: Labor relations (public service)
					Recommendation 159: Labor relations (public service)

Year	Women's Participation				Conference Action
	Governments	Employers	Workers	Visiting Ministers	
1979	97	9	14	4	Convention 152: Occupational health of dock workers Convention 153: Hours of work (road transport) Recommendation 161: Hours of work (road transport) Recommendation 162: Occupational health of dock workers
1980	107	21	47	4	Recommendation 162: Older workers (preliminary discussion of convention 156)
1981	113	19	47	5	Resolution Concerning Participation of Women in ILO Meetings Convention 154: Collective bargaining Recommendation 163: Collective bargaining Convention 155: Occupational safety Recommendation 164: Occupational safety Convention 156: Men and women workers with family responsibilities Recommendation 165: Same subject

Year	Women's Participation				Conference Action
	Governments	Employers	Workers	Visiting Ministers	
1982	114	19	36	2	Convention 157: Social security rights
					Convention 159: Termination of employment at initiative of employer
					Recommendation 166: Termination of employment
					Protocol to Plantations Convention
1983	118	13	39	5	Convention 159: Vocational rehabilitation and employment (disabled persons)
					Recommendation 167: International system for maintenance of social security rights
					Recommendation 168: Vocational rehabilitation and employment of disabled
1984	112	16	31	4	Recommendation 169: Employment policy
					resolution re employment policy and standards for labor statistics

Year	Women's Participation				Conference Action
	Governments	Employers	Workers	Visiting Ministers	
1985	153	23	60	5	Convention 160: Labor statistics
					Convention 161: Occupational health services
					Recommendation 170: Labor statistics
					Recommendation 171: Occupational health
					conclusions of the committee on equality in employment submitted to nairobi decade of women conference
					Resolution V: Equality of choice and treatment between men and women: reaffirmation of the 1985 plan of action
					Resolution re Apartheid: Productivity Statistics; African Action; Accident Prevention
1986	113	20	31	2	Convention 162: Asbestos
					Recommendation 172: Asbestos
					instruments to amend constitution (size; geographic distribution; no "industrial important" states)

Year	Women's Participation				Conference Action
	Governments	Employers	Workers	Visiting Ministers	
1987	121	23	28	6	Convention and Recommendation on Employment Priorities and Social Security (First Discussion)
					Resolution on International Year of Shelter for the Homeless
1987a	37	7	3	0	Maritime Code
1988	134	34	37	5	Convention 167: Safety and health in construction
					Recommendation 175: Safety and health in construction
					Convention 168: Employment promotion and protection against unemployment
					Recommendation 176: Employment promotion and protection against employment
					Resolution Concerning Rural Employment Promotion
					Revision of Declaration on Apartheid
1989	134	27	50	9	Convention 169: Revision of convention 107: indigenous and tribal population
					First Discussion of Revision of Convention 89, Night Work for Women
Total	2,681	368	892	80	

Total: (not counting visiting ministers): 3,941
Grand Total: 4,021

Appendix 2.

Women Participating in Annual Conferences by Country, 1919–89

Date of Entry	Country	Government	Employer	Worker	Total
1934	Afghanistan	5	0	1	6
1920–67	Albania	0	0	0	0
1962	Algeria	19	1	0	20
1976	Angola	10	0	8	18
1981	Antigua, Barbuda	0	0	0	0
1919	Argentina	33	1	2	36
1919	Australia	34	1	0	35
1919–38, 1947	Austria	55	1	15	71
1973	Bahamas	2	0	1	3
1974	Bangladesh	1	0	1	2
1967	Barbados	0	1	0	1
1919	Belgium	44	9	20	73
1981	Belize	0	0	1	1
1960	Benin	9	0	0	9
1919	Bolivia	15	1	0	16
1966	Botswana	5	0	3	8
1919	Brazil	34	3	3	40
1920	Bulgaria	8	17	26	51
1960	Burkina Faso	1	1	0	2
1948	Burma	0	0	0	0
1963	Burundi	0	0	2	2
1954	Byelorussia	8	0	7	15
1960	Cameroon	17	0	0	17
1919	Canada	60	8	29	97
1975	Cape Verde	3	0	0	3
1960	Central African Republic	4	0	1	5
1960	Chad	0	0	0	0
1919	Chile	11	0	6	17
1919	China	25	2	9	36
1919	Colombia	43	2	6	51
1975	Comoros	6	0	1	7
1960	Congo	14	0	1	15
1920–27, 1944	Costa Rica	13	4	0	17
1919	Cuba	35	1	2	38
1960	Cyprus	2	5	0	7
1919	Czechoslovakia	27	0	13	40

Date of Entry	Country	Government	Employer	Worker	Total
1969	Democratic Kampuchea	3	0	0	3
1965	Democratic Yemen	3	0	0	3
1919	Denmark	81	18	29	128
1977	Djibouti	4	0	0	4
1978	Dominica	0	0	0	0
1924	Dominican Republic	12	0	0	12
1934	Ecuador	9	0	0	9
1936	Egypt	12	0	3	15
1919–39, 1948	El Salvador	3	1	1	5
1968	Equatorial Guinea	0	0	0	0
1923	Ethiopia	13	0	0	13
1970	Fiji	2	0	2	4
1920	Finland	54	6	20	80
1919	France	151	41	40	232
1960	Gabon	15	0	6	21
1973	German Democratic Republic	11	1	4	16
1919–35, 1951	Federal Republic of Germany	20	7	50	77
1957	Ghana	8	0	1	9
1919	Greece	65	10	12	87
1974	Grenada	2	8	0	10
1919–38, 1945	Guatemala	29	0	6	35
1959	Guinea	2	0	0	2
1974	Guinea-Bissau	6	0	0	6
1966	Guyana	2	0	1	3
1919	Haiti	2	2	0	4
1919–38, 1955	Honduras	13	0	0	13
1922	Hungary	23	2	10	35
1945	Iceland	1	1	5	7
1919	India	20	0	7	27
1950	Indonesia	12	0	3	15
1919	Iran	8	3	6	17
1932	Iraq	13	1	3	17
1923	Ireland	30	0	7	37
1949	Israel	10	0	7	17
1919–39, 1945	Italy	47	23	31	101
1960	Ivory Coast	4	0	2	6
1962	Jamaica	25	0	8	33
1919–40, 1951	Japan	16	3	13	32

Date of Entry	Country	Government	Employer	Worker	Total
1956	Jordan	0	1	0	1
1964	Kenya	3	2	3	8
1961	Kuwait	5	0	0	5
1955	Lao People's Democratic Republic	0	0	0	0
1948	Lebanon	5	0	3	8
1966	Lesotho	2	0	2	4
1919	Liberia	31	4	11	46
1952	Libya	3	0	1	4
1920	Luxembourg	7	0	1	8
1960	Madagascar	8	0	1	9
1965	Malawi	0	0	0	0
1957	Malaysia	0	0	7	7
1960	Mali	8	0	0	8
1965	Malta	3	0	0	3
1961	Mauritania	0	0	2	2
1960	Mauritius	4	0	2	6
1931	Mexico	52	0	0	52
1968	Mongolia	32	0	3	35
1956	Morocco	0	0	0	0
1975	Mozambique	4	1	0	5
1978	Namibia	4	0	0	4
1966	Nepal	3	0	0	3
1919	Netherlands	78	25	12	115
1919	New Zealand	25	1	1	27
1919–38, 1957	Nicaragua	11	0	3	14
1961	Niger	0	0	1	1
1960	Nigeria	28	1	3	32
1919	Norway	84	17	51	152
1947	Pakistan	2	0	1	3
1919	Panama	47	2	1	50
1975	Papua New Guinea	5	0	0	5
1919–37, 1956	Paraguay	2	0	0	2
1919	Peru	18	0	1	19
1948	Philippines	86	1	6	93
1919	Poland	40	1	11	52
1919	Portugal	62	1	21	84
1971	Qatar	0	0	0	0
1919–42, 1956	Romania	6	0	11	17
1962	Rwanda	0	0	0	0

Date of Entry	Country	Government	Employer	Worker	Total
1979	Saint Lucia	0	0	0	0
1982	San Marino	9	0	0	9
1975	Sao Tome and Principe	1	0	0	1
1976	Saudi Arabia	0	0	0	0
1960	Senegal	21	0	0	21
1976	Seychelles	0	0	0	0
1961	Sierra Leone	5	0	0	5
1965	Singapore	6	0	4	10
1978	Solomon Islands	0	0	0	0
1960	Somalia	11	1	0	12
1919–66	South Africa	1	0	2	3
1919–41, 1956	Spain	26	6	23	55
1948	Sri Lanka	2	0	0	2
1956	Sudan	1	0	0	1
1975	Suriname	10	0	0	10
1968	Swaziland	1	0	1	2
1919	Sweden	71	19	51	141
1919	Switzerland	49	7	27	83
1947–58, 1961	Syrian Arab Republic	13	1	2	16
1962	Tanzania	3	0	2	5
1919	Thailand	8	9	2	19
1960	Togo	3	0	1	4
1963	Trinidad and Tobago	14	13	6	33
1956	Tunisia	14	0	0	14
1932	Turkey	16	8	0	24
1963	Uganda	8	1	1	10
1954	Ukrainian SSR	9	0	3	12
1934–40, 1954	USSR	36	0	22	58
1971	United Arab Emirates	9	0	0	9
1919	United Kingdom	104	10	66	180
1934–77, 1980	United States	136	22	22	180
1919	Uruguay	25	1	0	26
1919–57, 1958	Venezuela	77	7	14	98
1950–76, 1980–85	Vietnam	2	2	1	5
1965	Yemen	8	0	7	15
1919–49, 1951	Yugoslavia	50	1	24	75
1960	Zaire	7	0	2	9
1964	Zambia	1	4	4	9
1980	Zimbabwe	5	0	1	6

Appendix 3.

Visiting Women Ministers at Annual Conferences

Angola
Mrs. Da Silva Padre, Minister of Labor   1985
Austria
Mrs. Grete Rehor, Federal Minister for Social Administration   1966–69
Botswana
Mrs. Kebatshabile L. Disele, Minister of Home Affairs   1981–82
Brazil
Mrs. Dorothea Fonseca Furquim, Minister of State for Labor   1989
Canada
Mrs. Mary Beth Dolin, Minister of Labour and Manpower, Manitoba   1983
Colombia
Mrs. Maria Elena de Crovo, Minister of Labor and Social Security   1972
Congo
Mrs. Madeleine-Sophie Lihau-Kanza, Minister of State for Social Affairs   1970
Denmark
Miss Grethe Fenger Moller, Minister of Labor   1983–85
Federal Republic of Germany
Mrs. Anke Fuchs, Secretary of State, Federal Ministry of Labor and
   Social Affairs   1981
Finland
Mrs. Tyne Leivo-Larsson, Minister of Social Affairs   1955
Mrs. Vieno Simonen, Minister of Social Affairs   1960–61
Miss Kyllikki Pohjala, Minister of Social Affairs   1963
Mrs. Anna-Lüsa Tiekso, Minister of Social Affairs and Health   1968–69
Mrs. Alli Lahtinen, Minister of Social Affairs and Health   1970
Mrs. Seija Karkinen, Minister of Social Affairs and Health   1973–75
Mrs. Pirkko Tyolajarvi, Minister of Social Affairs and Health   1977–78
Ms. Sinkka Loja-Penttila, Minister of Social Affairs and Health   1980–81
Mrs. Eeva Kuuskoski-Vikatmaa, Minister of Social Affairs and
   Health   1983–86
Ghana
Miss Adisa Munkaita, Minister for Labor and Social Welfare   1981
Guinea-Bissau
Mrs. Henriqueta Godinho Gomes, Minister of Civil Service and
   Labor   1987–89
Iceland
Mrs. Johanna Sigurdardottir, Minister of Social Affairs   1987–89

Israel
Mrs. Golda Meir, Minister of Labor   1954
Mali
Mrs. Lalla Sy Diallo, Minister of Employment and Civil Service   1987, 1989
Malta
Miss Agatha Barbara, Minister of Labor, Culture and Welfare   1975, 1977–81
Mexico
Mrs. Gloria Brasdefer, Principal Officer, Ministry of Labor and
     Social Welfare   1982
Mongolia
Mrs. Myatavyn Lhamsuren, Chairman, State Committee on Labor and
     Social Services, Council of Ministers   1970–71, 1974
Norway
Mrs. Dergfrid Fjosc, Minister of Social Affairs   1973
Mrs. Ruth Ryste, Minister of Social Affairs   1977, 1979
Mrs. Inge Louise Valle, Minister of Local Government and Labor   1980
Ms. Astrid Noklebye Heiberg, Under Secretary of State, Ministry of Health
     and Social Affairs   1983
Ms. Vesla Vetlesen, Minister of Development Cooperation   1987
Poland
Mrs. Maria Milczarek, Minister of Labor and Social Policy   1979–80
Romania
Mrs. Aneta Spornic, Vice Minister of Labor   1979
Sweden
Mrs. Anna Greta Leijon, Minister of Labor   1975, 1983–86
Mrs. Ingela Thalen, Minister of Labor   1987–89
Turkey
Miss Imren Aykut, Minister of Labor and Social Security   1987–89
United Kingdom
Mrs. Shirley Williams, Parliamentary Secretary, Minister of Labour   1966
United States
Ms. Ann Dore McLaughlin, Secretary of Labor   1988
Ms. Elizabeth Dole, Secretary of Labor   1989
Venezuela
Mrs. Marisela Padron Quero, Minister of Labor   1987, 1989
Zaire
Mrs. Inyanza Muduka, Secretary of State of the Department of Labor
     and Social Welfare   1989

Appendix 4.

Women Attending Regional Meetings

The following table indicates, by region, the countries that have sent women to regional conferences and shows the number of women attending from each group (government, employer, worker) per conference and country.

	Countries	Government	Employer	Worker	Total
LATIN AMERICAN REGION					
Santiago 1936	Chile			1	
	Brazil	1			
	United States	1			
					3
Havana 1939	Cuba	1		3	
	Mexico			1	
	United States	1		3	
					9
Mexico City 1946	United States	2			
	Uruguay	1			
					3
Montevideo 1949	United States	2			
					2
Havana 1956	Cuba	1			
	Mexico	1			
	United States		1		
					3
Buenos Aires 1961	Argentina	1			
	Panama	1			
	United States	1			
					3
Ottawa 1966	Canada	1			
					1
Caracas 1970	Honduras	1			
	Trinidad		1		
	Uruguay	1			
	Venezuela	1			
					4

	Countries	Government	Employer	Worker	Total
Mexico City 1974	Argentina	1			
	Canada	1			
	Cuba	1			
	Jamaica	1			
	Mexico	1			
	Peru	1			
	Trinidad	1			
	Uruguay	1			
					8
Medellín 1979	Argentina	2		1	
	Brazil	2			
	Canada	1			
	Chile	1			
	Colombia	6	1	8	
	Costa Rica	1		1	
	Cuba	1			
	Granada		1	1	
	Haiti	1			
	Jamaica	1			
	Mexico	2		1	
	Panama	1			
	Paraguay	1			
	Suriname	1			
	United Kingdom:				
	observers	2			
	Uruguay	2			
	Venezuela	3	1		
					43
Montreal 1986	Argentina	2			
	Bahamas	1			
	Brazil	1			
	Canada	4			
	Colombia	1			
	Cuba	2			
	Dominican Republic	1			
	Dominica		1		
	Granada		1		
	Guatemala	3			
	Mexico	1			

	Countries	Government	Employer	Worker	Total
	Nicaragua		1		
	Spain: observer	1			
	Trinidad	1			
	United Kingdom:				
	observers	2			
	Uruguay	1			
	Venezuela	2			
					26
				Total	105
ASIAN REGION					
New Delhi 1947	China	1			
					1
Ceylon 1950	France	1			
	United Kingdom	1			
					2
Tokyo 1953	Hong Kong	1			
	Japan	1			
	United Kingdom	1			
					3
New Delhi 1957	Hong Kong	1			
	India			1	
	USSR	1			
					3
Melbourne 1962	Australia	1			
					1
Tokyo 1968	Hong Kong	1			
	Japan	2			
	Philippines	1			
	Mongolia	1			
	USSR	1		1	
					7
Teheran 1971	Hong Kong	1			
	Philippines	1			
	Mongolia	2			
					4

	Countries	Government	Employer	Worker	Total
Colombo 1975	Australia	1			
	Hong Kong	1			
	Philippines	1			
	Mongolia	2			
	Thailand	1			
					6
Manila 1980	Australia	1			
	France		1		
	Indonesia	1			
	Iran	1			
	Japan	1		2	
	Mongolia	1			
	Philippines	3		1	
					12
Jakarta 1985	China	1			
	Indonesia	1		1	
	Iran			1	
	Iraq	1			
	Japan			1	
	Malaysia		1	3	
	Mongolia	1		1	
	Philippines	6			
					18
				Total	57
AFRICAN REGION					
Lagos 1960	Nigeria	1	1		
	United Kingdom			1	
					3
Addis Ababa 1966	Burkina Faso	1			
	Central Africa	1			
	France	1			
	Gabon		1		
	Israel	1			
	Liberia		1		
	Malagasy			1	
	Nigeria		1	1	
	Tanganyika			1	
	Tunisia	1			
	USSR	1			
					12

	Countries	Government	Employer	Worker	Total
Accra 1969	Liberia	1			
					1
Nairobi 1973	Egypt	1			
	Ethiopia	2			
	Senegal	1			
					4
Abidjan 1977	Angola	1			
	Benin	1			
	Ivory Coast	2			
	Senegal	1			
					5
Tunis 1983	Algeria	1			
	Cameroon	3			
	Congo	1			
	Djibouti	1			
	Ethiopia	1			
	Mozambique	1			
	Nigeria	2			
	Tanzania	1			
	Tunisia	1			
					12
				Total	37

EUROPEAN REGION

Geneva 1955	Austria	1			
	Czechoslovakia			1	
	France		1	1	
	Norway			1	
	Poland	1		1	
					7

	Countries	Government	Employer	Worker	Total
Geneva 1974	Belgium	2			
	Bulgaria	1	1	1	
	Denmark	1	1		
	France		2		
	Germany (West)			1	
	Italy	1	1	1	
	Netherlands	1	1	1	
	Norway	1			
	Switzerland	1			
	United Kingdom	2			
	USSR	2			
					22
Geneva 1979	Austria	1			
	Belgium	3			
	Czechoslovakia	1			
	Finland	2		1	
	France		3	3	
	Greece	1	1		
	Ireland	1			
	Italy	2	1		
	Netherlands		2	1	
	Poland	1			
	Portugal	2			
	Sweden	2	2		
	USSR	2			
	Yugoslavia	2			
					34
				Total	63
			Grand	Total	262

Notes

Introduction

1. A provision regarding women was also included in the League Covenant. Article 23 provided that members "will endeavor to secure and maintain fair and humane conditions of labor for men, women and children." This was the subject of a vigorous lobby led by a Britisher, Lady Aberdeen. In fact, the subject became the responsibility of the ILO.

2. See Carol Riegelman in *The Origins of the International Labor Organization,* James T. Shotwell, ed. (New York: Columbia University Press, 1934), 1:55. Published for the Carnegie Endowment for International Peace.

3. Ibid., 59–76.

4. Extract from the General Principles (the Labor Charter), Article 427 of the Constitution and Rules of the International Labor Organization, 1919.

5. The powers and composition of the Governing Body have changed over the years. It now shares its financial powers with the Conference, acts through a series of committees, and determines policy to a degree not foreseen in the early years. Its membership has risen from the original twenty-four to fifty-six, and the methods for selecting its members have also changed. Thus, instead of a system of selecting eight government seats from states of chief industrial importance, all seats are to be selected on a regional basis by their respective groups in the Conference.

6. In 1947 the title of Director became Director-General to conform with UN practice.

7. From the text of the ILO Resolution on Equal Opportunities and Equal Treatment for Men and Women in Employment, adopted by the International Labor Conference at its 71st Session, Geneva, 1985.

8. In 1967 two covenants were adopted to implement the Declaration. Disagreements, largely between capitalist and socialist countries, had led to the adoption of two covenants rather than one—one on civil and political rights, and the other on economic, social, and cultural rights. Vastly differing opinions among states regarding specific provisions have often led to reluctance to assume these legal obligations. The former has been ratified by 89 and the latter by 94.

9. Gladys Boone, *The Women's Trade Union League in Great Britain and the United States of America* (New York: Columbia University Press, 1943), 15.

10. Louise A. Tilly, and Joan W. Scott, *Women, Work and Family* (New York: Holt, Rinehart and Winston, 1978), 2.

1. The Impossible Dream: Early Years

1. Mary Lynn McDougall in *Becoming Visible: Women in European History,* Renate Bridenthal and Claudia Koonz, eds. (Boston: Houghton Mifflin, 1977), 262.

2. See Tilly and Scott, *Women, Work and Family,* for a description of these developments.

3. Blanche Glassman Hersh, *The Slavery of Sex: Feminist-Abolitionists in America* (Urbana: University of Illinois Press, 1978), 56–58, 189, 196.

4. International Council of Women, *Women in a Changing World: The Dynamic Story of the International Council of Women Since 1888* (London: Routledge and Kegan Paul, 1966).

5. Bridenthal and Koonz, *Becoming Visible,* 332.

6. Ibid., 331.

7. See Mary Walker in *Women in the Labour Movement: The British Experience,* Lucy Middleton, ed. (London: Croom Helm, 1977), chapter 4, for a discussion of these developments. For a full description of the movement that led up to the ERA, see Nancy F. Cott, *The Grounding of Modern Feminism* (New Haven, Conn.: Yale University Press, 1981). For developments in the period from 1945–1968, see Cynthia Harrison, *On Account of Sex: The Politics of Women's Issues, 1945–69* (Berkeley: University of California Press, 1988).

8. Ray Strachey, *The Cause: A Short History of the Women's Movement in Great Britain* (London: G. Bell, 1928), 311–12.

9. Aileen S. Kraditor, *The Ideas of the Woman Suffrage Movement, 1890–1920* (New York: Anchor, 1971), 196–97.

10. For descriptions and analysis of the work of the temperance movement, the role of the suffragists, and the Socialist and Communist parties, see Rose Evans Pauson, *Women's Suffrage and Prohibition: A Comparative Study of Equality and Social Control* (Glenview: Scott, Foresman, 1973); and Kraditor, *The Ideas of the Woman Suffrage Movement.* For a comprehensive discussion of the various movements for women's rights, see Meredith Tax, *The Rising of the Women: Feminist Solidarity and Class Conflict, 1880–1970* (New York: Monthly Review Press, 1980).

See also Bridenthal and Koonz, *Becoming Visible.* This volume contains a series of essays seeking to understand the history of women and, using both chronological and thematic approaches, to bring the feminist movement into the "mainstream of Western civilization" (Preface, ix). Chapters by Barbara Corrado Pope,

Edith F. Hurwitz, and Renate Bridenthal, respectively, explore the role of leisured women in the nineteenth century, the development of "an international sisterhood," and "women between two World Wars."

A useful analysis of the life of Carrie Chapman Catt and of her contribution not only to the peace movement but to the establishment and role of the International Council of Women is included in a study by Arnold Whittick, *Woman into Citizen* (London: Atheneum, 1979). The study is primarily concerned with the life of Dame Margaret Corbett Ashby and the history of the International Alliance for Women, which evolved from the National Union of Suffrage Societies.

For the most authoritative history of the U.S. scene during this period see Philip S. Foner, *Women and the American Labor Movement,* vol. 1, *From Colonial Times to the End of World War I.* Vol. 2, *From World War I to the Present,* describes all the women's organizations (New York: Free Press, 1979).

11. Alice Kessler-Harris, *Out to Work—A History of Wage-Earning Women in the U.S.* (New York: Oxford University Press, 1982), 153.

12. See Val R. Lorwin and Sarah Boston in *Women and Trade Unions in Eleven Industrialized Countries,* Alice H. Cook, Val R. Lorwin, and Arlene Kaplan Daniels, eds. (Philadelphia: Temple University Press, 1984), 142.

13. Ibid. In the late 1920s a separate nonpolicymaking Women's TUC Conference was set up as a body without power that advises the TUC General Council. Servicing this conference is the Women's Advisory Committee made up of council members and members elected by the Women's Conference.

14. Foner, *Women and the American Labor Movement,* 1:129.

15. [Birmingham] *Evening Dispatch,* May 7, 1936; see also Middleton, *Women in the Labour Movement,* 23, 101.

16. Boone, *The Women's Trade Union League in Great Britain and the United States of America,* 31.

17. Sheila Lewenhak, *Women and Trade Unions: An Outline of Women in the British Trade Union Movement* (New York: St. Martin's, 1977), 114.

18. Margaret Bondfield has told her own story, based on letters and her diary, in *A Life's Work* (London: Hutchinson, 1948). The book includes 28 illustrations. It is dedicated to "The Younger Generation." The quotation cited appears on p. 28.

19. Norbert C. Soldon, *Women in British Trade Unions, 1874–1976* (Dublin: Gill and Macmillan; Totowa, N.J.: Roman and Littlefield, 1978), 160.

20. Cook, Lorwin, and Daniels, *Women and Trade Unions in Eleven Industrialized Countries,* 233.

21. Jennifer S. Uglow, ed., *The International Dictionary of Women's Biography* (New York: Continuum, 1982), 288.

22. Pauline S. Newman, "Labor's Unfinished Business," *Jewish Daily Forward,* New York. See also Barbara M. Wertheimer, *We Were There: The Story of Working Women in America* (New York: Pantheon, 1977), 293, for a full analysis

of the role of Pauline Newman in the ILGWU, the strikes, and the fire (including pictures).

23. Rose Schneiderman with Lucy Goldthwaite, *All for One* (New York: Paul S. Erikson, 1967). See also Tax, *The Rising of the Women*, for a full description of the fire and of the two strikes of the New York City garment workers (1909–10) and the Lawrence, Mass., textile workers; Carol Groneman and Mary Beth Norton, eds., *To Toil the Livelong Day: America's Women at Work, 1780–1980* (Ithaca, N.Y.: Cornell University Press, 1987), 141–60, for the role of Newman in both the New York strikes and the 1912 Kalamazoo strike; also Foner, *Women and the American Labor Movement.*

24. The demands of labor for representation at the Peace Conference and the provisions they wished to have incorporated in the peace treaties were developed in a series of international labor meetings, held in Leeds and Stockholm, and culminating in the session in Berne. They are analyzed in Riegelman in *The Origins of the International Labor Organization,* Shotwell, ed., 1:55.

25. See Harrison, *On Account of Sex,* for analysis of organizing problems in the United States.

26. See Minutes of the Labor Commission, reproduced in Shotwell, *The Origins of the International Labor Organization,* 2:219.

27. Ibid., 273–85.

28. In a discussion following the meeting, Mr. Barnes told James T. Shotwell, the U.S. member of the Commission, that he believed if the presentation of the group had been more cohesive it would have been more effective. See James T. Shotwell, *At the Peace Conference* (New York: Macmillan, 1937), 216. Footnote 1 summarizes the conversation with Barnes.

29. Ibid., 229; March 31, 1919.

30. Ibid., 244.

31. International Council of Women, *Women in a Changing World,* 45.

32. *Conflicting Perceptions of the Role of Women in International Politics During the Inter-War Years,* a paper prepared by Carol Miller (of St. Hilda's College, Oxford), for the Joint Annual Convention of the British International Studies Association, London, March 28–April 1, 1989.

2. Women's Role During the First Twenty Years

1. National Women's Trade Union League of America, *Life and Labor Bulletin* (Chicago, December 1919); see also Rose Schneiderman and Lucy Goldthwaite, *All for One* (New York: Paul S. Erikson, 1967).

2. Harrison, *On Account of Sex* (Berkeley: University of California Press, 1988), 8. The establishment of the Women in Industry Service during World War I was the result of pressure from the NWTUL and the National Consumers League. In 1920 the U.S. Congress transformed the service into a permanent agency—the Women's Bureau of the Department of Labor.

3. Foner, *Women and the American Labor Movement,* 2:129. Foner indicates that the expenses of the congress were underwritten by NWTUL and Mrs. Robins.

4. Twelve countries sent accredited delegates: Argentina, Belgium, the British Empire, Canada, Czechoslovakia, France, India, Italy, Norway, Poland, Sweden, and the United States. Seven additional countries sent technicians or observers: Cuba, Denmark, Japan, the Netherlands, Serbia, Spain, and Switzerland. The Netherlands delegate was Henriette Kuyper, daughter of a famous Dutch politician, who was also a government adviser at the International Labor Conference, as were the other women observing the women's congress.

5. Both Margaret Bondfield and Mary Macarthur also represented the British Standing Joint Committee of Women's Industrial Organizations, set up to coordinate the activities of the numerous women's groups in Great Britain.

6. Bridenthal and Koonz, *Becoming Visible,* 433.

7. Middleton, *Women in the Labour Movement,* 84–89.

8. International Labor Conference, 1st session, 1919, *Record of Proceedings* (Geneva: International Labor Office, 1919), 33. 50. In the early years the terms committee and commission were used interchangeably.

9. Ibid., 50.

10. The total participation comprised 73 government delegates and 71 advisers; 23 employer delegates with 32 advisers; and 24 worker delegates with 46 advisers. Of the 23 women, 14 were on the government delegations, 1 was an employer adviser, and 8 were workers.

11. On her return home Bouvier was made vice president of the French section of the International Federation of Workers.

12. Report of the Director, *The World of Industry and Labor* (Geneva: International Labor Office, 1939), 84.

13. See International Labor Conference, 1919, *Record of Proceedings,* 103.

14. See summary of proceedings, Second International Congress of Working Women, October 17–25, 1921.

15. Antony Alcock, *History of the International Labor Organization* (New York: Octagon, 1971), 24.

16. Blanche Wiesen Cook, ed., *Crystal Eastman on Women and Revolution* (Oxford: Oxford University Press, 1978), 162.

17. See John Mainwaring, *The International Labour Organization: A Canadian View* (Ottawa: Canadian Ministry of Labor, 1986), 48–50.

18. National Women's Trade Union League of America (NWTUL), *Life and Labor Bulletin,* vol. 2, no. 3, ser. 15 (Chicago, November 1923).

19. Agnes Nestor, in her *Woman's Labor Leader: An Autobiography of Agnes Nestor* (Rockford, Ill.: Bellevue, 1954), describing a visit to Britain in 1918 (with Melinda Scott, a labor organizer) tells of talks with Margaret Bondfield and with Mme Duchene "who had made the fight for equal pay in France." She later participated in several ILO meetings.

20. NWTUL, *Life and Labor Bulletin.*

21. Article 408 of the ILO Constitution deals with the application of conventions and recommendations.

22. Voting rights for women were first obtained in New Zealand (1893), Australia (1902), and Finland (1906). Other prewar successes were: Norway (1913), Denmark, Greenland, and Iceland (1915), USSR (1917), Luxembourg and Poland (1918), and Austria, Czechoslovakia, Germany, the Netherlands, and Sweden (1919); immediate postwar Canada and the United States (1920), Ireland (1922), Mongolia (1924), United Kingdom (1928), Ecuador (1929), Spain (1931), and Brazil and Uruguay (1932). France only gave women the right to vote in 1944, and Italy in 1945. For an analysis of the significance of the suffrage movement see Bridenthal and Koonz, *Becoming Visible.* In several European countries limited categories of women were accorded the vote. Austria in 1849 accorded proxy votes to women of the landed class and in the next fifteen years similar concessions were made in Brunswick, Prussia, and Schleswig-Holstein. See Joni Lovenduski, *Women and European Politics: Contemporary Feminism and Public Policy* (Amherst: University of Massachusetts Press, 1986).

23. Edith F. Hurwitz in *Becoming Visible,* Bridenthal and Koonz, eds., 325–41.

24. International Labor Conference, 11th session, 1928, *Record of Proceedings,* report of the Director, 60–61.

25. International Labor Conference, 32d session, 1949, *Record of Proceedings.* At the opening session the Conference president, introducing the president of the International Federation of Christian Trade Unions, stated: "To the representative of the non-governmental organisations with which we have entered into consultative relationship, I would also like to extend a warm welcome." He noted that the representative of the trade unions was speaking in accord with the amended Article 14, paragraph 9, of the Standing Orders of the Conference.

26. By contrast with Paul, Bondfield declared that protective legislation had always been initiated either by working women themselves or at their request.

27. See Harrison, *On Account of Sex,* for analysis of ERA and its history; also Nancy F. Cott, *The Grounding of Modern Feminism* (New Haven, Conn.: Yale University Press, 1987). See Alice Kessler-Harris, *Out to Work: A History of Wage-Earning Women in the United States* (New York: Oxford University Press, 1982) for a full examination of the controversies and players related to protective labor legislation.

28. Cook, *Crystal Eastman on Women and Revolution.*

29. International Labor Conference, 15th session, 1931, *Record of Proceedings.*

30. International Labor Conference, 16th session, 1932, *Record of Proceedings.*

31. Kessler-Harris, *Out to Work,* 250–51.

32. Ibid., 250–63.

33. Bridenthal and Koonz, *Becoming Visible*, 442–43.

34. Georgie Anne Geyer, *The New Latins: Fateful Change in South and Central America* (New York: Doubleday, 1970), 232.

35. Stuart Maclure, *If You Wish Peace, Cultivate Justice: The International Labour Organisation After Forty Years* (Geneva: World Federation of United Nations Associations, 1960), 15.

36. International Labor Conference, 18th session, 1934, *Record of Proceedings*.

37. The whole story of USSR relations with the ILO (up until 1969) is told in Alcock, *History of the International Labor Organization*.

38. Although there were no women among the four observer delegates, Mrs. Arthur Bullard (widow of a well-known journalist and a Geneva-based friend of Frances Perkins) was attached to the delegation with the specific responsibility of looking after John L. Lewis, president of the United Mine Workers Union and later a founder of the Congress of Industrial Organizations (CIO).

39. International Labor Conference, 21st session, *Record of Proceedings*, 464.

40. Interviewed in 1986, when she was 94, her mind and memory remained clear and accurate. Tall and straight, despite a cane, she still lived alone.

41. Three women who provided major technical backup, and carried out much of the research in the section were Mme Brun, a French woman who joined the staff under Thibert and stayed in the service until retirement; Melita Budiner, an Austrian who joined the staff in 1925 after winning a competition as a bilingual secretary, and who ultimately obtained (during the war) a degree from the University of Geneva which permitted her reemployment in the professional level; and Mme Janjić, who was the technical work-horse of the service until her retirement in 1983.

42. ILO, "Studies and Reports," ser. 1. *The International Protection of Women Workers* (Geneva, 1921); *Women's Work Under Labour Law: A Survey of Protective Legislation* (Geneva, 1932); and *The Law and Women's Work: A Contribution to the Study of Women's Work* (Geneva, 1939).

43. A. M. Allen, *Sophy Sanger: A Pioneer in Internationalism* (Glasgow: Glasgow University Press, 1958).

44. The ILO's international civil service was a compromise, developed by Royal Meeker, the first director of its research division—a former U.S. civil servant—between the differing concepts of the British and French services. The independence of the international civil service from national service and from national restrictions was symbolized by the loyalty oath taken by all members of the staff. (The Director and Assistant Directors take the oath orally before the Governing Body. The rest of the staff simply sign it.) See Staff Regulations of the International Labor Office. The regulations have been revised from time to time but the loyalty oath has remained the same. Most of the changes have dealt with the joint administration/staff machinery.

45. Carol Riegelman worked for Professor Shotwell in preparing the volumes on the origins of the ILO, and had thus come to know both Harold Butler and Edward Phelan. Immediately after the United States joined, she had been invited to accompany the first U.S. Assistant Director as his assistant, a position that did not in fact exist. In 1935, after a session of the Governing Body, when she was assigned to assist U.S. members, she was offered a bonus by the U.S. labor member. Fearing the political implications of accepting or refusing, she, on the advice of the U.S. employer member, gave the money to the staff union assistance fund. This experience was probably unique in staff history. She remained on the staff until 1952, when she married Isador Lubin, then U.S. member of the UN Economic and Social Council, and returned to the United States.

3. The War and Immediate Postwar Years

1. The decision was made to transfer the working headquarters out of Geneva initially to Vichy, France, but ultimately to Montreal, Canada. Those to go to the new headquarters (category A) comprised 40 individuals in the professional division, of which 4 were women, and 12 in the services division, of which 8 were women. Those subject to recall (category B) amounted to a total of 87: 49 men and 6 women in the professional division and 8 men and 30 women in the services division. The third division (category C) amounted to 95 individuals: 1 woman and 11 men in the professional category and 84 men and 50 women in services. Those remaining in the Geneva office (category D) consisted of 3 senior male officials and 17 men and 6 women to provide maintenance. As time went on most of those in category B and some in C and D were, in fact, brought to Montreal.

2. After marriage to another Montreal-recruited member of the staff, who ultimately became the legal adviser of UNESCO, Joan Riley resigned from the ILO but continued to work for the Office and other international bodies as a free-lance interpreter.

3. Carter Goodrich, then U.S. member of the Governing Body, was also a professor of economics at Columbia University.

4. Just prior to the outbreak of war, the Governing Body had appointed an Emergency Committee with authority to act in its place on most issues.

5. Participants were: Clement Attlee, lord privy seal and member of the war cabinet of the British Empire; Paul-Henri Spaak, minister of foreign affairs and of labor, who commented that he was speaking as the Belgian minister of labor, and Paul van Zeeland, former prime minister of Belgium, who served as the Belgian government member of the Governing Body; Jan Masaryk, deputy prime minister and minister of foreign affairs of Czechoslovakia, and Jaromis Necas, minister of state and former chairman of the Governing Body from Czechoslovakia (which had hosted a session in 1937); A. Dimitratos, minister of labor, agriculture, and cooperation of Greece; Garcia Tellez, secretary of labor and social

welfare of Mexico, as well as Pedro de Alba, former senator and member of the Governing Body; Pierre Krier, minister of labor of Luxembourg; J. van den Tempel, minister of social affairs of the Netherlands; Frank Langstone, minister of lands of New Zealand; C. J. Hambro, president of the Norwegian Storting, as well as Olav Hindahl, the minister of labor; Fernandez Stoll, director of labor of Peru; Jan Stanczyk, minister of labor and social welfare of Poland; and, from the ILO's host country, Norman McLarty, the minister of labor.

6. Transport and General Workers Union, *Minutes and Record of Proceedings of the National Delegate Conference of Women Members,* held October 7–8, 1943, in Conway Hall, London Transport House, London.

7. Bridenthal and Koonz, eds., *Becoming Visible,* 488, 390, respectively.

8. The information concerning the San Francisco conference is drawn from the papers of Dean Gildersleeve and Carter Goodrich contained in the Rare Manuscript collection at Columbia University.

9. The U.S. delegation found itself in a fortunate position because of the availability of a U.S. Army PX and occupancy of one of the few hotels with a good restaurant and hot water for baths. As a result, U.S. hospitality was very welcome—to delegates as well as to staff. Thus many of the conference negotiations took place in the halls of the California Hotel.

10. The Committee on Constitutional Change had held three meetings in Quebec, Canada, prior to the Paris Conference and its preliminary report had been included in the conference documentation.

11. On July 1, 1945, her resignation was accepted and Lewis Schwellenbach became secretary of labor. Truman had directly put her on the delegation. On September 12, 1946, he named her to the U.S. Civil Service Commission where she remained until Eisenhower's inauguration in 1953.

12. The term "full" as against "high levels" of employment has frequently been an issue. More conservative government and employer spokesmen consider that "full employment" is unrealistic except in wartime, and believe the flexibility provided by a pool of unemployed workers may be advantageous. Labor economists and trade unions, however, believe that this goal should not be neglected in setting policies. In 1964 the Conference called for "full, productive and freely chosen employment" as a major goal, thus ending the ILO debate on "high levels" as a goal.

13. The members of the Montreal meeting were: Marit Aarun, chief inspectorate, Norway; Isabelle Blume-Gregoire, M.P., Belgium; Mrs. Rex Eaton, assistant director, National Employment Service, Canada; Miss E. S. Fraser, assistant secretary, Ministry of Labour and National Service, Great Britain; Kirsten Gloer-Tarp, inspector of factories, Denmark; Kerstin Hesselgren, former chief inspector of factories, Sweden; Frieda Miller, director of Women's Bureau, Department of Labor, United States; and Krishnahbar Wagh, investigator, Labour Office, government of Bombay, India. Following the meeting, the Governing Body decided

to be represented with a tripartite delegation at future meetings. The December 1951 meeting was attended by similar experts from Australia, Chile, France, India, Italy, Great Britain, and the United States. Ana Figueroa of Chile (later to become a member of the ILO staff) was chairman, Angela Marie Cingolani of Italy was vice chairman, and Dame Mary Smieton of Great Britain was reporter.

14. Harrison, *On Account of Sex*, 3–23.

15. Clara Beyer of the U.S. delegation was primarily responsible for the changes affecting women migrants. The discussion at the session was one step leading to the migration conference.

4. The Ongoing Agenda: Setting International Standards

1. Committees are constituted by the standing Selection Committee—discussed in chapters 2, 7—on the basis of nominations by the government, employers, and workers groups, respectively. Each government which participates in a committee names its own representatives; the employers and workers groups, respectively, meet to select their individual members on each committee, and their selection is based on individual preferences, availability, and nationality.

2. This Recommendation has an unusual history. It came before the Conference three years in succession because of resistance by various governments as well as by all employers to any further instruments seeking to generalize lower hours of work. The final text was a compromise in order to achieve approval. The special provisions relating to women were part of the compromise.

3. International Labor Conference, 76th session, *Report V (1) Night Work, Fifth item on the Agenda* (Geneva, 1989). The Council of the European Communities adopted a directive on the implementation of the principle of equal treatment for men and women and went on to call for revision of conflicting laws and regulations. In 1987 the Council included the prohibition of night work in the list of instruments that should be abolished "with the introduction of a general improvement in working conditions including, if possible a reduction in night work."

4. From 1971 the Proceedings of the Conference list only governments which are members of committees, and do not provide the name of individual representatives. Employers and workers are listed by name, as are the officers of the committees. Thus it is not possible to provide exact figures as to the number of women on each committee after 1971. Estimates can be made from the listing in plenary when a roll call vote is taken. The total number of women in any session of the Conference is given in the list of delegates.

5. International Labor Conference, 76th session, 1989, *Provisional Record of Proceedings*, no. 30, fifth item on the Agenda: "Night Work: Report of the Committee on Night Work."

6. Alice Kessler-Harris, *Feminist Studies* 14, no. 2 (Summer 1988): 236–37.

7. GB.244/CD/4/5, 224th session of the Governing Body, Geneva, November 1989, *Committee on Discrimination*. Report of the Meeting of Experts on Special Protective Measures for Women and Equality of Opportunity and Treatment. The 24 experts who participated comprised 8 appointed by governments and 8 each after consultation with the respective employers and workers' groups of the Governing Body. All were women except for 1 government representative and 1 worker representative.

8. Two of the women signing the statement were Mary R. Macarthur, for the Women's Trade Union League and Margaret Bondfield for the National Federation of Women Workers. See chapters 1 and 2 for discussion of the role of both these women in the early British trade union movement and in the ILO.

9. *The Position of Women After the War: Report of the Standing Joint Committee of Industrial Women's Organisations,* presented to the Joint Committee on Labour Problems After the War (London: Cooperative Printing Society, 1916/1917).

10. In the United States the establishment of labor codes under the NRA frequently involved the setting of differentials which did little to help women's wages—and the establishment of minimum wage legislation was of assistance primarily to those in the least well paid occupations.

11. Transport and General Workers' Union, *Minutes and Record of the Proceedings of the National Delegate Conference of Women Members,* held on October 7–8, 1943, in Conway Hall, London Transport House, London.

12. Lovenduski, *Women and European Politics,* 10–11.

13. Speech by Edwige Avice, Ministry of Foreign Affairs, France, at New York University, October 3, 1989. Press release, Consulat General de France, Service de presse et d'information.

14. See *Equal Opportunities for Women,* Commission of the European Communities, Directorate-General Information, Communication, Culture, no. 10/87, 1984.

15. Indra Bose returned in 1970 as a full worker's delegate and sat on the Committee on Protection and Facilities for Worker Representatives in Undertakings. The following year she served both on the Committee on Benzine and that dealing with the World Employment Program. She said, in the plenary, that today society was broadly divided into three groups—administrators, managers of the means of production, and "people who work with their heads and hands for producing wealth for everybody to share." The ILO tripartite structure, she asserted, provided an excellent common platform for the three groups.

16. For a discussion of the convention see Mainwaring, *The International Labour Organization: A Canadian View,* 126–27. In the same volume Mainwaring credited Elizabeth Johnstone with having drafted the questionnaire and guided the convention through the Conference committees. When Canada ratified the convention in 1972, C. H. Wilfred Jenks, then Director-General, congratulated

her on the fact that her adopted country had just ratified her convention, and expressed the hope that "this ratification presages the ratification by the country of her birth" (p. 164). This hope is still unfulfilled.

17. See correspondence between Peterson and Johnstone and between Peterson and David Morse in the Peterson Papers at the Schlesinger Library (Radcliffe College, Cambridge, Mass.). In 1961 Peterson had written Morse protesting the lack of a "broad continuing program on the employment of women." Commenting on the postponement of a meeting of the panel of consultants on women's issues, she urged that there be at least "some long-term research" and "policy decisions" on the employment of women in newly developing and in industrialized countries.

18. Keyserling was the daughter of Louis Dublin, a famous labor economist, and she married Leon Keyserling, well-known New Deal lawyer. Throughout her career she has been a firm protagonist for child care and other support services, and for increasing minimum wages by legislation.

19. In 1972 Barbara Green objected to the detailed requirements for verifying the ages of younger workers which would, she declared, be a serious obstacle to ratification. In 1974 she objected to the proposal that there be a supplementary convention on equality of treatment and opportunity for migrant workers which would include an obligation to penalize employers for employing clandestine workers, even if they were not aware of the fact. Exploitation, she said, was certainly evil, but equality of treatment was another matter.

20. Clara Beyer worked closely with Carol Riegelman, the Office expert on migration. The conference action served as background for the Migration Conference in 1951, discussed in chapter 5.

21. Carol Groneman and Mary Beth Norton, eds., *To Toil the Livelong Day: America's Women at Work, 1780–1980* (Ithaca, N.Y.: Cornell University Press, 1987), 11.

22. A conference committee which drafted the Convention and Recommendation on Human Resources and that which drafted the declaration and plan of action sat together to work out a common text.

5. New Directions in Postwar Activities

1. See letter from David Morse to Aryness Wickens, October 1948, in the Morse Papers at Mudd Library, Princeton University, Princeton, N.J.

2. The first proposal for the new industrial committees was that they follow the bipartite pattern of the Maritime Commission, but governments insisted that ILO experience had proved the advantages of the tripartite structure.

3. A preparatory Maritime Conference, held in Copenhagen immediately after the postwar Paris session gave both delegations and staff an understanding of immediate needs for technical assistance. Most of the hotels were still being used for government offices, and the economic conditions were closely similar to

those of Paris. Aside from the senior staff, many of the men and all of the women were housed in excursion boats tied up to a pier, within walking distance of the conference session, and with strictly limited amenities.

4. At the Seattle session China sent as a female government adviser Chang Teh-Hsiuh, an expert in the Ministry of Social Affairs. Ireland sent Thekla J. Beere, from the Department of Industry and Commerce, who came as a full delegate. The United Kingdom sent as an adviser Margaret Bertha Alice Churchard, assistant secretary, Ministry of Transport. Three women came from the United States as government advisers: Ida C. Merriam of the Social Security Board; Dagney Johnson, office of the solicitor, Department of Labor; and Clara Beyer, the only old-timer among the women. By the 1976 session there were women representatives from 22 countries, including five altogether from South Africa, New Zealand, the Philippines, and Thailand, two from the Middle East, and three from Africa. Three of the women were employers. There were no workers, presumably because the number of women trade unionists in the industry was still small.

5. International Labor Conference, 75th session, 1988: Supplement to the report of the Director-General: documents of the 239th (February–March 1988) session of the Governing Body; *ILO medium-term plan, 1990–95: Report on Programme Implementation, 1986–87.*

6. Lourdes Beneria and Martin Roden, *The Crossroads of Class and Gender* (Chicago: University of Chicago Press, 1987).

7. Zubeida M. Ahmad and Martha F. Loutfi, *Women Workers in Rural Development: A Programme of the ILO* (Geneva: International Labor Organization, 1985). Much of the discussion on this issue is based on this publication.

8. UN Industrial Development Organization: UNIDO/NGO meeting on the Contribution of Women to Human Resource Development in Industry, Vienna, Austria, March 22–23, 1988. PPD.87, August 2, 1988, Report, 10–11.

9. Sometimes husbands pay their wives for their agricultural labor but since there is no standard, they are paid abysmally little. Sometimes women manage to sell a little from their own plots of land. For this analysis and what follows immediately see UNIFEM Occasional Paper no. 4 by Marilyn Carr and Ruby Sandhu, September 1987. Study commissioned by UNIFEM.

10. GB 239/8/35, 239th session, Geneva, February 29–March 4, 1988. Third report of the program, Financial and Administrative Committee.

11. *ILO: Women's Participation in Cooperatives,* "Women at Work," no. 1, 1987, ISSN 0378-477 (Geneva: International Labor Office, 1987).

12. Miranda Davies, *Third World—Second Sex: Women's Struggles and National Liberation: Third World Women Speak Out* (London: Zed, 1983), 127–28.

13. UNIDO/NGO Meeting on the Contribution of Women to Human Resources Development, 11.

14. These included: the World Young Women's Christian Association, the International Council of Women, the International Council of Nurses, the Women's International Democratic Federation, the International Federation of University Women, the International Federation of Women Executives, the Soroptimist International, the International Federation of Business and Professional Women, the International League for Peace and Freedom, and Zonta International. The International Council for Social Welfare was also represented by women.

15. An evaluation unit brings together information collected by the various technical units (both at headquarters and in the field). These studies normally do not distinguish between projects dealing with men and women. In 1985 the theme of the evaluation was women and an updated assessment was made of 10 selected projects dealing with women. The basic 1985 document (GB231/OP/2/5) is an analysis of 60 projects dealing specifically with women and 17 projects with specific women's components.

16. International Labor Conference, 73d session, 1987, Report 6: *The Role of the ILO in Technical Co-operation.*

17. UNIFEM Occasional Paper no. 6, 54.

18. Ahmad and Loutfi, *Women Workers in Rural Development.*

19. Ibid.

20. The statements above are from GB 234/16/29, the 1986 Report of the Committee on Operational Programs of the Governing Body.

21. International Labor Conference, Geneva, 1987, Record of Proceedings, Report of the Committee on Technical Assistance, Item 6, 28/1/29.

22. GB 235/11/21, Report of the Committee on Discrimination, March 2–6, 1987.

23. Ibid.

24. Ibid.

25. GB 292/PFA/3/1, Director-General's Program and Budget Proposals 1990–91 (December 1988).

26. From a statement made to the UN Commission on the Status of Women (22d session, January–February 1969) on the occasion of the fiftieth anniversary of the ILO. Elizabeth Johnstone, then coordinator of women and young persons on the ILO staff, made a comprehensive review of the advances of women, including changes of attitudes.

27. *World Employment Programme: Research in Retrospect and Prospect* (Geneva: International Labor Office, 1976, third impression with modifications 1979), 29.

28. Groneman and Norton, eds., *To Toil the Livelong Day: America's Women at Work, 1780–1980,* 17.

29. The *Christian Science Monitor,* March 3, 1988.

30. UNIDO/NGO Meeting on the Contribution of Women to Human Resource Development, 11.

31. The report of the Tripartite World Conference on Employment, Income Distribution, and Social Progress and the International Distribution of Labor, Geneva, June 4–17, 1976. A number of women were officers of the conference or on its committees.

32. *World Employment Programme: Research in Retrospect and Prospect*, 47. The report is the fourth comprehensive report on research activities within the framework of the WEP. The report reviewed the objectives of the WEP, summarized the steps taken through missions and projects of various kinds to implement the program, primarily in developing countries but also in some developed countries facing employment problems, and described the many research studies completed or under way.

33. A paper issued by the Office of Women Workers in May 1982 (ILO/W.1/ 1982) lists major ILO instruments and documents concerning women workers. The list includes—in addition to conventions and recommendations, declarations, and resolutions adopted by the annual conferences—the resolutions adopted by regional meetings, industrial committees, and similar groups; studies and reports; periodical reports on the working of conventions, regional meetings, and advisory committees; meetings of consultants, seminars, and symposia; WEP monographs and studies; reports made for other UN agencies; and specific articles published in the *International Labour Review,* the *Social and Labour Bulletin,* and in *Women at Work,* as well as relevant studies made by the International Institute for Labor Studies and the International Social Security Association (which works in conjunction with the ILO).

34. See medium-term plan for 1982–87, which includes GB 236/CD/2/1, 236th session of the Governing Body, Geneva, May 1987. The document contains a list of ILO activities proposed in the plan of action and, in a parallel column, those to be undertaken in the 1988–89 biennium. Those listed in the plan are expected to cover a period going beyond the 1988–89 biennium.

35. *Women at Work*, no. 1, 1988, foreword by Bertil Bolin, then Deputy Director-General responsible for the office for women worker's questions.

36. GB 292/PFA/3/1: Director-General's Program and Budget Proposals (December 1988), Major Program 55, Promotion of Equality.

6. The Regional Approach: Women's Role

1. See Appendix 2 for chart indicating numbers of women by country, indicating breakdown by groups in government, employers, and workers.

2. International Labor Office, Report 2, *Labour Policy in General, Including the Enforcement of Labour Measures* (New Delhi, 1947), 180–202. The 1948 Conference was not held and the preparatory conference was in fact the first Asian Conference, followed by the second session held in Ceylon.

3. ILO ASIA/75/Conf/2: Report, *Japan/ILO Asian Regional Workshop on*

Administrative Arrangements for the Exercise of Responsibilities of Labour Departments with Regard to Women Workers (Tokyo, November 18–29, 1974).

4. Rural Development and Women in Asia: Proceedings and Conclusions of the ILO Tripartite Asian Regional Seminar (Mahabaleshwar, Maharashtra, India, April 6–11, 1981).

5. Report: Regional High-Level Consultation of Senior Government Officials in Labor Departments and Women's Bureau/Ministries Concerned with Women Workers (Bangkok, January 26–29, 1983).

7. Women Policymakers in the ILO

1. Lunsingh-Meijer, the only daughter of a wealthy wine importer, studied law at Utrecht, spent two years at the Ecole Libre des Sciences Politiques in Paris, and joined the Foreign Office in 1936.

Warburton served in Geneva from 1971 to 1985, rising from the rank of counselor to that of ambassador. She left the Foreign Office in 1986 to become president of the Lucy Cavendish College of Cambridge University, a residential college for women 25 years or older who sought new jobs and new interests.

Another example was Sylva Gelber of Canada, who first spent sixteen years in the Department of Labor in Palestine dealing both with labor inspection and maternity issues. In 1968 she became chief of the Women's Bureau in the Canadian Department of Labor, and in that post became deeply involved in relations with ILO.

2. This committee had before it proposals from a small meeting of members of the Governing Body. Based on the committee's conclusions the Governing Body convened, in Zambia, in cooperation with the Organization for African Unity and the UN Special Committee Against Apartheid, a tripartite meeting to plan a joint international program of action. As a result of this meeting, the Governing Body requested the conference to establish a Committee on Apartheid to update the 1964 Declaration on Apartheid. Three years later another tripartite conference was held in Lusaka, and a third in Harare in 1988, which set priorities for the ILO's Plan of Action in Africa.

3. See appendix 3 for a complete list of visiting ministers.

4. Lovenduski, *Women and European Politics,* 153.

5. Women serving on the Governing Body in this period included: from Togo, Dackey; from the USSR, both Nina Ivanova Pilipchuk and Mrs. Mironova; Mrs. A. F. W. Lungsingh-Meijer from the Netherlands; Anna Maria Zaefferer de Goyenche and Perla del Valle Roque de Marinelli from Argentina; Barbara Green of the United Kingdom; and a substitute employer member from the United States, Sybil Patterson.

6. N. D. Aleksandrova and V. A. Nikiforova were both government advisers from the USSR; Helen Dalleau from France, Anneli Vuorinen from Finland, and

Yang Biwen from China all served in this capacity. Substitute delegates for full government members were Mary Batista and Jenny Clauwaert Gonzales of Venezuela, Hanna Gutema of Ethiopia, Wiwiek Setyawati of Indonesia, and Maria Simo of Hungary. Holmboe Ruge of Norway, Sara Jorda Fernandez of Spain, and Ana Maria Luettigen de Lechuga were substitute deputy government members. Henriette Munkebye and Torild Skard of Norway were both deputy government advisers.

7. GB 235/PFA/7/7, 235th session, Geneva, February–March 1987. The report, *Composition and Structure of the Staff and Work of the Selection Board,* also provides information by place of assignment, by regions, by nationality, age and sex, type of contract, and recommendations for promotion.

8. Walter Galenson, *The International Labor Organization: An American View* (Madison: University of Wisconsin Press, 1981), 113–39. The background of the Soviet claim, and the pressure on Morse to make the appointment, was part of the reason Morse had resigned, even though his term had two years left.

9. See papers of David Morse, Mudd Library, Princeton University, Princeton, N.J.

10. The role of the staff union and the various joint committees is described more fully in chapter 8.

11. For many of the immediate postwar years a British woman, Violet Ogden, who had joined the staff in the 1930s, was chief of the personnel services but her responsibilities were primarily with the clerical staff, and in processing rather than determining personnel policy. There has never been a woman chief of headquarters administration, though as was seen in chapter 7 there have been some in branch Offices and in the field Offices.

12. When civilians were not permitted to go to Germany, Lansdorp was assigned by the army to UNRRA (UN Relief and Rehabilitation Agency) which sent her to The Hague. In 1947 she was made responsible for recruitment of Dutch staff, then in Paris and Geneva. She subsequently joined IRO (the International Refugee Organization) where she stayed until it closed down. In 1952 she went to UNESCO where she worked in personnel administration.

13. Another branch chief with DI status is Gabrielle Stoikov, a citizen of the Federal Republic of Germany, who was promoted to become chief of a new industrial activities branch. Stoikov has been recognized by both the employers' and workers' groups as a woman with a high leadership potential.

Inez Holmes, an Irish national who has been a DI for some time, is chief of the Translation and Meetings branch, responsible for the varied group of translators working under her as well as for servicing the innumerable meetings held by the ILO.

14. Information from a letter in the files of the Paris Office, dated October 25, 1944, from Morel to Edward Phelan, ILO Director, in Montreal.

15. From time to time there have been women deputy directors or adminis-

trators in several branch offices, but at the present time the only woman in this category is Monique Theodore-Morin who worked in the Paris Office for nearly twenty years in the general service grade and was upgraded to the professional level in 1983. (To meet some of the women's family responsibilities, a flexible work schedule permits some to come early and leave early and others to arrive late and stay late.)

16. The earliest senior branch office official was Alice S. Cheyney, educated at Vassar and Bryn Mawr colleges and at the University of Pennsylvania, where she received a Ph.D. Prior to her service at the ILO, she had been employed by the New York and Massachusetts minimum wage boards and the federal Department of Labor. She had spent many summers in Geneva, working as a volunteer, helping visitors to understand the ILO. For several years she served as second-in-command of the ILO's Washington Office. In 1935 she was detached to the women's service in Geneva. She resigned from the ILO shortly after the outbreak of war in 1939, and subsequently married a Pennsylvania businessman.

At an early period the Japanese Office had a woman Deputy Director—Tamako Naganashi. Prior to her employment by the ILO, she had worked with Chester Hepler when he was a senior officer in the Allied Occupation Forces in Asia. His recommendation, when he joined the ILO in Geneva (first as director of the manpower division and then of the personnel division), had led to her appointment.

17. The editor of *Women at Work* from 1976–86 was an Indian woman, Krishna Ahooja-Patel, who was subsequently detached to INSTRAW (International Research and Training Institute for the Training of Women) in Santo Domingo.

8. Women Organizers Within the Office

1. The story of the early days of the staff union, including the correspondence between the Director and the initial members of the first staff committee, as well as the "staff charter" are published in a pamphlet prepared by the staff union in 1973 as a contribution to the 50th anniversary of the ILO.

2. Henri Reymond, and Sidney Mailick, *International Personnel Policies and Practices* (New York: Praeger, 1985), 37.

3. See Article 10.1 (chapter 10) of the Staff Regulations, defining the role of staff representatives, and Article 10.2, describing the Administrative Committee's composition and functions. A number of hours are allocated to the union to be distributed by the staff committee as it sees fit.

4. See Annex 1 of the current Staff Regulations, "Recruitment Procedures," and procedures for both internal and external competitions. Joint juries of the administration and staff are appointed by the Administrative Committee after consultation with the staff representatives.

5. International Labor Office, Staff Regulations, May 1939, chapter 3, p. 8.

6. Survey conducted by E. Hopkins and A. Korten for the staff union, *Equal-*

ity of Opportunity and Treatment for Women in the ILO (Geneva, November 1976).

7. See report of working party on equality of opportunity and treatment for women in the ILO, March 9, 1979, distributed by the staff union. Excluded from consideration were experts assigned to the field under the Technical Assistance Program; locally recruited nonprofessional staff in the field structure (since conditions might not be comparable); short-term officials, i.e., those not possessing either fixed term contracts or indefinite contracts. In addition to the final report, the working party issued an interim report covering some of the recommendations listed.

8. Report of the ad hoc committee on the status of women in the international civil service: CPG/28/IB/3, July 2, 1975. The participants were: E. Ambler (WHO/Washington), P. Attree (IAEA/Vienna), R. Bell (WHO/Geneva), C. Carmona (UNESCO/Paris), O. Cutullic (UN/Geneva), R. Cuvillier (ILO/Geneva), S. Donohue (Union Sindicale, FAO/Rome), K. Dube (ECA/Addis Ababa), E. Epstein (ILO/Geneva), J. Jaccard (WHO/Geneva), C. Lankester (UNDP/New York), J. Lasserre-Bigorry (ILO/Geneva), I. Lorenzo (UNIDO/Vienna), P. Merlet (ITU/Geneva), R. Molineaux (UN/New York), S. Morrison (ITU/Geneva), A. Quintano (ITU/Geneva), H. Schebesta (UNIDO/Vienna), M. Schwab (UN/Geneva), L. Smith (FAO/Rome), J. Taillafer (UNESCO/Paris), J. Taylor (UN/Geneva), and P. Thompson (UN/New York).

9. "Report on Women in the Professional Category and Above in the United Nations System," prepared by Earl D. Sohn, JIU/REP/77/7; see also "Status of Women in the Professional Category and Above: Second Progress Report," prepared by Earl D. Sohn, JIU/REP/82/4, Geneva, March 1982.

10. See reports of the Subcommittee on Equal Opportunity, established by the Administrative Committee, completed in 1982 and 1983, respectively. As indicated, the second report updates the statistics used in the first and provides a discouraging but still fairer picture, since the 1979 figures were somewhat "out of pattern" in consequence of the financial crisis caused by the absence of the United States. The promotion of Béguin to Assistant Director-General in 1981 and her retirement in 1983 altered the number of women at the top—and was not compensated for by additional appointments of women either as Assistant Directors-General or D2 until 1989.

11. See H. Pour, "Femmes au BIT: un entretien avec Antoinette Béguin," *Union* (new series) 131, May 1983.

12. See *Union*, 158:9, February 1986, Periodical of the ILO staff union, article by Margaret Cove Christiansen concerning the employment of women and their position on the staff. See also notes of the second meeting on equal opportunity and treatment at the ILO, attended by 30 staff members on January 14, 1986.

13. Newsletters and notes of meetings of the action group for equality.

14. See SU/AGM/1986/D.3, September 1986, ILO Staff Union, Annual General Meeting, October 7, 1986: Report of the Committee 1985–86; SU/AGM/1986/R.5, adopted resolution concerning equal opportunity and treatment.

---

15. Governing Body, GB 232/7/29, 232d session, Geneva, March 3–7, 1986, seventh item on the agenda.

16. Reymond and Mailick, *International Personnel Policies and Practices,* 54.

17. See Governing Body, GB 242/PFA/5/6, 242d session, Geneva, February–March 1949, Program, Financial, and Administrative Committee, fifth item on the agenda, composition and structure of the staff.

18. *Union* (new series) 186:4–6, December 1988, interview by Mario Trajtenberg.

19. ILO press release, October 25, 1989. Trained in Ghana, London, and Dublin, she entered the civil service of Ghana and rose to be principal secretary to the ministry of finance and economic planning. She joined the UN Development Program in 1981; her most recent employment was as UN coordinator and UNDP resident representative in Uganda.

9. The International System and Nongovernmental Organizations

1. See ILO Constitution. The ILO was to be located at the seat of the League, its membership to be coterminous, its budget to be paid out of the general funds of the League, and its conference instruments registered there.

2. UNESCO assumed the activities of the Committee on Intellectual Cooperation; the WHO those of the health section of the League; and the FAO those of the International Institute of Agriculture.

3. See reports of sessions of the Commission on the Status of Women.

4. The last effort of the commission in 1948 to dominate was quietly ignored. It had asked, insofar as practicable, to be given the opportunity to comment on ILO proposals before they were adopted. This was an effort to take relations one step further than the agreement between the United Nations and the ILO which provided for exchanges of information and reciprocal representation without vote in their respective meetings.

5. The WHO report is cited in *Worldwide News,* October 1987 (a publication of World Wide, Washington, D.C.). The UNICEF report was cited in Carr and Sandhu, UNIFEM Occasional Paper no. 6, September 1987.

6. For the above discussion on population questions, see Richard Symonds and Michael Carter, *The United Nations and the Population Question* (New York: McGraw-Hill, 1973), 165–69. See also 1986 report by the executive director of UN Fund for Population Activities (87/32001/E/8000).

7. See E/1987/15 (E/CN.6/1987/6) Commission on the Status of Women, Report on the 1987 session (January 12–16, 1987), Economic and Social Council, Official Records, 1987; Supplement 2.

8. Article 71 of the UN Charter established the basic principles for cooperation with nongovernmental organizations which was subsequently followed by the specialized agencies. The article provides that "the Economic and Social Council

may make suitable arrangements for consultations with non-governmental organizations which are concerned with matters within its competence."

9. Compilation prepared by WWB. According to the *Toronto Star* of March 7, 1987, UNDP provided support for the initial research and CIDA (Canadian International Development Agency) has provided $3 million to be paid over five years.

10. Cited in *Trickle Up Program, Inc.: The TUP Decade 1979–1989*. The founders and operators of the program are Glen and Mildred Leet; he was a former member of the UN staff and she was a former president of the National Council of Women, and subsequently vice president of the International Council.

11. See Report, *UNIDO/NGO Meeting on the Contribution of Women to Human Resource Development in Industry*, Vienna, Austria, March 22–23, 1988. UNDP, PPD.87, August 2, 1988.

12. *Economic and Social Council: United Nations Children's Fund, Executive Board, 1988 Session*, "Medium-Term Plan for the Period 1987–1991." E/ICF/1988/3 (March 18, 1988):38.

13. See *Equal Opportunities for Women*, Commission of the European Communities, Directorate-General Information, Communication, Culture, no. 10/87, Brussels.

14. International Labor Conference, 73d session, 1987. Report of the Director-General, Part 2, Activities of the ILO in 1986, p. 15.

15. *Working Women: ICFTU policies and programmes* (Brussels: ICFTU).

16. See decisions of the 14th World Congress, March 14–18, 1988, Melbourne.

17. See Pamela Roby in *Another Voice: Feminist Perspectives on Social Life and Social Science*, Marcia Millman and Rosabeth Moss Kanter, eds. (New York: Octagon, 1976), chapter 7.

18. For a fuller description of women in the labor movement between the 1960s and the 1980s, see Ruth Milkman in *Women, Work and Protest: A Century of US Women's Labor History*, Ruth Milkman, ed. (Boston: Routledge and Kegan Paul, 1985). She concludes that the revitalization of the labor movement could become the basis of a full-scale alliance between the nation's women workers with "their own distinctive consciousness" and organized labor.

19. *Reflections on the Future of Multilateral Cooperation: the ILO Perspective*. Report of the Director-General to the 73d session of the International Labor Conference, 1987 (Geneva: ILO, 1987), 17.

Index

The Authors

Carol Riegelman Lubin (Mrs. Isador Lubin) is a consultant for U.S. social welfare organizations concerned with women, children, housing, and unemployment. She represents the International Federation of Settlements and Neighborhood Centers at the United Nations. She served in a variety of positions on the ILO professional staff from 1935 to 1952.

Anne Winslow has served as Editor-in-Chief at the Carnegie Endowment for International Peace and as Fellow of the United Nations Institute for Training and Research. Professionally involved in UN affairs since World War II, she is the author of many studies and reports on the UN's social and economic activities.